A TREASURY

of

HUMOR

A

TREASURY

o f

HUMOR

Thousands of humorous **stories**, **jokes**,
anecdotes and **one-liners**, up-to-date
and categorized for ease of use.

Lowell D. Streiker

 HENDRICKSON
PUBLISHERS

A Treasury of Humor
Copyright © 2000 by Lowell D. Streiker, Ph.D.
Published by Hendrickson Publishers, Inc.
P.O. Box 3473
Peabody, Massachusetts 01961-3473

Disclaimer: The names of persons, businesses, and churches used in this collection are mostly fictitious. Any resemblance to businesses, churches, or persons living or dead is, for the most part, purely coincidental.

Printed in the United States of America

ISBN 1-56563-457-8

First Printing—July 2000

Cover design by Richmond and Williams, Nashville, Tennessee
Interior design by Scott Pinzon, Kirkland, Wash.
Edited by Peggy Anderson, Cynthia Beach, Scott Pinzon, and Heather Stroobosscher

Library of Congress Cataloging-in-Publication Data
    A treasury of humor / Lowell D. Streiker.
        p. cm.
    ISBN 1-56563-457-8 (cloth)
      1. American wit and humor. I. Streiker, Lowell D.
    PN6162.T69 2000
    818'.60208--dc21

                                                    00-029553

Dedication

To Betty Johnson,
whose memory always brings a smile

Acknowledgements

Special thanks to my special angels—
Aggie, Elizabeth, and Connie

Contents

Introducing Lowell Streiker

Lowell D. Streiker is an ordained minister in the United Church of Christ and holds a Ph.D. in religion from Princeton University. He has written, co-authored, compiled, edited, and contributed to more than twenty books. He has co-produced and moderated the television series *Counterpoint* for CBS. He has appeared on numerous radio and television programs including *The Oprah Winfrey Show, The Merv Griffin Show,* and CBS *Morning News.*

Visit his website, Reverend Lowell's Electronic Congregation, at http://www.revlowell.com. Your humorous contributions and comments are always welcome.

MEET LOWELL IN PERSON!

Share Lowell's "good clean fun" words of inspiration with your business, church, or other audience. Lowell is available for speaking engagements, workshops, conferences, and preaching. During the past four years, he has spoken, sung, preached, and entertained in the United States, Norway, Germany, Holland, Finland, Russia, Poland, and Hungary. For more information, contact Lowell today:

3309 El Camino Dr.
Cottonwood, CA 96022
Phone: (530) 347-1948
Fax: (530) 347-5617
E-mail: revlowell@earthlink.net

■ Accountants

My accountant is worth every penny he charges because of the time he saves me. This year, for example, he probably saved me five to ten years in prison.

—Speaker's Idea File

When he was an accountant, my brother Scott had a consulting contract with a big electronics firm in Houston. At the completion of the contract, he received a large check for services rendered, but discovered that it was one cent short. A stickler for detail, he insisted that the discrepancy be repaired, and in due course, received another check for a single penny. When he presented it for payment at his bank, the teller examined it closely and asked him, "How would you like this, sir? Heads or tails?"

An angry worker goes into her company's payroll office to complain that her paycheck is fifty dollars short.

The payroll supervisor checks the books and says, "I see here that last week you were overpaid by fifty dollars. I can't recall your complaining about that."

Replied the worker, "Well, I'm willing to overlook an occasional error, but this is two in a row!"

—Paul Dickson

■ Actors and Acting

Comedienne/actress Beatrice Lillie (whose marriage to Robert Peel made her Lady Peel) was showing off the family pearls.

A malicious rival murmured, "I can't believe those pearls are genuine, my dear. They say you can always tell by biting them. Would you let me try?"

"Certainly," said Lillie promptly. "But remember, my sweet, that you can't tell real pearls with false teeth."

James Whistler made a brilliant remark at a London club, and poet Oscar Wilde murmured, "Gad, I wish I'd said that!"

Whereupon Whistler responded, "Don't worry, Oscar, you will."

The late Gertrude Lawrence was one of those irreplaceables who seldom had an understudy. If she was sick, the show was off. An aspiring actress discovered this, to her dismay, when she auditioned before Moss Hart for a part in a play he was producing. She announced that, among her other credits, she had been the understudy in *Susan and God*, one of Miss Lawrence's great hits.

"Interesting," murmured Hart. "I take it you were understudying God?"
—Art Linkletter

Checking into a small motel, Boris Karloff explained, "My demands are modest. I just want a small place to hang my hat and a few friends."

In 1926, Groucho Marx was playing in *The Coconuts* at the National Theater in Washington, and President Calvin Coolidge made one of his rare visits to the playhouse. The whole cast was abuzz with the event—the President of the United States was right there in the third row! Groucho behaved as long as he could. But shortly after the second-act curtain rose, he stopped right in the middle of a comedy song, loped to the footlights, and said, "Calvin, aren't you up beyond your bedtime?"
—Art Linkletter

My friend's son is a freshman at college. The boy, it seems, is deeply interested in the theater.

Recently the proud papa received a letter from his son in which the lad enthusiastically announced that he'd landed a part in a school play. "I play a man who's been married for twenty years," the boy wrote.

"Good luck, son," his old man wrote back. "Keep up the good work, and before you know it, they'll be giving you a speaking part."

—Myron Cohen

Actor Blair Underwood relates: "I remember asking my mother one time, 'Who do you pay to get on television?'

"And she said, 'Oh, no, no, baby, they pay you.'

"And I said, 'Oh yes, this is what I want to do!'"

When Carol Channing was touring in *Hello, Dolly!* on the West Coast, there was the inevitable cocktail party for the press in each city. Carol is a journalist's delight—they know they can ask her anything and get an entertaining reply. That is, almost anything. At one party, a lady reporter chirped up, "Miss Channing, do you remember the most embarrassing moment of your life?"

"Yes, I certainly do," said Carol. "Next question?"

A naive reporter asked actor Howard Lindsay, who was the original father in *Life with Father*, the customary question: "Mr. Lindsay, can you remember the best piece of advice that you ever received?"

"Oh, yes," the actor replied enthusiastically. "It was the time many years ago that I was advised to marry my lovely wife, Dorothy Stickney."

"Sir, do you remember who gave you that advice?"

"Certainly! She did."

Whatever you have read I have said is almost certainly untrue, except if it is funny, in which case I definitely said it.

—Tallulah Bankhead

ACTOR FINDS "ORPHANAGE" IS NO PLACE FOR LOLLIPOPS

San Francisco (AP)—Don Frederick, an actor, received a call to report to The Orphanage on Montgomery Street to work on a television series. En route, he stopped at a candy store and bought several dozen lollipops for the kids. He belatedly discovered that The Orphanage was a night club.

—cited by Bud and Lolo Delaney, *The Laugh Journal*

Fan club: A group of people who tell an actor he's not alone in the way he feels about himself.   —Jack Carson

The great husband-and-wife acting team of Alfred Lunt and Lynn Fontanne made just one motion picture, *The Guardsman*. On the day of the premiere, Lunt was sick in bed and couldn't go. Miss Fontanne went alone and returned distraught.

She was already talking as she came in and almost weeping with despair. "Alfred," she said, "it was a total disaster. I cannot imagine what the photographer can have been thinking of, or the director. For some reason I came out as an ugly witch, with my makeup all wrong, my cheeks cadaverous, my hair a mess. The sound system managed to make my voice sound half a squeak and half a groan. You at least were fine in every respect, except for a tendency to have thin lips for some reason, but I was impossible. The close-ups were invariably taken at such an angle that all you could see of me were my nostrils, or else my eyelashes cast such shadows that I looked as though I had large bags under both eyes. I shall certainly never be able to hold up my head again in public, and I intend to go into retirement at once."

And, thoughtfully, Lunt said, "Thin lips, eh?"   —Isaac Asimov

Further Reading:
My Life with Annette, Amos Kateer

■ Advertising

Remember those famous Burma Shave roadside signs? Here are a few collected by Frank Rowsome Jr. in his book *Verse by the Side of the Road*:

• His face was smooth and cool as ice, and oh, Louise, he smelled so nice.
• He had the ring; he had the flat—but she felt his face, and that was that.
• The bearded lady tried a jar: she's now a famous movie star.
• No lady likes to dance or dine, accompanied by a porcupine.
• The whale put Jonah down the hatch, but coughed him up because he scratched.

Dick Jacobs of the Joseph Jacobs Organization has a great way of convincing you of the importance of advertising. He says, "Doing business without advertising is like winking at a pretty girl in the dark. You know what you're doing, but nobody else does."

—Joey Adams

In the *Cleveland Plain Dealer* classifieds: "Unmotivated? Looking for ten people to ruin my business."

Ad spotted in the Eau Claire, Michigan, *Trade Lines Shopper's Guide*: "Rapid Weight Loss. Lose 305 pounds a week. Guaranteed!"

Posted on a bulletin board at a Virginia health club: "Free to good homes—six adorable puppies, all shots. Mother is a Champion AKC Registered Golden Retriever. Father is also a dog."

ACTUAL CLASSIFIED ADS

• In a Los Angeles daily: "Wanted: man to work on nuclear fissionable isotope molecular reactive counters and three-phase cyclotronic photosynthesizers. No experience necessary."

- In the Southern Illinois University student newspaper: "Sweet little old lady wishes to correspond with S. I. U. undergraduate. Prefers six-foot male with brown eyes answering to initials J. D. B. Signed, His Mother."
- From a Miami Beach weekly: "Having trouble with your husband coming home late—or not at all? Let us make a confidential investigation for you. Special discount if your husband is over seventy-five years of age."
- Found in the Mount Pleasant, Michigan, *Morning Sun*: "Models needed. Have your hair done by world-renounced artists."
- An ad in the *Saturday Review*: "For sale, genuine kid gloves for practically nothing due to computerized sewing error. We have 50,000 pairs with three thumbs on each hand. Bids welcomed."

POP N. FRESH DOUGH BOY DIES AT 71

Veteran Pillsbury spokesman Pop N. Fresh died Wednesday of a severe yeast infection. He was seventy-one. He was buried Friday in one of the biggest funerals in years. Dozens of celebrities turned out including Mrs. Butterworth, the California Raisins, Hungry Jack, Betty Crocker and the Hostess Twinkies. The graveside was piled high with flours.

Longtime friend, Aunt Jemimah, delivered the eulogy, describing Fresh as a man who "never knew how much we kneaded him."

Fresh rose quickly in show business, but his later life was filled with turnovers. He was not considered a smart cookie, and wasted much of his dough on half-baked schemes. Still, even as a crusty old man, he was a roll model to millions.

Fresh is survived by his second wife. They had two children—and one in the oven.

Let advertisers spend the same amount on improving their product that they do on advertising and they wouldn't have to advertise it.

—Will Rogers

When I first got into the business, they told me I needed a press agent. So I hired one, for a hundred dollars a week. The first week, no press at all. I called my agent and said, "What's happening?"

He said, "They're talkin' about ya, baby, they're talkin' about ya!"

Two more weeks go by, two hundred bucks more, and no press. I'm pretty mad. I called my agent and said, "Hey, what's happening here?"

He said, "They're talkin' about ya, baby, they're talkin' about ya!"

Five weeks go by. Five hundred bucks down the drain and not a thing to show for it. I was so mortified and angry that I went down to his office, barged right in, and said, "What's happening? What've I got to show for my five hundred bucks?"

He said, "They're talkin' about ya, baby, they're talkin' about ya!"

I said, "Yeah? So what're they saying?"

He said, "They're saying, 'Whatever happened to Will Jordan?'"

—Will Jordan

The value of advertising is that it tells you the exact opposite of what the advertiser actually thinks. For example:

If the advertisement says, "This is not your father's Oldsmobile," the advertiser is desperately concerned that this Oldsmobile, like all other Oldsmobiles, appeals primarily to old farts like your father.

If Coke and Pepsi spend billions of dollars to convince you that there are significant differences between these two products, both companies realize that Pepsi and Coke are virtually identical.

If the advertisement strongly suggests that Nike shoes enable athletes to perform amazing feats, Nike wants you to disregard the fact that shoe brand is unrelated to athletic ability.

If Budweiser runs an elaborate advertising campaign stressing the critical importance of a beer's "born-on" date, Budweiser knows this factor has virtually nothing to do with how good a beer tastes.

If an advertisement shows a group of cool, attractive youngsters getting excited and high-fiving each other because the refrigerator contains Sunny Delight, the advertiser knows that any real youngster who reacted in this way to this beverage would be considered by his peers to be the world's biggest [dipstick].

And so on. On those rare occasions when advertising dares to poke fun at the product—as in the classic Volkswagen Beetle campaign—it's because the advertiser actually thinks the product is pretty good. If a politician ever ran for president under a slogan such as "Harlan Frubert: Basically, He Wants Attention," I would quit my job to work for his campaign.

—Dave Barry

The owner of a prosperous department store in a medium-sized Midwestern town was a firm believer in the power of advertising—and every one of his ads for years on end featured the line, "The owner of this store is a decorated veteran of World War II." A new agency, anxious to get the account, assured the owner he could cut his ad appropriation by 10 percent and no loss of business by simply eliminating this slogan, but was met with an adamant, "Nothing doing. I'm convinced it increases sales."

"Humph," snorted the agency man. "I'll bet you weren't even in World War II."

"I certainly was," the owner answered angrily.

"What branch of service?" persisted the agency man.

Replied the owner, "The Luftwaffe."

—Bennett Cerf

■ Advice

If you don't find it in the index, look very carefully through the entire catalogue.

—"Consumer's Guide," Sears, Roebuck and Co. (1897)

In my opinion, the only time it's better to give than to receive is if the commodity that's being given is advice.

—Ron Dentinger

If your eyes hurt after you drink coffee, try taking the spoon out of the cup.

—Norm Crosby

If somebody tells you that you have ears like a donkey, pay no attention. But if two people tell you, buy yourself a saddle.

—Sholem Aleichem, Jewish novelist

My uncle Jack, a traveling salesman, was driving through Missouri, when he found the bridge over a stream washed away by a recent storm. A native sat whittling a stick by the side of the wreckage. "How deep is this stream?" asked Uncle Jack.

"Dunno."

"Think I can drive through it?"

"Sure thing. Why not?"

Uncle Jack drove head-on into the stream. His car promptly sank out of sight, and he barely got out with his life. "What do you mean by telling me I could drive through that stream?" he cried furiously. "Why, it's ten feet deep if it's an inch!"

The native scratched his head. "Can't understand it," he admitted. Then, pointing to his own waist, he added, "The water's only up to here on the ducks!"

I have found the best way to give advice to your children is to find out what they want and then advise them to do it.   —Harry S Truman

■ Aging

If you want to know how old a woman is, ask her sister-in-law.

—E. W. Howe

I can define "middle-aged." That's when you're faced with two temptations and you choose the one that'll get you home at nine o'clock.

—Ronald Reagan at the annual Salute to Congress Dinner, February 4, 1981

BUMPER STICKERS ON AGING

Wrinkled was not one of the things I wanted to be when I grew up.

My wild oats have turned to shredded wheat.

You know you are getting old when people tell you how good you look.

—Alan King

The secret of staying young is to live honestly, eat slowly, and lie about your age.

                                                    —Lucille Ball

My wife never lies about her age. She just tells everyone she's as old as I am. Then she lies about my age.

                                         —Joan Rivers' husband

On signing the Alternative Motor Fuels Act of 1988 on October 14, 1988, President Reagan said, "And believe me, when you're my age, you just love hearing about alternative sources of energy."

Poking fun at himself, President Reagan declared: "There was a Democrat during the campaign who told a large group, 'Don't worry, I've seen Ronald Reagan, and he looks like a million.' He was talking about my age."

Nothing is more responsible for the good old days than a bad memory.

                                         —Franklin P. Adams

A big-time celebrity was doing a benefit at a senior citizens' home. He went up to one of the elderly ladies, sat down beside her, and said, "Do you know who I am?"

She said, "No, but go to the front desk. They'll tell you who you are."

                                         —Norm Crosby

The aging rock group the Rolling Stones is again touring the United States. "Each show will include three encores," remarks Conan O'Brien, "and two naps."

                            —*Late Night with Conan O'Brien*, NBC

I don't find that I get mellower as I get older. It's just that I don't have the energy to sustain the rages for as long as I used to.

                                         —Betsy Salkind

THE WISDOM OF SENIOR CITIZENS

- I started with nothing. I still have most of it.
- When did my wild oats turn to prunes and All-Bran?
- I finally got my head together. Now my body is falling apart.
- Funny, I don't remember being absent-minded.
- All reports are in. Life is now officially unfair.
- If all is not lost, where is it?
- It is easier to get older than it is to get wiser.
- If at first you do succeed, try not to look astonished.
- The first rule of holes: if you are in one, stop digging.
- I tried to get a life once, but they told me they were out of stock.
- I went to school to become a wit. I only got halfway through.
- It was so different before everything changed.
- Some days you're the dog, and some days you're the hydrant.
- Nostalgia isn't what it used to be.
- A day without sunshine is like a day in Seattle.
- I wish the buck stopped here! I could use a few.
- It's not the pace of life that concerns me; it's the sudden stop at the end.
- It's hard to make a comeback when you haven't been anywhere.
- Living on Earth is expensive, but it does include a trip around the sun.
- The only time the world beats a path to your door is if you're in the bathroom.
- If God wanted me to touch my toes, He would have put them on my knees.
- Never knock on Death's door. Ring the bell and run (he hates that).
- When you are finally holding all the cards, why does everyone else decide to play chess?
- If you are living on the edge, make sure you wear your seat belt.
- There are two kinds of pedestrians: the quick and the dead.
- A closed mouth gathers no feet.
- Health is merely the slowest possible rate at which one can die.
- It's not hard to meet expenses; they are everywhere.
- Jury: Twelve people who determine which client has the better attorney.

—Lowell Bowman

At a signing ceremony for the legislative agenda and the economic report of the president on February 6, 1986, Ronald Reagan said, "I did turn seventy-five today, but remember, that's only twenty-four Celsius."

It's hard for me to get used to these changing times. I can remember when the air was clean and sex was dirty. —George Burns

My, my sixty-five! I guess this marks the first day of the rest of my life savings. —H. Martin

A woman past forty should make up her mind to be young, not her face. —Billie Burke

Nothing so dates a man as decrying the younger generation. —Adlai Stevenson

President Lincoln once rejected a person recommended for a position because he didn't like his face. One of his cabinet staff disagreed with the president. He said that he didn't think not liking someone's appearance was enough explanation for turning down an applicant. Lincoln shook his head. He said, "Every man over forty is responsible for his face."

> **I** like my bifocals,
> My dentures fit just fine,
> My hearing aid is perfect,
> But how I miss my mind! —Carol Rumsey

You know you're getting old when you walk into a record store and everything you like has been marked down to $1.99.
—Jack Simmons, Showtime Comedy Cable

My grandmother's ninety. She's dating. He's ninety-three. It's going to be great. They never argue. They can't hear each other.

—Cathy Ladman

One windy day, octogenarian Oliver Wendell Holmes was walking down a Washington street with nonagenarian Chauncey Depew when the wind whisked up the skirts of a pretty young pedestrian. Sighed Chief Justice Holmes, "Oh, to be seventy again!"

—Art Linkletter

THEN AND NOW: A GUIDE FOR AGING BOOMERS

Old and new concerns for people of the Baby Boom generation.

Then: Long hair.	Now: Longing for hair.
Then: Keg.	Now: EKG.
Then: Acid rock.	Now: Acid reflux.
Then: Moving to California because it's cool.	Now: Moving to California because it's hot.
Then: Watching John Glenn's historic flight with your parents.	Now: Watching John Glenn's historic flight with your kids.
Then: Trying to look like Marlon Brando or Elizabeth Taylor.	Now: Trying not to look like Marlon Brando or Elizabeth Taylor.
Then: Our president's struggle with Fidel.	Now: Our president's struggle with fidelity.
Then: Paar.	Now: AARP.
Then: Killer weed.	Now: Weed killer.
Then: The Grateful Dead.	Now: Dr. Kevorkian.
Then: Getting out to a new, hip joint.	Now: Getting a new hip joint.
Then: Hoping for a BMW.	Now: Hoping for a BM.

I know a guy who looks forty years younger than he is. When he's not working, his wife must put a slipcover over him.

—H. Aaron Cohl

As we grow older, our bodies get shorter and our anecdotes longer.

—Robert Quillen

SIGNS YOU ARE GETTING OLD

- You don't hold in your stomach when someone young and attractive enters the room.
- You can live without sex but not without glasses.
- Your best friend is dating someone half his age, but is not breaking any laws.
- You sing along with elevator music.
- People call at 9 P.M. and ask, "Did I wake you up?"

When I turned sixty, I finally decided what I want to be. I want to be twenty-one.

Always be nice to your children because they are the ones who will choose your rest home.

—Phyllis Diller

I said to my old husband, "I'm gonna take you out into the country for a picnic. Do you like the country?"

He said, "Sure I do. When I was a little boy, I used to live in the country."

I said, "When you was a little boy, everybody lived in the country."

—Moms Mabley

I'm now at the age where I've got to prove that I'm just as good as I never was.

—Rex Harrison (attributed)

You know you're getting old when you answer the phone and a woman asks, "Do you know who this is?" and you say no and hang up.

—Franklin P. Adams

She was so old that when she went to school, they didn't have history.
—Rodney Dangerfield

Senile: But see Naples first.

I'm beginning to appreciate the value of naps. Naps are wonderful, aren't they? Sometimes now I have to take a nap to get ready for bed.
—Marsha Warfield

When I admire a pretty girl, I feel like a dog who barks at passing cars but who wouldn't know what to do with one if he caught it.

I've reached that age when a good day is one when you get up and nothing hurts.
—H. Martin

My wife says that I'm at that age where if I go all out, I end up all in.

My wife claims that I no longer have to worry about avoiding temptation. At my age, she says, temptation is avoiding me!

Life begins at forty, but so does arthritis and the habit of telling the same story three times to the same person.
—Sam Levenson

At a Harvard class reunion, humorist Robert Benchley exclaimed, "Except for an occasional heart attack, I feel as young as I ever did."

The four stages of man are infancy, childhood, adolescence, and obsolescence.
—Art Linkletter

AN APPROPRIATE PRAYER FOR SENIOR CITIZENS

Lord, Thou knowest better than I know myself that I am growing older.

Keep me from getting too talkative, and thinking I must say something on every subject and on every occasion.

Release me from craving to straighten out everybody's affairs.

Teach me the glorious lesson that occasionally it is possible that I may be mistaken.

Make me thoughtful, but not moody; helpful, but not bossy. Thou knowest, Lord, that what I want most is a few friends at the end.

George Bernard Shaw in an elevator with fellow attendees at his six-tieth college class reunion: "John? Is that you? I thought we were both dead!"

He's so old that when he orders a three-minute egg, they ask for the money up front.

—Milton Berle

"**H**ow do you account for your longevity?" asked a reporter on the day Harvey turned 110.

"You might call me a health nut," Harvey replied. "I never smoked. I never drank. I was always in bed and sound asleep by ten o'clock. And I've always walked three miles a day, rain or shine."

"But," said the reporter, "I had an uncle who followed that exact routine and died when he was sixty-two. How come it didn't work for him?"

"All I can say," replied Harvey, "is that he didn't keep it up long enough."

—Quoted in *Lutheran Digest*

From birth to age eighteen, a girl needs good parents; from eighteen to thirty-five, she needs good looks; from thirty-five to fifty-five, she needs a good personality; and from fifty-five on, she needs cash.

—Sophie Tucker

He's so old his blood type was discontinued.
—Bill Dana

Further Reading:
One Hundred Years Old, Abbie Birthday
Inflammation, Please!, Arthur Itis
How I Broke My Hip, Eileen Dover and Phil Down

■ Air Travel

There's lots to be afraid of about flying. For example, why is it that the first word you see when you arrive at an airport is "terminal"? Couldn't they call it something else? Why must flight attendants always point out, your seat cushion may be used as a flotation device? A flotation device! If I'd wanted to float to Dallas, I would've chartered a canoe.
—Lewis Grizzard

Why is it . . . that there are bargain air fares to every destination except yours?
—James Holt McGavran in *Good Living*

I had the chance to go to London a couple of months back. Had kind of a weird flight over, though, because one of the flight attendants got very angry with me. I didn't eat all of my dinner. She said, "Sir, you really shouldn't waste all that food. There are people starving on Air India."
—Tim Cavanagh

The Federal Aviation Agency's rules for takeoffs and landings of jet-powered transports include this sentence: "The takeoff distance shall not be greater than the length of the runway."

When I have a choice, I prefer to fly with the airline that has had the most recent crash. I figure the odds are in my favor.
—Lewis Grizzard

Two wrongs do not make a right. Two Wrights made an airplane.

My flight to Louisville was experiencing serious engine trouble, and the pilot instructed the cabin crew to have the passengers take their seats and prepare for an emergency landing. A few minutes later the pilot asked the flight attendants if everyone was buckled in and ready.

"All set back here," came the reply, "except for one lawyer who's still passing out business cards."

I was on a nonstop flight from Atlanta to Los Angeles. The fellow sitting next to me said, "Going to Los Angeles?"

"I hope so," I answered. "I really hope so."   —Lewis Grizzard

Some people carry on so much baggage, you're not sure whether they're flying to Oakland or about to climb the south face of Mt. Everest.

Flight attendants are usually bright and cheery. That's because they don't have to eat the airline food.

A small plane with an instructor and student on board hit the runway and bounced repeatedly until it came to a stop. The instructor turned to the student and said, "That was a very bad landing you just made."

"Me?" replied the student. "I thought you were landing!"

                                       —*The Cockle Bur*

Flying doesn't thrill me. . . .We don't know how old the planes are, and there's really no way for us to tell, 'cause we're laymen. But I figure if the plane smells like your grandmother's house, get out. That's the bottom line.   —Garry Shandling

The Concorde was great. It travels at twice the speed of sound. Which is fun except you can't hear the movie till two hours after you land.

—Howie Mandel

Have you noticed that most flight attendants look young? It's because they keep losing the bags under their eyes.

—Nazareth

In today's world, most of us get on and off airplanes so often we don't think about the process anymore. We tune out the flight attendants and their pre-take-off announcement about seat backs and tray tables, forgetting this speech is done for our safety.

A flight attendant for Southwest Airlines, who chooses to be called Joanne, uses humor to regain the attention of frequent flyers. Here's what I heard Joanne say on a recent Southwest flight:

"Ladies and gentlemen, if you could please give your attention to the other flight attendants, who include my husband Dave and his ex-wife Susan, they'd like to point out the safety features of the aircraft. For those of you who haven't been in an automobile lately and used your seat belt, slide the flat end into the buckle. To release, lift up on the flip-latch, and it will separate. Tying the belts together is not acceptable.

"I know they've told you there are fifty ways to leave your lover. Unfortunately, we have only six ways on this aircraft: two forward entry doors, two over the wing exits and two aft exit doors. All are clearly marked with red EXIT signs, and the disco lighting along the aisle will lead you to them.

"In the seat back pocket in front of you, or to the side if you are sitting in one of our plush lounge areas, you should find an emergency briefing card that further supplements this information on our safety features. Of course, there's no telling what you'll find in those pockets—gum wrappers, candy wrappers, empty cups or cans—and if you dig deep enough, possibly a dirty diaper.

"Since we will be flying over pools, puddles, and hot tubs on our way to Albuquerque today, you'll note your seat bottom cushion may be used as a flotation device in the event of a water evacuation.

"Flight attendants are now walking through the cabin, checking to make sure seat belts are fastened, tray tables are up and locked, that seats are in the forward and most uncomfortable position, and that the carry-on luggage you wished you had checked, is crammed all the way under the seat in front of you.

"We certainly don't anticipate a change in the cabin pressure, but should one occur, four margarine cups will magically appear overhead. When they do, stop screaming, place the cup over your nose and mouth and breathe normally until notified by crew members, or until Susan comes by offering mouth-to-mouth. In that case, preferential treatment will be given to those gentlemen with Rolex watches.

"There's no smoking at all on board this aircraft. We prohibit smoking in the lavatories, and if we find you doing so, Dave will ask you to step out on the wing, where you can also enjoy our patio furniture and the movie *Gone with the Wind*.

"Now that we have all the rules and regulations out of the way, sit back, relax, and enjoy your hour flight. If there's anything else you need during your flight, *forget about it!* . . . Just kidding. Don't hesitate to call on Dave. Susan and I will be in the back, finishing our nails."

Joanne had plenty to say when the plane landed as well:

"On behalf of Southwest Airlines and this flight crew, we'd like to be the first to welcome you to Albuquerque. Do us one last favor: keep your tush to the cush, your seat belt fastened, and the luggage right where it is until Captain America and Boy Wonder pull this aircraft up to the gate and turn off the fasten seat belt signs. That will be your only indication that it's safe to jump up, grab all of your luggage, and go absolutely nowhere.

"Thanks for choosing Southwest today. Go out, have a great week, and do come back and see us again, because no one loves you more than us. Oh, one more note. We have a special gentleman on board today celebrating his ninety-eighth birthday and his first flight. [Everyone on the plane began to applaud.] Do me a big favor and wish our captain a happy birthday on your way out and let him know he doesn't look a day over fifty. [Moans and groans from the passengers.] I can't believe you all fell for that." —David Naster

Groucho Marx was traveling by air and requested permission to smoke a cigar. There's a fairly hard-and-fast regulation on commercial airlines against this particular aromatic indulgence. But the hostess felt that perhaps in the case of a passenger as famous as Groucho Marx the rules might be relaxed. "I suppose you can smoke a cigar if you don't annoy the lady passengers," she said.

To which Groucho quickly replied, "You mean I've got a choice?"

—Art Linkletter

I took an economy flight. There wasn't any movie, but they flew low over drive-ins. —Red Buttons

I like to look out the windows when I'm up in an airplane. When you fly over Colorado, you see the Rocky Mountains. When you fly over Arizona, you see the Grand Canyon, and when you fly over Los Angeles, you see a bunch of people lying on the ground spelling out the word, "HELP!"

Orville Wright said to his brother, Wilbur, "You were only in the air for twelve seconds. How could my luggage be in Cleveland?"

—Red Buttons

Trains stay on the ground as God intended. Remember: "Lo, I will be with you always." He never mentioned "high." —Lewis Grizzard

Hard to believe, but Paul Sirks was preparing to take off from an airport in Urbana, Ohio, when the engine of his private plane stalled, so he got out and re-started it by turning the propeller with his hand. The aircraft then taxied down the runway and took off without him. The empty plane flew all over Ohio for two hours before it ran out of gas and crashed into a farmer's field ninety miles away.

In this classic story, it was a flight attendant who brought down the great boxer Mohammed Ali.

As the jet was rolling down to the runway, the flight attendant instructed the heavyweight champion that he needed to fasten his seat belt. He looked at her, smiled, and bragged, "Superman don't need a seat belt."

She gave him an even bigger smile and said, "No, Superman don't need an airplane, either. Will you buckle up please?"

Ali laughed as he fastened his seat belt.

In the Middle Ages, men of science tried to recreate bird wings. They strapped their devices onto the shoulders of daredevils and found a tall cliff. Within a hundred years, daredevils were almost extinct.   —Lewis Grizzard

Further Reading:
What Makes Airplanes Go, Jeff Fuel
Fighting Jet Stream Winds, Gail Force
Parachuting, Hugo First
Long Way Down, Rip Cord Broke

■ Animals

Actual classified ad from Salt Lake City: "Livestock for sale—Mexican burro, very gentle, friendly. Can be seen at Creek Road in Union, or heard within a radius of three miles any morning from 6:00 A.M. on."

Helena, Montana (AP)—Ranchers have frequent skirmishes with naturalists over the value of coyotes in sheep country, but at least one Helena-area rancher can still see humor in the situation. The rancher erected this sign along Route 12:

"Eat American lamb. Ten million coyotes can't be wrong."
                                      —cited by Bud and Lolo Delaney, *The Laugh Journal*

I had a linguistics professor who said that it's man's ability to use language that makes him the dominant species on the planet. That may be. But I think there's one other thing that separates us from animals. We aren't afraid of vacuum cleaners.   —Jeff Stilson

The electric eel in the aquarium became depressed, and his keeper asked if there was anything that could be done. "I'm unhappy because I have no wife," said the eel. The next day the keeper dropped a female eel into the tank, returned an hour later, and was shocked to find the male eel just as depressed as he had been before.

"What's the matter now?" he asked.

"Just my luck," he said turning toward the intended mate. "DC."

—Paul Dickson

There's a perky little lady who lives on Fire Island—and loves it. When the beach in front of her house gets too crowded for her own comfort, she simply circulates quietly among the sun worshippers and bathers, shades her eyes, and exclaims, "Goodness, isn't that a fin out there?" In no time flat, she has the beach to herself.

—Bennett Cerf

Carl Sagan observes, "It is of interest to note that while some dolphins are reported to have learned English—up to fifty words used in correct context—no human being has been reported to have learned dolphinese."

A man comes into a bar with a small white mouse in his pocket. He puts the mouse on the bar and orders a martini for himself and a thimbleful for the mouse.

After downing the drink, the mouse stands on its hind legs and sings a medley of songs: "I Could Have Danced All Night," "I've Grown Accustomed to Her Face," "The Rain in Spain Stays Mainly in the Plain," and more.

The bartender is amazed.

"Listen," says the man, "buy us a round of drinks, and you can keep the mouse."

The bartender serves them and then says, "I can't believe that you're giving away a gold mine like that for a few drinks."

"Heck," says the mouse's former owner, "all he knows is *My Fair Lady*."

—Paul Dickson

A lady came up to me on the street and pointed at my suede jacket. "You know a cow was murdered for that jacket?" she sneered.

I replied in a psychotic tone, "I didn't know there were any witnesses. Now I'll have to kill you too."

—Jake Johanson

 Edna Patterson and her husband came into sudden wealth as the result of Mr. Patterson's investments in Internet stocks. Edna loved surprises, and her husband was rich enough to indulge her every whim. For a birthday present he found her a parrot that spoke eleven languages and that cost him exactly one thousand dollars for each language. When he got home, he asked, "What d'ya think of that wonderful bird I sent you?"

"It was elegant," she answered. "It's in the oven right now."

The husband's face turned purple. "In the oven?" he shouted. "Why, that bird could speak eleven languages!"

The wife asked, "Then why didn't it say something?"

Actress/comedienne Bea Lillie was giving a small dinner party at her East Side apartment, when suddenly there was the sound of fluttering wings at the open window. A stray pigeon had landed on the ledge and was eyeing the group curiously. "Oh, hello," ad libbed Bea. "Any messages?"

From a "Fun Facts" column in Andalusia, Alabama, *Star-News*: "River hippos travel in herds of five to thirty animals. Pygmy hippopotamuses live alone or in paris."

Further Reading:

The Monkey Cage, Jim Panzee

Monkey Shines, Bob Boone

The Lion Attacked, Claudia Armoff

Meals on Safari, Lionel Eecha

A Whole Lot of Cats, Kitt N. Caboodle

I Like Fish, Ann Chovie

Snakes of the World, Anna Conda

Crocodile Dundee, Ali Gator

Greeting Sheep Strangers, Hugh R. Ewe

Silly Rabbit, Trixie R. Forkids

Los Angeles Pachyderms, L. A. Funt

Sea Birds, Al Batross

Animal Scents, Farrah Mones

The Unknown Rodent, A. Nonny Mouse

Turtle Racing, Eubie Quick

Animal Illnesses, Ann Thrax

Kangaroo Illnesses, Marcus Wallaby, M.D.

■ Applications and Forms

The business manager of a Philadelphia newspaper, checking office life-insurance applications, came across one in which an employee named his wife beneficiary and then filled out the space headed, "Relationship to you," with the word, "Nice."

The personnel man received a questionnaire which asked, among other things: "How many people do you have, broken down by sex?"

His answer: "Liquor is more of a problem with us."

The employment clerk, checking over the applicant's papers, was amazed to note the figures 107 and 111 in the spaces reserved for "Age of Father, if living" and "Age of Mother, if living."

"Are your parents that old?" asked the surprised clerk.

"Nope," was the answer, "but they would be if living."

A laborer applying for a factory job struggled through an application form and came to the query: "Person to Notify in Case of Accident." He wrote: "Anybody in sight."

One of the queries on the questionnaire sent by the summer camp director was "Is your daughter a leader or a follower?"

My husband described our energetic seven-year-old thus: "She is a leader without any followers."

From an auto-accident report to an insurance company: My car sustained no damage whatsoever and the other car somewhat less.

A young man applying for a teaching position, in response to a query about marital status: Eligible.

The application blank sent in by a woman trying for a teaching job in a Texas school system had a very flattering picture attached with this note: I don't have a recent photograph of myself, but am enclosing one of my high-school daughter. We look very much alike.

From a benefits notice: Medicare does not pay for this service because it is part of another service that was performed at the same time or is another service that cannot be performed at the same time as that other service.

The Victoria, B.C., *Times* instructs the carrier boy to interview people who quit the paper and send in the reason for their cancellation. One boy submitted this message: "The news upsets Mrs. Smardon."

Insurance salesperson to customer: "You've filled in this application all right except for one thing, Mr. Perkins—where it asks the relationship of Mrs. Perkins to yourself, you should have put down 'wife,' not 'strained.'"

A Topeka, Kansas, assessor recently ran across the best answer yet to the question on the tax assessment blank: "Nature of taxpayer." The answer: "Very mean."

In Northampton, Massachusetts, a Smith College freshman scrawled as her denominational preference: I like to be called Betty.

■ Art and Artists

Headline on a *New York Daily News* review of a museum art collection: "Make La Trek to See Lautrec—Met's exhibit opens today and there's no time Toulouse."

Sign in an art gallery: We hung this picture because we couldn't find the artist.

In my youth I wanted to be a great pantomimist—but I found I had nothing to say.
—Victor Borge

Further Reading:
Misunderstood: My Personal Expression, Art Tistic

■ Atheists and Agnostics

Most people past college age are not atheists. It's too hard to be in society, for one thing. Because you don't get any days off. And if you're an agnostic you don't know whether you get them off or not.

—Mort Sahl

My uncle Frank was an insomniac dyslexic agnostic. He stayed up all night wondering if there really was a dog.

The atheists have produced a Christmas play. It's called *Coincidence on 34th Street.*

—Jay Leno

Hypocrite: One who writes a book praising atheism and then prays it will sell.

—Jim Reed, *A Treasury of Ozark Country Humor*

Heck is where people go who don't believe in Gosh.

Further Reading:

I'm an Atheist, Noel Noheaven

■ Automobiles

Automobile: A machine that runs up hills and down people.

Ad found among the miscellaneous listings in the *Stanwood/Camano News*, in Washington state: "Caution! Homeowners between Warm Beach and Stanwood— Daughter will be learning how to drive. Use caution after leaving garage or porch. Farmers advised to place hay bales around barns, farm equipment, and slow-moving livestock. She will be driving white sedan with frightened father aboard."

Spare tire: The one you check the day after you have a flat.

Short cut: A route on which you can't find anybody to ask where you are.

Sign at auto repair shop: Try us once, you'll never go anywhere again!

Aunt Aggie has found a foolproof way to avoid parking tickets. She just removes the windshield wipers!

They have a car that runs on solar energy. It'll kill romance—how can a guy tell his date he ran out of sun?

He bought one of these new sub-subcompacts. It saves him a fortune in gas—he can't get into it.

If you want to bring your family closer together, buy a smaller car.

After driving for fifty years, my aunt Lou explained: "The thing I dislike most about parking is that noisy *crash!*"

Television sets are becoming very popular in automobiles these days. My uncle has a television set in his automobile, but it led to a little trouble. You see, he was sitting in the car watching television while his wife was driving on the throughway at sixty miles per hour. And then the commercial came on, and he stepped out to go to the bathroom.

—Jackie Clark

A hundred years ago we were much smarter; then you lived until you died and not until you were just run over.   —Will Rogers

A lot of friction is caused by half the drivers trying to go fast enough to thrill their girlfriends and the other half trying to go slow enough to placate their wives.   —Bill Vaughan

Gas prices are outrageous. I saw a bum with a sign: Will Work for Unleaded.   —Scott Wood

Overheard: "I told the guy at the auto parts store that I wanted a windshield wiper for your Yugo. He said, 'That sounds like a fair exchange.' "   —*Executive Speechwriter Newsletter*

The most dangerous part of a car is the nut that holds the steering wheel.   —"Senator" Ed Ford

A firm believer in seat belts, a Mr. Koshland of the Southampton Koshlands drove to church one recent Sunday morning, jammed into the one remaining space in the parking lot, hurriedly unbuckled his belt, stepped out of his car—and his pants fell off.   —Bennett Cerf

Why do they call it rush hour when nothing moves?   —Robin Williams

Rolls-Royce has announced it has a new car it will sell for $216,000. Reports Jay Leno, "It's so fancy that the cup holder is a guy named Charles."   —*The Tonight Show*, NBC

Further Reading:

Life Before Cars, Orson Buggy
I Must Fix the Car!, Otto Doit
Car Repairs, Axel Grease
Hertz, Don't It?, Lisa Carr
I Need Insurance, Justin Case
I Lived in Detroit, Helen Earth
Car Capital of the World, Mitch Egan
A History of Gas Stations, Phil Errup
Stranded by a Lonely Highway, M. T. Tank
How to Tune Up Your Auto, Carl Humm
French Cars, Myra Neault
The Auto Salvage Business, Rex Toad

■ Babies

A baby is God's opinion that the world should go on.

—Carl Sandburg

People said I'd slim down quickly. Nobody told me it was because I'd never have time to eat.

When your first baby drops her pacifier, you sterilize it. When your second baby drops her pacifier, you tell the dog: "Fetch."

—Bruce Lansky

A crying baby is the best form of birth control.   —Carole Tabron

Childbirth classes neglect to teach one critical skill: How to breathe, count, and swear all at the same time.   —Linda Fiterman

Mother Nature, in her infinite wisdom, has instilled within each of us a powerful biological instinct to reproduce; this is her way of assuring that the human race, come what may, will never have any disposable income.   —Dave Barry

Seen on a baby-size T-shirt: Party at my crib—2:00 A.M.

You know that having a baby has drastically changed your life when you and your husband go on a date to Wal-Mart on double coupon day.
—Linda Fiterman

People who say they sleep like babies usually don't have them.
—Leo J. Burke

Life is tough enough without having someone kick you from the inside.
—Rita Rudner

I was a tiny baby when I was born. Really tiny. I was breast fed intravenously. I had to have a special nurse 'cause I was so little. She didn't like to touch me. She used to put Q-tips in my ears and use them as handles . . . My folks used to go out to shows, go out to eat. I never had a baby-sitter. They used to sit me down on a piece of flypaper.
—Lenny Rush

His mother's eyes,
His father's chin,
His auntie's nose,
His uncle's grin,

His great-aunt's hair,
His grandma's ears,
His grandpa's mouth,
So it appears . . .

Poor little tot,
Well may he moan.
He hasn't much
To call his own.
—Richard Armour

If men had babies, maternity leave would be in the Bill of Rights.

—Corky Sherwood Forest on *Murphy Brown*

Whatever is on the floor will wind up in your baby's mouth. Whatever is in your baby's mouth will wind up on the floor.

—Bruce Lansky

Now why did you name your baby John? Every Tom, Dick, or Harry is named John.

—Samuel Goldwyn

Did you know that babies are nauseated by the smell of a clean shirt?

—Jeff Foxworthy

Taking care of a baby is easy—if you have nothing else to do.

—Bruce Lansky

"This baby of mine will someday become president."
"Whoever heard of a baby president?"

We've decided to name our child "Doctor" to save on tuition.

—Liya and Jens Oertel

I always wondered why babies spend so much time sucking their thumbs. Then I tasted baby food.

—Robert Orben

■ Banks

These are tough times. But I'm not the only one with problems. My bank returned a sixty-five dollar check marked "INSUFFICIENT FUNDS." I can't believe they don't have sixty-five dollars.

—Ron Dentinger

A bank is where you borrow when you can't get a loan from a friend.

A record number of savings and loan failures left America with a nationwide shortage of flimsy toaster ovens, cheap pocket calculators, and ugly dinnerware.   —P. J. O'Rourke

The banks have a new image. Now you have "a friend." Your friendly banker. If the banks are so friendly, how come they chain down the pens?   —Alan King

Burglars broke into a bank after hours and found a lone teller trying to balance his books. After forcing him to open the vault, they tied and gagged him. Quickly tossing all the cash into a duffel bag, they were about to leave when they heard the teller making noises through his gag. Curious, they loosened it and asked what he was trying to say. "Take my daily balance sheet too," he gasped. "I'm short seven hundred dollars!"   —*Tai Pan*, Manila

This little old lady was held up by a rough character with a gun. She wasn't a bit scared. "You should be ashamed of yourself, robbing a poor little old lady like me," she protested. "A man your size should be robbing a bank."   —Joey Adams

I don't even have a savings account because I don't know my mom's maiden name and apparently that's key to the whole thing there. I go in every few weeks and guess.   —Paula Poundstone

Texas Senator Lloyd Bentsen, chairman of the Senate Finance Committee, observed, "The thrift industry is in terrible shape. It has reached the point where if you buy a toaster, you get a free savings and loan."   —Quoted by Clyde Farnsworth in the *New York Times*

The banks are giving absolutely nothing away for free. My local branch now has coin-operated ball-point pens.

—Gene and Linda Perret

A story from the late Speaker of the House, Tip O'Neill:

An Irishman went into the local bank to get a loan to buy a house. The Yankee banker looked up the record of the Irishman's bank account, then he looked over the application for the loan, and then he addressed the applicant. "I have a standard test," he said. "I have one glass eye and one real eye. I'll give you the loan if you can tell me which is my glass eye and which is my real eye."

The Irishman studied each of the banker's eyes carefully. "The glass eye is the left eye," he finally said.

"You're correct," said the banker. "But how could you tell?"

"It was easy," said the Irishman. "The left eye had warmth in it."

The fees for withdrawing from your ATM are expected to double or even triple. Basically the ATMs have become full-service. Instead of getting robbed at the ATM, the ATM robs you. You eliminate the middle man.

—Jay Leno

Gracie: Where do you keep your money?
George: In the bank.
Gracie: What interest do you get?
George: Four percent.
Gracie: Ha! I get eight.
George: You get eight?
Gracie: I keep it in two banks.

—George Burns and Gracie Allen

■ Baseball

Baseball has been called the national pastime. It's just the kind of game anyone deserves who has nothing better to do than try to pass his time.

—Andy Rooney

When Philadelphia Phillies "good-hit, no-field" star Gregg Jefferies had the thrill of watching his wife give birth to their first daughter, he was sure to leave all the important work to the experts. "The doctor asked me if I wanted to catch the baby," Jefferies reported. "I said, 'Obviously, you haven't seen me play defense.'"

—Quoted by Tom FitzGerald in the *San Francisco Chronicle*

One afternoon in St. Louis, Stan "The Man" Musial was having a field day against the Chicago pitcher, crusty Bobo Newsome. Stan first slammed a single, then a triple, and then a homer. When Stan came up to bat for the fourth time, the Chicago manager decided to yank Bobo and take a chance on a rookie relief pitcher.

The rookie trudged in from the bull pen and took the ball from Bobo. "Say," he murmured, "has this guy Musial got any weaknesses?"

"Yeah," grunted Bobo, "he can't hit doubles."   —Art Linkletter

Definition of baseball: Three minutes of action crammed into three hours.   —Terry Marchal in the Charleston, West Virginia *Gazette*

I understand that the Cub's Web page had more hits in one day than the whole team had all year.

Years ago, when the Dodgers were still in Brooklyn and Leo Durocher was the team's manager, a horse wandered up to Leo and said, "Why don't you use me on your team? I can hit and field as well as anyone you've got."

"Get lost! I've got enough troubles."

"Come on, Leo, give me a chance; try me in the field."

"Okay. Just for laughs."

The horse went into the field and made one spectacular catch after another.

"Amazing," said Durocher. "Come on in and bat." The horse hit one ball after another over the fence, and Durocher signed the horse on the spot.

The next day, the Dodgers were playing the Giants. The first three Giants were put out by the dazzling fielding of the horse. The Dodgers came to bat, and the first three men reached base. With all the bases loaded the horse came to bat, and he blasted the first ball over the Ebbets Field wall.

"Run, run!" Durocher yelled.

But the horse just stood there. "Are you kidding?" he said. "If I could run, I'd be racing at Jamaica."

—Paul Dickson

Further Reading:

Woulda Been a Great Shortstop, Kent Hitt

Poetry in Baseball, Homer

■ Beauty

He took my glasses off and said, "Without your glasses, why, you're beautiful."

I said, "Without my glasses, you're not half bad either."

—Kit Hollerbach

I don't have anything against face lifts, but I think it's time to stop when you look permanently frightened.

—Susan Forfleet

The most common error made in matters of appearance is the belief that one should disdain the superficial and let the true beauty of one's soul shine through. If there are places on your body where this is a possibility, you are not attractive. You are leaking.

—Fran Lebowitz

I'm tired of all this nonsense about beauty being only skin deep. That's deep enough. What do you want—an adorable pancreas?

—Jean Kerr

"**W**e used to play spin the bottle when I was a kid," says comedy writer Gene Perret. "A girl would spin the bottle, and if the bottle pointed to you when it stopped, the girl could either kiss you or give you a nickel. By the time I was fourteen, I owned my own home."

—*Classic One-Liners*

Further Reading:
Swedish Perfumeries, Ole Factory
The History of Rouge, Rosie Cheeks
Look Younger, Fay Slift

■ Bible

So . . . after Adam was created, there he was in the Garden of Eden. Of course it wasn't good for him to be all by himself, so the Lord came down to visit. "Adam," He said, "I have a plan to make you much, much happier. I'm going to give you a companion, a help-mate for you—someone who will fulfill your every need and desire. Someone who will be faithful, loving, and obedient. Someone who will make you feel wonderful every day of your life."

Adam was stunned. "That sounds incredible!"

"Well, it is," replied the Lord. "But it doesn't come for free. In fact, this is someone so special that it's going to cost you an arm and a leg."

"That's a pretty high price to pay," said Adam. "What can I get for a rib?"

—H. Aaron Cohl

THE BIBLE IN FIFTY WORDS
God made
Adam bit
Noah arked
Abraham split
Joseph ruled
Jacob fooled
Bush talked
Moses balked

Pharaoh plagued
People walked
Sea divided
Tablets guided
Promise landed
Saul freaked
David peeked
Prophets warned
Jesus born
God walked
Love talked
Anger crucified
Hope died
Love rose
Spirit flamed
Word spread
God remained.

■ Birth

Sign seen on a maternity-ward door: "Push! Push! Push!"

Sign outside a maternity shop: "We provide the accessories after the fact."

When I was born, I was so surprised I didn't talk for a year and a half.

—Gracie Allen

The old system of having a baby was much better than the new system, the old system being characterized by the fact that the man didn't have to watch.

—Dave Barry

The latest fad, giving birth under water, may be less traumatic for the baby, but it's more traumatic for the other people in the pool.

—Elayne Boosler

51

What they put women through today when they're having a baby! They don't want to medicate them as compared to previous generations. When my mom had me, she had so much medication that she didn't wake up till I was seven.

—Dennis Wolfberg

Telegram to Mary Sherwood after the birth of her child: "Dear Mary, we all knew you had it in you."

—Dorothy Parker

■ Birthdays

Seen on a bumper sticker: Finally 21, and Legally Able to Do Everything I've Been Doing Since 15.

I never know what to get my father for his birthday. I gave him a hundred dollars and said, "Buy yourself something that will make your life easier." So he went and bought a present for my mother.

—Rita Rudner

Birthday parties are a lot like childbirth. After both events you solemnly swear that you'll never make that mistake again.

—Linda Fiterman

What's the best way to have your husband remember your anniversary? Get married on his birthday.

—H. Aaron Cohl

My neighbor Sarah is a wise and experienced mother. Last week, she announced to a gaggle of young children at her son's seventh birthday party, "Now remember, kids, there will be a special prize for the little boy who goes home first."

Every morning before starting her class, the teacher would write the date on the blackboard, and if it had any significance in history, she would add a comment. On October 12, she knew that simply writing "Columbus Day" would be an insult to her students' intelligence. Instead she wrote, "It all started over 500 years ago today." Then she went out into the hall to monitor students on the way to class. As the starting bell rang, she stepped back into the room—and was greeted by a chorus of twenty-seven voices singing "Happy Birthday to You."

—*Quote Magazine*

And I have what every man who has that many candles on his birthday cake needs around him—a large group of friends and a working sprinkler system.

—Ronald Reagan, February 6, 1984

Further Reading:
Things to Do at Parties, Bob Frapples

■ Books

The difference between literature and journalism is that journalism is unreadable and literature is unread.

—Oscar Wilde

Everything comes to him who waits. Except a loaned book.

—Kin Hubbard

 A rare-book collector met a guy who said he'd just thrown out an old Bible that had been packed away for generations. "Somebody named Guten-something had printed it," the man explained.

"Not Gutenberg!" gasped the book collector. "You've just thrown away one of the most famous books every printed. One copy recently sold at auction for over $4 million!"

The other man was still unmoved. "My copy wouldn't have brought a dime," he said. "Some guy named Martin Luther scribbled notes all over it."

—Tal D. Bonham

Rare volume: A borrowed book that comes back.

I just got out of the hospital. I was in a speed-reading contest. I hit a bookmark.
—Steven Wright

TOP 24 SHORTEST BOOKS IN THE WORLD

A Guide to Arab Democracies
A Journey through the Mind of Dennis Rodman
Amelia Earhart's Guide to the Pacific Ocean
America's Most Popular Lawyers
Bob Dole: The Wild Years
Career Opportunities for History Majors
Career Opportunities for Liberal Arts Majors
Detroit: A Travel Guide
Different Ways to Spell "Bob"
Dr. Kevorkian's Collection of Motivational Speeches
Easy UNIX
Everything Men Know about Women
Everything Women Know about Men
French Hospitality
George Foreman's Big Book of Baby Names
How I Became Charismatic, by Al Gore
How to Sustain a Musical Career, by Art Garfunkel
Human Rights Advances in China
Spotted Owl Recipes, by The Sierra Club
Staple Your Way to Success
The Amish Phone Book
The Difference between Reality and Dilbert
The Engineer's Guide to Fashion
The Book of Virtues, by Bill Clinton

Why pay a dollar for a bookmark? Use the dollar as a bookmark.
—Fred Stoller

A librarian pointed proudly to a patron exiting with four books under her arm. "That lady," boasted the librarian, "gets more out of a mystery novel than any other reader in town. She begins every whodunit in the middle, so she not only wonders how it will come out, but also how it began."
—Bennett Cerf

Further Reading:
How to Read a Book, Paige Turner
Holmes Does It Again, Scott Linyard
Boy Scout's Handbook, Casey Needzit
I Read You Like a Book, Claire Voyant

■ Bosses

To make a long story short, there's nothing like having the boss walk in.
—Doris Lilly

Boss: I've decided to use humor in the workplace. Experts say humor eases tension, which is important in times when the work force is being trimmed. Knock-knock.
Employee: Who's there?
Boss: Not you anymore.
—Scott Adams, *The Dilbert Principle*

If you really want a job done, give it to a busy important man. He'll have his secretary do it.
—Calvin Coolidge

"I'm planning a salary increase for you," the boss told an employee. "When does it become effective?"
"Just as soon as you do."
—Dennis Fakes, *Points with Punch*

■ Bugs, Frogs, and Small Creatures

A company found that it could make a new and remarkable line of cosmetics from the skins of bullfrogs. Immediately it began advertising for frog skins, and one of the first replies was a telegram from a farmer in Texas who stated:

CAN SEND ANY QUANTITY UP TO 100,000. ADVISE.

A telegram was sent back asking for the full hundred thousand. A week later a small box arrived from the farmer with one dried bullfrog and a note: "This is all there was. The noise sure had me fooled."

—Paul Dickson

A frog telephones a psychic hotline and is told, "You are going to meet a beautiful young girl who will want to know everything about you."

"Great," says the frog. "Will I meet her at a party?"

"No," said the psychic. "Next year—in a biology class."

—H. Aaron Cohl

A huge, swarthy-complexioned man walks into a bar with a frog growing out of his ear. "When did you first notice that?" the bartender asks.

"It started as a wart," replies the frog.

A grasshopper hops onto a bar, and the bartender turns to him and says, "Hi, little fellow, did you know that we serve a drink here that's named after you?"

The grasshopper looks at him with surprise and says, "You mean to say you have a drink named Irving?"

—Paul Dickson

A bee's stinging apparatus measures less than one thirtieth of an inch. The other two feet are pure imagination.

—Will Rogers

"I don't kill flies, but I like to mess with their minds. I hold them above globes. They freak out and yell, 'Whoa, I'm way too high!'"

—Bruce Baum

Further Reading:
Beekeeping, A. P. Arry
Chirpin' and Jumpin', Katie Didd
Little Bitty Froggies, Tad Pole
Mosquito Bites, Ivan Awfulitch

■ Bumper Stickers

There are so many religious bumper stickers. I think some people will be surprised when their bumpers make it into heaven and they don't.

—Adam Christling

Seen on cars and motor homes around the country:
- Forget about world peace—Visualize using your turn signal!
- Why do psychics have to ask your name?
- Well, Bill, it all depends upon what the definition of "forgiveness" is. —God
- My kid beat up your honor student
- D.A.R.E. to Keep Cops Off Donuts
  (Donut Abuse & Rotundity Elimination)
- Eliminate and abolish redundancy
- If a woman's place is in the home
  WHY AM I ALWAYS IN THIS CAR!
- He who dies with the most toys is nonetheless dead

Seen on T-shirts and bumpers in San Jose, California:
- Time's fun when you're having flies. —Kermit the Frog
- HAM AND EGGS: A day's work for a chicken;
  a lifetime commitment for a pig
- Ever stop to think . . . and forget to start again?
- I'm not a brat. I'm not, I'm not, I'm not!
- Dare to be naive
- My child was inmate of the month at the county jail.

■ Bureaucrats

Although I can accept talking scarecrows, lions, and great wizards of emerald cities, I find it hard to believe that there is no paperwork involved when your house lands on a witch.

—Dave James

Steve Tatham, on Treasury Secretary Robert Rubin continuing to borrow for the federal government in defiance of the debt ceiling: "Who can pass up all these after-Christmas bargains?"

He uses statistics as a drunken man uses lampposts—for support rather than for illumination.

—Andrew Lang

You may be a bureaucrat if:
- you've counted the pencils in your desk drawer.
- you know your exact retirement date even though it's more than five years away.
- you believe that the more employee rules there are, the fewer employee problems.
- co-workers set their watches by your morning trip to the rest room.

—Dale Dauten, King Features

The only thing that saves us from bureaucracy is its inefficiency.

—Eugene McCarthy

■ Buses

Now all the buses want exact change. I figure if I give them exact change, they should take me exactly where I want to go.

—George Wallace

When I was a teenager in Chicago, there was one bus driver on the Washington Boulevard route who had hung one of those shrunken heads over his coin box. He explained to curious passengers, "He wouldn't move to the rear of the bus."

A bus repairman was filling out a report on a highway accident. Then he came to the question, "Disposition of passengers?" He wrote, "Mad as can be."

■ Business

Interviewer to job applicant: "Can you come up with any reason you want this job other than your parents want you out of their house?"
—Mike Shapiro in *The Wall Street Journal*

One of my first office jobs was cleaning the windows on the envelopes.
—Rita Rudner

The closest to perfection a person ever comes is when he fills out a job application.
—Ken Kraft

Husband, returning home after a hard day at the office: "Dexter got a gold parachute, Nolan got a golden handshake, and I got a golden retriever."

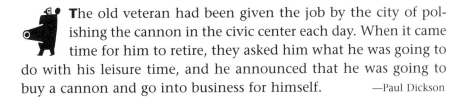 **T**he old veteran had been given the job by the city of polishing the cannon in the civic center each day. When it came time for him to retire, they asked him what he was going to do with his leisure time, and he announced that he was going to buy a cannon and go into business for himself.
—Paul Dickson

When my aunt Maude was a secretary at the Board of Trade in Chicago, her boss would send her out without fail every working day about noon to a deluxe delicatessen down the block to order him a turkey club sandwich and a container of nonfat milk. After her first year on the job, Maude took to making the club sandwich at home, and bringing a container of milk to the office. She cleared five dollars every day on the transaction.

There's a trick to not being late. Just set your clock fifteen minutes ahead, and you'll never be late. Of course, you may get fired for leaving early.

An executive approached a mason and asked him what he was doing. The mason replied, "I'm mixing mortar that is going to tenderly and devotedly hold each of these bricks in place. And one by one, I'm going to set these bricks until they begin to take shape. They will rise row by row toward the heavens and eventually form a tall tower—the tower of a court building. It will stand for years and years as a symbol of truth and justice. This edifice will stand as a beacon, representing all that is right in America."

"You idiot!" the executive bellowed. "This is supposed to be a garage!"
                                                              —Gene Perret

An expert is somebody who is more than fifty miles away from home, has no responsibility for implementing the advice he gives, and shows slides.   —Edwin Meese III, the *New York Times*, January 24, 1984

After eight months in the Belgian Congo filming *Roots of Heaven*, Darryl Zanuck collected a trunkful of shrunken heads from one of the cannibal tribes. When he returned, he decided they might be worth something and called up Saks Fifth Avenue, Beverly Hills. He asked the switchboard operator, "To whom do I speak about selling some shrunken heads?"

"One moment please."

There was a clicking sound, then a firm, businesslike voice: "This is the head buyer speaking."

One New York shoe store ordered a large consignment of shoes from a manufacturer in Buffalo. A week later the store manager received a letter saying, "Sorry, we cannot fill your order until full payment is made on the last one."

The manager wrote back, "Please cancel the new order. I can't wait that long."
                                                              —Joey Adams

A traveler stopped to observe the curious behavior of a farmer who was plowing his field. A single mule hitched to the plow was wearing blinders, and the farmer was yelling, "Giddyap, Pete! Giddyap, Herb! Giddyap, Ol' Bill! Giddyap, Jeb!"

After watching the farmer carry on like this for a while, the traveler asked, "Say, mister—how many names does that mule have?"

"Just one—his name is Pete."

"Then why do you call out Herb and Bill and—"

"It's like this," explained the farmer. "If Ol' Pete knew he was doing this work alone, I couldn't make him do it. But if he thinks he's got three other mules workin' alongside of him, he does the job all by himself."

"What a marvelous idea!" exclaimed the traveler.

And when he got back to his corporate office in New York, he invented the committee.

Workplace jargon inspired by the daily cartoon *Dilbert:*

Adminisphere: The rarefied organizational layers beginning just above the rank and file. Decisions that fall from the adminisphere are often profoundly inappropriate or irrelevant to the problems they were designed to solve.

Alpha Geek: The most knowledgeable, technically proficient person in an office or work group.

Blamestorming: Sitting around in a group discussing why a deadline was missed or a project failed and who was responsible.

Body Nazis: Hard-core exercise and weightlifting fanatics who look down on anyone who doesn't work out obsessively.

CLM (Career Limiting Move): Used among microserfs to describe ill-advised activity. Trashing your boss while he or she is within earshot is a serious CLM.

Chainsaw consultant: An outside expert brought in to reduce the employee headcount, leaving the brass with clean hands.

Chips and Salsa: Chips refers to hardware, salsa refers to software, as in, "Well, first we gotta figure out if the problem's in your chips or in your salsa."

Cube Farm: An office filled with cubicles (alternate: veal pens).

Deinstalled: Euphemism for being fired. Heard on the voice mail of a vice president at a downsizing computer firm: "You have reached the number of a deinstalled vice president. Please dial our main number and ask the operator for assistance." (See also "Decruitment.")

Dilberted: To be exploited and oppressed by your boss. Derived from the experiences of Dilbert, the geek-in-hell comic strip character. "I've been Dilberted again. The old man revised the specs for the fourth time this week."

Flight Risk: Used to describe employees who are suspected of planning to leave the company or department soon.

404: Clueless. From the World Wide Web error message "404 Not Found," meaning that the requested document could not be located. Usage: "Don't bother asking him; he's 404, man."

Generica: Features of the American landscape that are exactly the same no matter where one is, such as fast food joints, strip malls, subdivisions. Usage: "We were so lost in generica that I forgot what city we were in."

GOOD Job: A "Get Out Of Debt" job. A well-paying job people take in order to pay off their debts, which they will quit as soon as they are solvent again.

Idea Hamsters: People who always seem to have their idea generators running.

Irritainment: Entertainment and media spectacles that are annoying but you find yourself unable to stop watching them. The O. J. trials were a prime example.

Mouse Potato:The on-line generation's answer to the couch potato.

Ohno-second: That minuscule fraction of time in which you realize that you've just made a *big* mistake.

Percussive Maintenance: The fine art of whacking an electronic device to get it to work again.

Prairie Dogging: When someone yells or drops something loudly in a cube farm, and people's heads pop up over the walls to see what's going on.

Seagull Manager: A manager who flies in, makes a lot of noise, craps over everything and then leaves.

SITCOM: What a yuppie couples turn into when they have children and one of them stops working to stay home with the kids. Stands for Single Income, Two Children, Oppressive Mortgage.

Stress Puppy: A person who seems to thrive on being stressed out and whiney.

Swiped Out: An ATM or credit card that has been rendered useless because the magnetic strip is worn away from extensive use.

Tourists: People who take training classes just to get a vacation from their jobs. Example: "We had three serious students in the class; the rest were just tourists."

Treeware: Hacker slang for documentation or other printed material.

Vulcan Nerve Pinch: The taxing hand position required to reach all the appropriate keys for certain commands. For instance, the warm re-boot for a PC involves simultaneously pressing the Control key, the Alt key, and the Delete key (also known as the "three-finger salute").

Xerox Subsidy: Euphemism for swiping free photocopies from one's workplace.

"Business ethics," the lawyer told his son, "is something you couldn't do without. Take today for instance. A man comes in and gives me a hundred-dollar bill to clear up his account. After he leaves, I find two bills stuck together. He has paid me two hundred instead of one. Here, my son, enters the question of business ethics. Should I tell my partner or shouldn't I?"

PLEASE NOTICE:

You may have noticed the increased amount of notices for you to notice. Some of our notices have not been noticed. This is very noticeable. It has been noticed that the responses to the notices have been noticeably unnoticed. This notice is to remind you to notice the notices and respond to the notices because we do not want the notices to go unnoticed. Signed, The Department of Notification.

Businessman, kneeling at feet of young woman: "Marry me, Judith—with the understanding, of course, that past performance is not a guarantee of future results." —Cheney in *The Wall Street Journal*

There was a silk manufacturer who had really prospered. He had started off as a cutter, taken courses in business administration at night school, jumped to the rank of executive, and eventually reached the top as a full partner in the firm. When his partner died, he was head man. One morning, near the end of his most profitable year, his secretary brought in checks for him to sign.

"This one," she explained, "is for the house you're buying in Long Island. It's for $200,000."

"That's wonderful," said the manufacturer, scrawling his name.

"This one for $825,000 is for the office we're opening in Paris."

"Good."

"This one covers your son's wedding present. It's for $125,000."

"He deserves it. He's a good boy."

"And now," said the secretary, "I'd like to ask for a raise. I've been with you for more than two years. Would fifteen dollars be all right?"

"Fifteen dollars!" shouted the manufacturer. "What do you think I am, a millionaire?"

—Myron Cohen

Signs that your company has gone too far with its cost cutting:
- The head of purchasing goes to employees' homes and steals back office supplies.
- Water coolers are coin-operated.
- To get paid company life insurance, you have to sell ten policies to relatives.
- You have to call in sick on a 900 number.
- Company blood drives are now considered a profit center.

—Dale Dauten, King Features

A Rochester, New York, firm posted a notice announcing it would pay a hundred dollars to anyone who came up with an idea that could save the company money immediately. The first winner was an employee who suggested that the award be cut to fifty dollars.

—*Executive Speechwriter Newsletter*

Further Reading:
The Sweat Shop, Hiram Cheap
Employment Handbook, Ernie Living

C

■ California

He's from California. Now, California isn't for everybody. As Fred Allen said, "California is a fine place to live—if you happen to be an orange."

The California school system leaves a lot to be desired. A few years ago, my daughter brought home this as her first reader: "See Spot. See Spot run. Spot is a totally awesome dog. See Dick and Jane. See them catch a gnarly wave. 'Tubular,' says Dick. 'Fer sher,' says Jane." If I thought that her teacher could read, I would have written a nasty letter.
—Robert G. Lee

So you call this California, the land of golden sunshine, do you? Well, let me tell you something. Every day of every year the sun shines on New York three hours before it shines on you, so all California gets is New York's secondhand sunshine. Think that one over.
—James Thornton

California is crowded with condos. One student was asked by his teacher, "What happened in 1492?"

The kid answered, "How would I know? I live on the twelfth floor!"

Ronald Reagan, speaking to an audience in Minnesota: "I feel very much at home here in your lovely farm and dairy country. I'm a rancher myself. I take a little kidding now and then in Washington about our ranch. But you know, even some Midwesterners admit that cattle fit right into the California scene. They stand around all day in the sun, no clothes on, eating salad. I just want to assure you that cows in California are the same as cows in Minnesota. Except, of course, in California they have their teeth capped."

Hear about the New Age church in California? It has three commandments and seven suggestions.

—H. Aaron Cohl

The only difference between California and yogurt is that yogurt has active culture.

—Woody Allen

"I really loved my vacation in California," said the lady on the plane to the man sitting next to her.

"Where did you stay?" he asked.

"San Joe-Say."

"Madam, in California we pronounce the 'J' as 'H.' We say 'San Hosay.' How long were you there?"

The woman thought for a moment, then responded carefully, "All of Hune and most of Huly."

In California, we have a different kind of police. You get stopped in West Hollywood, "Stop! Those shoes don't go with those pants."

—Robin Williams

The mayor of Foster City, California, had just called the city council to order, when a violent earthquake occurred. The mayor dove out of the nearest window, closely followed by the council members. The faithful secretary noted in the record, "Upon motion of the city hall, the meeting was unanimously adjourned."

Tourist: I'm here for the winter.
Californian: You've come to the wrong place. We don't have one!

Everybody in Los Angeles is in therapy. It's a good thing they don't have parking spaces for the emotionally handicapped. There'd be no place to park.
—Jackson Perdue

A Californian went to Texas to attend a funeral. Unfortunately, no one was willing to speak for the deceased. Nobody had a kind word about him. After a long period of silence, the Californian stood up and said, "If nobody's going to say anything about that poor guy, I'd like to say a few words about California."

"I'm going to be a big star!" In California, we call that sort of statement creative visualization. In the other forty-nine states, it's called self-delusion.
—Maureen Brownsey

A mind reader moved to California. In two weeks he almost died because he had nothing to do!

California has some of the richest areas in the country. In one town near Hollywood at Christmas, they give baskets of food to people with only one Mercedes!

A pair of New York dockworkers were having their vacation in Southern California. While they were out playing tennis, one said to the other, "Whew, it's hot here, isn't it?"

"Of course it is," said his companion. "Are you forgetting how far we are from the ocean?"

■ Camps and Camping

Sherlock Holmes and Watson were camping in the forest. They had gone to bed and were lying beneath the night sky. Holmes said, "Watson, look up. What do you see?"

Watson obliged and answered, "I see thousands of stars."

"And what does that mean to you?" Holmes asked.

"I suppose it means that of all the planets in the universe, we are truly fortunate to be here on Earth. We are small in God's eyes, but should struggle every day to be worthy of our blessings. In a meteorological sense, it means we'll have a sunny day tomorrow. What does it mean to you, Holmes?"

"To me, it means someone has stolen our tent."

Hung across the gate of a Montana nudist camp: Clothed for the winter.

NATIONAL PARK SURVEYS

The following are actual comments received in 1996 from the Bridger-Teton National Forest registration sheets and comment cards:

- Trails need to be wider, so people can walk while holding hands.
- Instead of a permit system or regulations, the Forest Service needs to reduce world-wide population growth to limit the number of visitors to wilderness.
- Ban walking sticks in wilderness. Hikers that use walking sticks are more likely to chase animals.
- Trail needs to be reconstructed. Please avoid building trails that go uphill.
- Too many bugs and leaches and spiders and spider webs. Please spray the wilderness to rid the area of these pests.
- Please pave the trails, so they can be plowed of snow during the winter.
- Chairlifts need to be in some places, so that we can get to wonderful views without having to hike to them.
- The coyotes made too much noise last night and kept me awake. Please eradicate these annoying animals.
- A small deer came into my camp and stole my jar of pickles. Is there a way I can get reimbursed?

- Reflectors need to be placed on trees every fifty feet, so people can hike at night with flashlights.
- Escalators would help on steep uphill sections.
- Need more signs to keep area pristine.
- A McDonald's would be nice at the trailhead.
- The places where trails do not exist are not well marked.
- I brought lots of sandwich makings, but forgot bread. If you have extra bread, leave it in the yellow tent at V Lake.

■ Catholicism

Nancy Williamson, a young Catholic of good breeding, shocked her family by falling in love with Norman Worthington, a loudmouthed stockbroker who happened to be a Baptist. The young lovers married and lived happily ever after—as long as they did not discuss religion. Norman, it seems, would from time to time make rather disparaging remarks about Nancy's childhood faith, his strong opinion in no way influenced by any knowledge of Catholicism.

One fateful year, the couple decided to go on vacation to Ireland. Quite concerned about Norman's outspokenness, Nancy extracted a promise from him that he would not say anything critical of the Catholic church.

One evening they were playing darts in the local pub when news came over the radio that the Pope was ill. Immediately everyone crowded around the radio to listen.

"Oh, to heck with the Pope," said Norman. "Let's get on with the game."

He woke up in the hospital in a full body cast, and there was his sobbing wife sitting next to him. "Oh, Norman," she cried, "didn't I warn you not to say anything about their religion?"

"Yeah," said Norman. "But you didn't tell me the Pope was a Catholic."

John F. Kennedy employed humor to dispose of the religious issue in the 1960 campaign. "The reporters are constantly asking me my views of the Pope's infallibility," he declared. "And so I asked my friend Cardinal Spellman what I should say when reporters ask me whether I feel the Pope is infallible. And Cardinal Spellman said, 'I don't know what to tell you, Senator. All I know is that he keeps calling me Spillman.'"   —Bob Dole

Paddy O'Casey was on his death bed when his wife Colleen tiptoed into the bedroom and asked if he had any last requests. "Actually, my dear, there is one thing I really would like before I go off to that great shamrock patch in the sky," Paddy whispered. "A piece of that wonderful chocolate cake of yours."

"Oh, but you can't have that," his wife exclaimed. "I'm saving it for the wake."   —H. Aaron Cohl

Poor Walter Johnson had spent his life making wrong decisions. If he bet on a horse, it would lose; if he chose one elevator rather than another, it was the one he chose that stalled between floors; the line he picked before the bank teller's cage never moved; the lane he chose in traffic crawled; the day he picked for a picnic was the day of a cloudburst. In his twenties, he dated identical twin sisters, finally choosing one over the other. After graduating from law school, he married her, and she turned into a horrible shrew while her sister remained sweet and cheerful. And so it went, day after day, year after year.

Then, once, it became necessary for Johnson to travel to Bogata, Columbia immediately on company business. He was relieved to discover that only one airline had a flight that would get him there on time. So not having to risk a decision, he booked a reservation. Since he had made no decision, how could he possibly come to grief? He boarded the plane. Imagine his horror when, somewhere over treacherous mountains, the plane's engines caught fire, and it became obvious the plane would crash in moments.

Johnson broke into fervent prayer to his favorite saint, Francis.

He pleaded, "I have never in my life made the right choice. Why this should be, I don't know, but I have borne my cross and have not complained. On this occasion, however, I did not make a choice; this was the only plane I could take and I had to take it. Why, then, am I being punished?"

He had no sooner finished when a giant hand swooped down out of the clouds and snatched him from the plane. There he was, miraculously suspended two miles above the earth's surface, while the plane spiraled downward far below.

A heavenly voice came down from the clouds. "My son, I can save you, if you have in truth called upon me."

"Yes, I called on you," cried Johnson. "I called on you, Saint Francis."

"Ah," said the heavenly voice, "Saint Francis Xavier or Saint Francis of Assisi?"

A rabbi went to a racetrack for the first time in his life. As he walked in he couldn't help but notice a Catholic priest there. He figured: If I stay close to him, I'll learn what to do.

The first race was about to start. The rabbi watched the priest. The priest looked over the horses, came to Number 3, and made a few signs over it. Later, in the first race Number 3 came in and paid $27. The rabbi thought: This is really something.

The second race was about to start. The priest went over, examined the horses, picked out Number 7, made a few signs over it, and sure enough, Number 7 came in and paid $48. It was wonderful.

So when the third race was about to start, the rabbi said, "This is for me!" When the priest made a few signs over Number 9, the rabbi went and put all the money he had on Number 9.

Needless to say, Number 9 never showed up in the field. So after the race the rabbi went over to the good father and explained that he saw him give a blessing, he'd lost all his money, and he didn't understand what had happened.

And the priest said, "Sorry I am that you lost all your money. But 'tis a shame you don't know the difference between a blessing and the last rites."

—Hal McKay

My mother is Jewish; my father is Catholic. I was brought up Catholic, but with a Jewish mind. When I went to confession, I always brought a lawyer with me. "Bless me, Father, for I have sinned . . . I think you know Mr. Cohen?"

—Bill Maher

■ Cats

I gave my cat a bath the other day. . . . He sat there, he enjoyed it, it was fun for me. The fur would stick to my tongue, but other than that it was OK.   —Steve Martin

My elderly aunt Sally had a wonderful, faithful cat. One fateful day, a neighbor accidentally ran over the cat while backing out of his driveway. The man went to Aunt Sally and said, "I'm terribly sorry about your cat. I'd like to replace him."

"That's so nice of you!" said the old woman, deeply touched. "How good are you at catching mice?"

A man who carries a cat by the tail learns something he can learn in no other way.   —Mark Twain

■ Charity

A good deed never goes unpunished.   —Gore Vidal

Hear about the great bank robbery in Israel? They got ten thousand dollars in cash and more than sixty million dollars in anonymous pledges.   —Gene Baylos

Physical fitness was an important goal for President Kennedy. In line with this, he told a story about Arthur Goldberg, his secretary of labor: Goldberg went mountain climbing. But up near the peak, he got separated from all the others. The Red Cross sent climbers to try to find him. As they roamed over the mountain they shouted, "Goldberg! Goldberg! It's the Red Cross."

Finally a distant voice echoed down the mountain, saying, "I gave at the office!"   —Melvin Berger

Further Reading:
Good Works, Ben Evolent
Volunteer's Guidebook, Linda Hand
Rules for Living, Sharon Sharalike

■ Christmas

I haven't taken my Christmas lights down. They look so nice on the pumpkin.
—Winston Spear

One Christmas eve, I stopped in a small Southern town on my way to visit cousin Bobby Lee. I needed some air in my tires, but when I explained this to the service station owner, he couldn't understand a word I was saying. So I wrote him a note. "Oh," he exclaimed, "You all wah-ahnt aaah in your tahaahs!"

I also needed to have my oil checked, but I was too chicken to ask. When a Southerner says the words "oil" and "all," they sound different to him but not to me.

I stayed overnight at a Motel 6 but before I went to bed, I wandered over to the Baptist church for the annual town Christmas pageant. It was produced with great skill, talent, and creativity. But one small feature bothered me. The Three Wise Men were wearing firemen's helmets. Totally unable to come up with a reason or explanation, I left. At a 7-Eleven on the edge of town, I asked the lady behind the counter about the helmets. She exploded into a rage, yelling at me, "Don't y'all evah read the Baaah-bul?"

I assured her that I did, but simply couldn't recall anything about firemen in the Bible.

She said, "That just shows how ignorant y'all are. Ever'body knows it says in the Bahbul, 'The three wise men came from afaaahr!'"

While the art class was setting up a Christmas scene on the school lawn, one of the boys asked uncertainly, "Where should I put the three wise guys?"

In a California town, a resident set up on his lawn a floodlighted, paper-maché Santa Claus in an elaborate sleigh drawn by six reindeer, and had all his trees and shrubs festooned with varicolored lights. The man who lived directly opposite contented himself with a single wreath in his window and a sign on his gate reading: "See our display across the street."

—Bennett Cerf

Chuck Bridwell is the minister of the University Baptist Church of Coral Gables, Florida. Each year, he directs the Miami Christmas Pageant, which is held in the twenty-four hundred seat Dade County Auditorium. All eight performances are sold out every year. The cast numbers over four hundred people and includes live animals. There are camels for the three wise men, sheep for the shepherds, and a donkey for Mary and Joseph to use on their journey to Bethlehem. I'll let Chuck take the story from here:

"One year our seasoned donkey died, so we were forced to find another one. Our animal trainer found a replacement, but this donkey had never been on stage before. Our last dress rehearsal was a bit shaky; however, the new donkey managed to successfully carry Mary, with Joseph by her side, across the stage.

"On opening night, the time came for Mary and Joseph to make their journey to Bethlehem. With Mary on its back, the donkey came about fifteen feet on stage, stared up at the spotlight and started backing up towards the painted hills of Judea. When his rear end touched the backdrop, he froze.

"I was on the headset yelling for the lighting director to cut the spotlight. A few more actors joined Joseph in trying to encourage the donkey to complete his journey across the stage. When the spotlight was finally cut, the regular stage lights revealed a half-dozen actors pulling the donkey across the stage, a very shaken Mary still clinging to his back.

"That's when the narrator delivered his next line, which brought a roar of laughter and applause. He said, 'Yes, it was a l-o-o-o-o-ng journey to Bethlehem.'"

—David Naster

In Salt Lake City a dilatory housewife bought a last-minute box of one hundred identical Christmas cards, and, not even pausing to read the message inscribed thereon, feverishly dispatched them to the ninety-nine relatives and acquaintances whose own greetings already were displayed on her piano top and mantel. Some days later she accidentally picked up the one card left, and read what it said in a state of shock: "This little card is just to say, 'A gift you'll love is on its way.'"

—Bennett Cerf

Further Reading:
Christmas for Baldies, Yule Brynner
Stunned Over Christmas, Holly Daze
Playing with the Christmas Fire, Yule B. Sari
Happy New Year!, Mary Christmas

■ Church

The parking lot at Little Brown Church was so small that the first thing each parishioner prayed for when he or she got to church on Sunday morning was a place to park the car.

Malcolm Diamond, an amiable and well-respected elderly African American who had been highly successful in business, decided that he wanted to become a member of an Episcopal church near his home. He called on the pastor of this fashionable church and expressed his desire. "My dear fellow," said the rector, "I don't think you would be happy here. You would be most uncomfortable among my people and I am afraid it would be quite embarrassing to you and perhaps to them. I suggest you pray and meditate and see if God does not give you some direction."

A week later, Diamond met the rector on the street. "Reverend," he announced, "I took your advice and prayed and meditated and finally God sent me word. He said I shouldn't bother any more trying to join your church; he said he's been trying to get in there for years without success."

Small town: Where people go to church on Sunday to see who didn't.

—Larry Wilde

Taken to church for the first time, a four-year-old girl was mystified when the entire congregation knelt. "What are they doing?" she asked her mother.

"Ss-s-h," cautioned the mother. "They're praying."

"What?" exclaimed the four-year-old. "With their clothes on?"

—Bennett Cerf

Bob Brown shared the story of his father's embarrassing mishap in church. When finished helping with communion, his father sat down beside Bob's mother and did what he always did when he sat down beside her—gave her a hug and a little peck on the cheek. Then he looked up and saw his wife in the row in front of him

—Stephen Douglas Williford

Bennett Cerf reported that back in the 1950s a beatnik wandered into church, and on the way out, told the Reverend, "You were swinging, Daddy-o. You were way out."

"What was that again?" inquired the Reverend, knitting his brow.

"I mean," amplified the cat, "I dug your jive. I read you so good I put fifty big fish in your collection plate."

"Ah," beamed the Reverend, grasping the beatnik's hand. "Cool, man, cool!"

Once my wife was asked to host the monthly meeting of the women's fellowship. Instead of their planned discussion of world missions, the ladies spent most of the time chattering about their arthritic aches and pains, their children's or grandchildren's' tonsils and adenoids, and their husbands' enlarged prostates, slipped discs, and weak hearts. When my wife returned home, I asked her how the meeting had gone. "Well," she said, "it was not so much a study of missions as an organ recital!"

When I was holding the 9:30 service one Sunday morning, I noticed that one parishioner was very late. To my surprise, he was at the 11 o'clock service as well. But when the congregation rose to sing the hymn before the sermon, he left, murmuring to the usher: "This is where I came in."

In the midst of a sermon, a man jumped up. "Brethren!" he shouted. "I have been a miserable, contemptible sinner for years, and never knew it before tonight—"

A man in the nearby pew announced, "Sit down, Brother. The rest of us knew it all the time."

After Bob, the guest preacher, finished his sermon, he was asked to baptize a woman, so he did. Since the stairs were slippery, he held the woman's arm and walked the steps with her to her dressing room. However, he couldn't stay over there. He had to go to his dressing room on the other side of the baptistery, quickly get dressed, go downstairs, and shake hands with congregation members as they left. Normally, all he would have to do is re-enter the baptistery and walk to the other side, behind the closed curtains. But this baptistery didn't have curtains. Just some artificial plants at the front of the baptistery. Bob was stuck.

So, he did what seemed to be the most logical thing to do. During the announcements, he slithered back down the stairs and swam underwater to the other side. As he was swimming underwater, he happened to look at the wall of the baptistery facing the auditorium. It was then that Bob made the discovery.

What Bob saw when he looked at the wall was hundreds of people looking back at him. The wall was glass. Bob's mouth dropped like a big-mouthed bass, and he about drowned. It's a good thing he didn't. Everyone was laughing too hard to help.

—Stephen Douglas Williford

Herbert Tarr, author of *For Heaven's Sake*, received a letter from a Long Islander stating that her church was in a hopeless financial mess.

"We've tried bingo games, grab-bags, box socials, benefit movie openings—everything," she complained. "Can't you suggest something, no matter how drastic, to keep our church afloat?"

Mr. Tarr answered, "Try religion."   —Bennett Cerf

The services at the Little Brown Church always include a group reading of the Twenty-third Psalm. One Palm Sunday a visitor with a shrill, penetrating voice got about ten words ahead of the rest of the congregation at the beginning and resolutely maintained her lead to the very end.

At the end of the services, one longtime member asked another, "Who was that irritating lady who was always by the still waters while the rest of us were lying down in green pastures?"

At the Harvest Festival in church the area behind the pulpit was piled high with tins of fruit for the old-age pensioners. We had collected the tinned fruit from door to door. Most of it came from old-age pensioners.   —Clive James

Philadelphia (UPI)—Parishioners entering the Tindley United Methodist Church for Sunday services thought they were passing a handyman working on a stained-glass window in the back of the church. It wasn't until one hour later, when the pastor, the Reverend Maron O. Ballard, asked why part of the window was missing, that they discovered the man was a thief. "We've never had anything like this happen before," Reverend Ballard said. "People have broken windows, and we've had burglars, but no one has ever stolen a window." —cited by Bud and Lolo Delaney, *The Laugh Journal*

Church sign: "This is a Ch—ch. What is missing?"

On a church bulletin board in Fairbury, Illinois: "Even moderation ought not to be practiced to excess."

 A chap named Charlie took an active part in just about everything that was going on in his pleasant little home town, except church services. Try as she would, his wife just couldn't talk him into attending services on Sunday morning.

One Sunday, however, she broke down his resistance, and even persuaded him to greet people at the door. He hailed almost everybody by their first name, until the church was filled and the services about to begin. At the last moment a straggler appeared. Charlie shook his hand, told him how glad he was to see him in church, and expressed the hope he'd be back the following Sunday.

"I'll be back all right," the straggler assured him cheerfully, then walked down the aisle and up into the pulpit to start the services.

—Bennett Cerf

Just as the preacher was about to enter the pulpit, a woman in the congregation handed him a note about her husband. It read: "Bill Adams having gone to sea, his wife desires the congregation's prayers for his safety." The preacher, pressed for time, read the note too hastily, telling the congregation, "Bill Adams, having gone to see his wife, desires the prayers of the congregation for his safety."

Nurse: What church do you belong to?
Patient: None.
Nurse: Well, what church do you go to when you go?
Patient: If you must know, the church which I stay away from most of the time when I don't go is the Baptist.

"Nice to see you're attending church again," I said to crotchety Mr. Walters, when I ran into him at the local grocery store. "Is it because of my sermons?"

"Not yours," was the reply. "My wife's."

The following Sunday, Mr. Walters got up and walked out right in the middle of my sermon. I asked his wife if I had somehow offended him. Her reply: "It was nothing personal, Reverend. He was just sleepwalking."

I have noted in my travels that many people have nothing but praise for the church—especially when the collection plate is passed around!

As rector in an Episcopalian church, Father Terrance C. Roper understands the congregation's anxiety when it comes to the business affairs of the church. The need for more funds is never an easy subject to discuss. Keeping that in mind, Father Roper approached his flock with the following during one of his Sunday sermons. "It is time now to make a joyous noise unto the Lord," he said. "Now remember the Lord can clearly hear this joyous noise, and the Lord wants to hear this joyous noise.

"You all look confused. Allow me to explain. What is that joyous noise? Why that joyous noise is simply the glorious sound of hundreds of checks being simultaneously ripped from your checkbooks."

—David Naster

■ Church Bulletins

The order of service of the Congregational Christian Church of Red Cloud, Nebraska, listed the sermon topic "Gossip." Immediately following was the hymn "I Love to Tell the Story."

Writing in *The Christian Century*, Martin E. Marty shares some gleanings from church bulletins, sent in by readers:
- "'Surly the Presence of the Lord' by: Chamber Choir." (God as grump?)
- "Leader: The Living God send us froth to serve." (On the menu at the megachurch?)

- "Solo: 'The Solid Rock/'Tis So Sweet to Rust in Jesus.'" (Especially oily in the morning.)
- "Births: Stewart and Amy had a baby girl on August 7 in Wisconsin. Material grandmother is Mary." (A real Madonna, that old girl.)
- Assembly of God report on church attendance: "A very sweet presence of the Ford was in our praise and worship service." (Better than a sour old Olds.)
- Independence Day announcement: "Long ago, canons were fired on this day." (Today it's hard even to get rid of subdeacons.)
- *The Disciple* magazine reported that "five Disciples . . . were indicted into the Disciples Society for Faith and Reason this spring." (They had a cloud of witnesses as uninducted co-conspirators.)
- "People: Christ dwells in our hearts through faith that we may be rotted and grounded in love." (In that great compost heap of the human heart.)
- Financial announcement: "We exceeded our mission giving goal and our weekly budget was suppressed." (Henceforth to be regarded with unsurpassed secrecy.)
- Rochester, Minnesota, Meadow Park Church of Christ advertisement: "Good Friday Worship: 'This Blood's For You!'" (The Lite of the World.)
- Trustees' report, a church in Connecticut: "The eves of the education wing need repair." (Adam needed work too.)
- "Mission and Service Commission wants to thank all those who participated in the food panty drive." (For undercover needs.)
- Announcement of a high school youth event: "There is a big teat in store for everyone who comes to the meeting tonight." (Don't be cowed by that.)
- Presbyterian Church (USA) news: "The 205th General Assembly . . . calls on Congress and the Clinton administration to give priority to a single-prayer system [in the health bill]." (Enough of this trifaith invocation stuff.)
- "Congregation: A city set on a hill cannot be had." (Never heard of Rome or Boston?)
- Lutheran church announcement: "The Associated Ministries will hose Dr. Liebenow in an informal 'Coffee and Conversation.'" (Let us spray.)

MORE CHURCH BULLETIN BLOOPERS

- "Scouts are saving aluminum cans, bottles, and other items to be recycled. Proceeds will be used to cripple children."
- "The Ladies Bible Study will be held Thursday morning at 10. All ladies are invited to lunch in the Fellowship Hall after the B. S. is done."
- "The Pastor would appreciate it if the ladies of the congregation would lend him their electric girdles for the pancake breakfast next Sunday morning."
- "The audience is asked to remain seated until the end of the recession."
- "Low Self-Esteem Support Group will meet Thursday at 7 to 8:30 P.M. Please use the back door."
- "Pastor is on vacation. Massages can be given to church secretary."
- "The third verse of 'Blessed Assurance' will be sung without accomplishment."
- "The Rev. Merriwether spoke briefly, much to the delight of the audience."
- "The pastor will preach his farewell message, after which the choir will sing, 'Break Forth into Joy.'"
- "Next Sunday Mrs. Vinson will be soloist for the morning service. The pastor will then speak on 'It's a Terrible Experience'."
- On a church bulletin during the minister's illness: "God is good —Dr. Hargreaves is better."
- "The outreach committee has enlisted twenty-five visitors to make calls on people who are not afflicted with any church."
- The Hampton United Methodist Church will sponsor a Harvest Supper on Saturday, October 1. The menu for the evening will be a traditional New England boiled sinner, rolls, homemade apple pie, coffee, tea, and cider.

The parish bulletin for Blessed Virgin Mary Help of Christians church in Woodside, New York, included a notice for a "Trip to Rome, Assisi & Venus."

■ Clichés and Proverbs

Where do clichés come from? My grandfather says [in wonder], "You just tell a couple of jokes, and you're riding the gravy train?" First of all, it's hard to write jokes. Second of all, what is a gravy train? I didn't know they were actually hauling gravy by rail. People gather around big mounds of mashed potatoes waiting for the 5:15 gravy train to show up?
—Rich Hall

You can lead a horse to water. If he drowns, never give him mouth to mouth.
—Scott Wood

You've buttered your bread—now sleep in it.
—Gracie Allen

Some see the glass as half-empty, some see the glass as half-full. I see the glass as too big.
—George Carlin

Show me a man with both feet on the ground, and I'll show you a man who can't put his pants on.
—Joe E. Lewis

On the other hand, you have different fingers.
—Steven Wright

I made quite a name for myself back home. I left when I found out what it was.
—Herb Shriner

Where there's a will, I want to be in it.

At one point we decided to fight fire with fire. Well, basically . . . your house burned even faster.
—Anonymous firefighter

After Quasimodo's death, the bishop of the cathedral of Notre Dame sent word through the streets of Paris that a new bellringer was needed. The bishop decided to conduct the interviews personally and went up into the belfry to begin the screening process. After observing several applicants demonstrate their skills, he was about to call it a day when a lone, armless man announced that he was there to apply for the bellringer's job.

The bishop was incredulous. "You have no arms!" he said.

"No matter," said the man, "observe!" He then began striking the bells with his face, producing a beautiful melody on the carillon.

The bishop listened in astonishment, convinced that he had finally found a suitable replacement for Quasimodo.

Suddenly, rushing forward to strike a bell, the armless man tripped, and plunged headlong out of the belfry window to his death in the street below.

The stunned bishop rushed to the street. By the time he reached the man's side, a crowd had gathered around the fallen figure, drawn by the beautiful melody they had heard only moments before. As they silently parted to let the bishop through, one of them asked, "Bishop, who was this man?"

"I don't know his name," the bishop replied thoughtfully. "But his face rings a bell."

SAME STORY, PART 2

The following day, despite the sadness weighing on his heart due to the unfortunate death of the armless campanologist, the bishop continued interviewing for the bellringer of Notre Dame.

The first man to approach him said, "Your excellency, I am the brother of the poor, armless wretch that fell to his death from this very belfry yesterday. I pray that you honor his life by allowing me to replace him in this duty."

The bishop agreed to give the man an audition, but as the armless man's brother stooped to pick up a mallet to strike the first bell, he groaned, clutched at his chest, and died on the spot.

Two monks, hearing the bishop's cries of grief at this second tragedy, rushed up the stairs to his side. "What has happened?" the first breathlessly asked. "Who is this man?"

"I don't know his name," sighed the distraught bishop. "But he's a dead ringer for his brother."

A first grade teacher collected well-known proverbs. She gave each child in her class the first half of a proverb and had them come up with the rest. Their insights may surprise you:

- As you shall make your bed so shall you . . . mess it up.
- Better be safe than . . . punch a 5th grader.
- Strike while the . . . bug is close.
- It's always darkest before . . . daylight savings time.
- Never under estimate the power of . . . termites.
- You can lead a horse to water but . . . how?
- Don't bite the hand that . . . looks dirty.
- No news is . . . impossible.
- A miss is as good as a . . . mister.
- You can't teach an old dog new . . . math.
- If you lie down with dogs, you'll . . . stink in the morning.
- Love all, trust . . . me.
- The pen is mightier than the . . . pigs.
- An idle mind is . . . the best way to relax.
- Where there is smoke there is . . . pollution.
- Happy the bride who . . . gets all the presents.
- A penny saved is . . . not much.
- Two is company, three is . . . the Musketeers.
- Don't put off until tomorrow what . . . you put on to go to bed.
- Laugh and the whole world laughs with you, cry and . . . you have to blow your nose.
- None are so blind as . . . Helen Keller.
- Children should be seen and not . . . spanked or grounded.
- If at first you do not succeed . . . get new batteries.
- You get out of something what you . . . see pictured on the box.
- When the blind leadeth the blind . . . get out of the way.
- There is no fool like . . . Aunt Edie.

■ Clothes

When a woman goes to her closet and says, "I don't have anything to wear," she really means, "I don't have anything new to wear." When a man goes to his closet and says, "I don't have anything to wear," what he really means is, "I don't have anything clean to wear." —Diana Jordan and Paul Seaburn, *A Wife's Little Instruction Book*

I've got a shirt for every day of the week. It's blue.   —Ron Dentinger

Men believe they already have all the clothes they will ever need, and new ones make them nervous. For example, your average man has eighty-four ties, but he wears, at most, only three of them. He has learned, through humiliating trial and error, that if he wears any of the other eighty-one ties, his wife will probably laugh at him.

—Dave Barry

The favorite tie attracts the gravy.

If the shoe fits, buy it.

—Imelda Marcos

Those stretch pants so many young ladies are sporting these days come in three sizes: small, medium, and don't bend over.

—Tony Randall

My whole freshman year I wore brown and white shoes. Actually they were impractical, because the white one kept getting dirty.

—Dick Cavett

Further Reading:
I Was a Cloakroom Attendant, Mahatma Coate
Artificial Clothing, Polly Ester
Fallen Underwear, Lucy Lastic
Yoko's Robe, Kim Ono
Foot Coverings, Susan Socks
Tight Situation, Leah Tard

■ College
When my niece Laurel was a junior in high school two years ago, she had a hard time deciding which college to attend. When she finally made a choice, I asked her what had most influenced her.

She explained to me: "Uncle Lowell, I wrote to eleven colleges and this one had the best rating: 1,832 boys and 193 girls."

I went to college and majored in philosophy. My father said, "Why don't you minor in communications so you can wonder out loud?" So I did. I got out of school, landed a job as a morning DJ on an all-philosophy radio station, WYMI. "Good morning, it's 8:05 on YMI. For those of you just waking up, what's the point, really?"

—Mike Dugan

When I was a freshman at Temple University, I took a course in elementary zoology with Professor Elbert Windermeier. "I have brought a frog," said the professor, beaming at his class. "It is a fine specimen, fresh from the pond on my rural home. And now let us study its outer appearance and later dissect it."

He carefully opened a paper bag and unwrapped the package only to discover a neatly prepared ham sandwich. Windermeier stared at it with astonishment. "That's strange," he said. "I distinctly remember having eaten my lunch."

A question on a history exam at Harvard University: "For what was Louis XIV chiefly responsible?"

One smart aleck replied, "Louis XV."

During my graduate school days at Princeton University, all us guys thought that our friend Harry was the world's greatest Romeo. As proof we exhibited his little black book—alphabetically arranged. The fifty-third entry was a beautiful Norwegian exchange student named Anna Aaberg.

Seen on a T-shirt: I have a degree in Liberal Arts—Do you want fries with that?

There are more students in Columbia University than there are in any other in the world. . . .Thirty-two hundred courses are offered there. You spend the first two years deciding what courses to take, the next two years finding the buildings these are given in, and the rest of your life wishing you had taken another course.
—Will Rogers

Further Reading:
West Coast Universities, Stan Ford
East Coast Universities, Cora Nell
College Athletics, Nancy Dubblelay
Life in the Sorority House, Carrie Onn

■ Committees

Not even computers will replace committees, because committees buy computers.
—Edward Shepherd Mead

If you want to kill any idea in the world today, get a committee working on it.
—C. F. Kettering

A conference is a gathering of important people who singly can do nothing, but together can decide that nothing can be done.
—Fred Allen

■ Communicating

An American visiting England walked into a hotel lobby and pushed a button for elevator service. "The lift will be down presently," said a nearby clerk.

"The lift?" said the American. "Oh, you mean the elevator."

"No, I mean the lift," replied the Englishman, annoyed by the American's arrogance.

"I think I should know what it's called," said the American. "After all, elevators were invented in the United States."

"Perhaps," retorted the Englishman. "But the language was invented here."

—Roland Giduz in The Rotarian

Before the United Kingdom adopted the decimal system, Jack Paar seemed distressed by having to understand the British system of currency. He admitted that he uses only paper currency and never the coins: "If the taxi driver names a sum I haven't got, I drive around some more until he comes to the notes I have."

"Number twenty-three," yelled the man from the bar at a night-club. It was followed by a roar of laughter from around the room.

A newcomer asked one of the regulars what was going on. "Well, it's like this, we've all been together for years, and we know each other's jokes. A while back we decided to compile a numbered list of our favorites, so that all you have to do is mention the number and everyone can recall the story."

"That's great," said the newcomer. "Let me see the list and try one out."

He looked at the list, spotted the funniest joke, and shouted out, "Number eleven!"

There was a deathly silence, so he tried again. "Number eleven."

The silence continued.

"Why did they laugh at twenty-three and not at eleven?" he asked the old-timer.

"Well, you see," said the older man, "It isn't the joke so much as the way you tell it."

—Paul Dickson

Prime Minister Macmillan has been both the author and the butt of a good deal of political wit and invective. Perhaps the best-known example of his wit occurred when his speech before the United Nations on September 29, 1960, was interrupted by the Russian Premier, Khrushchev, who took off his shoe and pounded on the table with it. In the best tradition of British unflappability, Macmillan remarked calmly, "I'd like to have that translated, if I may."

—Art Linkletter

Back in medieval times, a thoroughly apocryphal story tells us that the Roman Pope was persuaded by some of his more conservative advisors to endure no longer the presence of Jews in the very heart and core of world Christianity. The Jews of Rome were, therefore, ordered evicted from their homes by a certain date.

To the Jews of Rome this was a great tragedy, for they knew no refuge where they might not expect worse treatment than in Rome. They appealed to the Pope for reconsideration, and the Pope, a fair minded man, suggested a sporting proposition. If the Jews would appoint one of their own number to engage in a debate with him, in pantomime, and if the Jewish representative were to win the debate, the Jews might remain.

The Jewish leaders gathered in the synagogue that night and considered the proposition. It seemed the only way out, but none of their number wished to volunteer to debate. Then the chief rabbi said, "It is impossible to win a debate in which the Pope will be both participant and judge. And how can I face the possibility that the eviction of the Jews will be the result of my specific failure?"

The synagogue janitor, who had been quietly sweeping the floor through all this, suddenly spoke up. "I'll debate," he said. They stared at him in astonishment.

"You, a cheap janitor?" said the chief rabbi. "Debate with the Pope?"

"Someone has to," said the janitor, "and none of you will."

So the janitor was made the representative of the Jewish community to debate with the Pope.

The great date came. In the square before St. Peter's was the Pope, surrounded by the College of Cardinals in full panoply, with crowds of bishops and other churchly functionaries. Approaching was the Jewish janitor, surrounded by a few of the leaders of the Jewish community in their somber black garb and their long gray beards.

Pope faced janitor, and the debate began.

Gravely, the Pope raised one finger and swept it across the heavens. Without hesitation the janitor pointed firmly toward the ground. The Pope looked surprised.

Even more gravely, the Pope raised one finger again, keeping it firmly before the janitor's face. With the trace of a sneer, the janitor raised three fingers, holding the pose just as firmly. A look of deep astonishment crossed the Pope's face.

Then the Pope thrust his hand deep into his robes and produced an apple. The janitor thereupon opened a paper bag that was sticking out of his hip pocket and took out a flat piece of matzo. At this, the Pope exclaimed in a loud voice, "The Jewish representative has won the debate. The Jews may remain in Rome."

The janitor backed off, the Jewish leaders surrounded him, and all walked hastily out of the square.

They were no sooner gone than the church leaders clustered about the Pope. "What happened, your Holiness?" they demanded. "We could not follow the rapid give-and-take."

The Pope passed a shaking hand across his brow. "The man facing me," he said, "was a master at the art of debate. Consider! I began the debate by sweeping my hand across the sky to indicate that God ruled all the universe. Without pausing an instant, that old Jew pointed downward to indicate that nevertheless the Devil had been assigned a domination of his own below.

"I then raised one finger to indicate there was but one God, assuming I would catch him in the error of his own theology. Yet he instantly raised three fingers to indicate that the one God has three manifestations, a clear acceptance of the doctrine of the Trinity.

"Abandoning theology, I produced an apple to indicate that certain blind upholders of so-called science were flying in the face of revealed truth by declaring the Earth was as round as an apple. Instantly, he produced a flat piece of unleavened bread to indicate that the Earth, in accord with revelation, was nevertheless flat. So I granted him victory."

By now, the Jews and the janitor had reached the ghetto. All surrounded the janitor, demanding, "What happened?"

The janitor said indignantly, "The whole thing was nonsense. Listen. First the Pope waves his hand like he's saying, 'The Jews must get out of Rome.' So I pointed downward to say, 'Oh yeah? The Jews are going to stay right here.' So he points his finger at me as if to say, 'Drop dead, but the Jews are leaving.' So I pointed three fingers at him to say 'Drop dead three times, the Jews are staying.' So then I see he's taking out his lunch, so I take out mine."

—Isaac Asimov

Our dog Duffy had a great-grandfather who once scampered into a telegraph office, took out a blank form, and wrote a message to his mother in Scotland which read, "Woof, woof, woof, woof, woof, woof, woof, woof, woof."

The clerk looked at it and said, "There are only nine words here, you could send another 'woof' for the same price."

"But," the dog replied, "that would be silly."

Further Reading:
How to Explain It Better, Clara Fie

■ Complainers

After the warning bell announced the Louvre's closing, one old museum guard grumbled to another as they shepherded the crowds out, "Every day for twenty years it's been the same. There's always somebody who's the last to leave."

Toward the end of the deer season last year, a "Deer Crossing" sign on a California highway had another sign fastened to it, evidently by a disappointed hunter. It read, "Promises, promises!"

Whining is anger through a small opening.

—Al Franken as Stuart Smalley

A hotel guest was a real pain in the neck, and gave none of the help a moment's rest. No matter what he got, he wasn't satisfied. When it came time for him to check out, no one was sorry. However, the entire staff was concerned about the size of the tips he would leave.

One bellhop, who didn't like to leave anything to chance, decided to give the guest a tactful reminder about tipping.

"You won't forget me, sir, will you?" he asked.

"Of course not," smiled the guest. "I'll write you every day."

—Myron Cohen

A sales representative stops at a small manufacturing plant in the Midwest. He presents a box of cigars to the manager as a gift.

"No, thanks," says the plant manager. "I tried smoking a cigar once, and I didn't like it."

The sales rep shows his display case and then, hoping to clinch a sale, offers to take the manager out for martinis.

"No, thanks," the plant manager replies. "I tried alcohol once, but didn't like it."

"I suppose you play golf," says the salesman. "I'd like to invite you to be a guest at my club."

"No, thanks," the manager says. "I played golf once, but I didn't like it."

Just then a young man enters the office. "Let me introduce my son, Bill," says the plant manager.

"Let me guess," the salesman replies. "An only child?"

Happiness isn't something you experience. It's something you remember.
—Oscar Levant

An English teacher calls the National Broadcasters Association office to complain. She says, "I cannot believe that in your industry some of the top people can't pronounce simple words properly. Tom Brokaw can't say his *R*s correctly. Barbara Walters has trouble with her *L*s, and Chris Wallace can't say *W*s. Let me talk to whomever is in charge."

The call is transferred to the CEO, who answers, "Hawwoe?"
—Ron Dentinger

Lincoln had in his Cabinet one maverick who was against every move proposed and automatically disputed every statement the President made. Lincoln, however, was adamant when advisors begged him to get rid of the dissenter.

In explanation, Lincoln told about a farmer he once encountered who was trying to plow with a decrepit horse. Lincoln noticed a big horsefly on the flank of the animal and was about to brush it off when the farmer cried, "Don't you bother that fly, Abe! If it wasn't for that fly this danged old hoss wouldn't move an inch!"

—Bennett Cerf

Remember this before you burden other people with your troubles. Half of them aren't the least bit interested, and the rest are delighted that you're getting what they think is coming to you.

—Vance Packard

■ Computers

A man wanted to know about mind, not in nature, but in his private large computer. He asked it, "Do you compute that you will ever think like a human being?"

The machine then set to work to analyze its computational habits. Finally, the machine printed its answer on a piece of paper. The man ran to get the answer and found, neatly typed, the words: "That reminds me of a story."

Surely the computer was right. This is indeed how people think.

A company we know is encountering so many errors it's thinking of buying a computer to blame them on.

I press the CONTROL key, but it's not giving me any.

Computers aren't smart, but they do have their own form of common sense. You never notice a computer making a dummy of itself at the office Christmas party.

President Clinton, as part of his goal to increase technical awareness and interest in the sciences, asked the various major computer companies to cooperate in a large multimedia publishing project. The general theme was "Elephants."

Apple submitted two pieces: "User Friendly Elephants and Their Friend, the Mouse" and "Think Different. No One Really Needs an Elephant."

IBM: "How to Sell an Elephant to Someone Who Wants a Race-horse."

Novell: "Connecting Elephants."

Borland: "All Elephants Should Cost $99."

NeXT: "Painting an Elephant Black."

Microsoft: "Why You Should Buy Microsoft Windows."

Failure Is Not an Option. It comes bundled with the software.

If at first you don't succeed, you must be installing Windows.

An accounting company bought a huge computer. It took up a whole wall in the small company. Two of the accountants gave it a trial run. They fed a complex accounting problem into the computer, and in a few minutes the answer spit out on a small piece of paper. They studied the paper gravely. One guy turned to the other and said, "Do you realize that it would take 400 ordinary accountants 350 years to make a mistake this big?"

The executive world is challenging. After four years of college and an M.B.A., they put you behind an impressive desk, face-to-face with a tiny little machine that's more intelligent than you are.

A picture is worth a thousand words. But it uses up a thousand times the memory.

With a computer we can now do a full eight hours of work in just an hour. Of course, it takes seven hours to discover what we did.

"I've just created a computer that's almost human."

"You mean, it can think?"

"No. But when it makes a mistake it can blame another computer."

The problem with computers is that they do exactly what we tell them. It's like the general who issued an order to all the guards on base that no vehicle was to be allowed to enter or leave the premises without an official identification seal. One young soldier was on detail duty when the general's car parked along the gate. It didn't have an identification seal, so the youngster followed orders and refused to let it pass.

The general was very angry. He said, "Young man, I'm the highest ranking officer on this base. Let this vehicle pass."

The soldier did not budge.

The general said, "I'm the general who issued this order. Now let us drive on through."

The soldier said, "No, sir."

Finally the general said, "I'm in charge on this base, and I'm giving my driver an order to go right on through! Do you understand that? Do you have any questions?"

The kid said, "Just one, sir. Who do I shoot first, you or your driver?"

Never let a computer know that you're in a hurry.

The computer will never fully replace humans. It may one day be capable of artificial intelligence, but it will never master real stupidity like we have.

In the computer age, it is disturbing to realize that a machine has your number.

I don't see why religion and science can't cooperate. What's wrong with using a computer to count our blessings?

Years ago, science fiction writer Isaac Asimov despaired of the ability of computers to act as linguistic translators. He noted:

Computers have been developed which can translate one language into another. Ideally, if the translated passage were then translated by computer back into the first language, the original words ought to be regained. This, however, does not allow for the ambiguity of languages.

Thus, there is the story of the computer that was ordered to translate a common English phrase into Russian and then translate the Russian translation back into English. I understand the expression, "The spirit is willing, but the flesh is weak," came back from Russian into English as "The vodka is cooperative, but the meat is inferior."

Computers come in two varieties: the prototype and the obsolete.

LAWS OF COMPUTING

- No matter how much you know about computers, you can find an expert who renders everything incomprehensible.
- You never run out of disks or printer ribbons [or toner] during business hours.
- The price of software is in inverse proportion to the readability of its manual.
- The size of a computer error is in direct proportion to the importance of the data lost.
- For every computer error there are at least two human errors, one of which is blaming it on the computer.
- No matter how long you delay the purchase of a computer product, a faster, cheaper, and more powerful version will be introduced within forty-eight hours.
- The power never fails at the beginning of a computing session.
- If you back up your disk, the original will not fail.
- Printers do not work when first set up. If they do, it is because you didn't follow instructions.
- You never lose data you don't need.

—Joel Makower, *Personal Computing A to Z*

If you put tomfoolery into a computer, nothing comes out but tom-foolery. But this tomfoolery, having passed through a very expensive machine, is somehow ennobled, and no one dares criticize it.

—Pierre Gallois

A teacher made an inquiry to the Internal Revenue Service and got a reply that hardly answered her question. After several follow-up inquiries with the same futile response, she wrote a letter that began, "Dear Computer: Please have your mother call me." Within a week, she received a handwritten note telling her exactly what she wanted to know.

When the computer arrived at a large business concern, the movers found it wouldn't fit into the elevator. The deliveryman asked, "How are we going to get this thing to the third floor?"

His manager answered, "Plug it in and let it figure it out for itself."

Interactive computers were becoming popular in some schools, as was the idea that children should be respected for themselves and not for their performance. Young Harry was striking the keys and seeing his answers on the screen. Once, the computer was heard to say, "Wrong. Try again. But remember, just because I said you were wrong doesn't mean I don't love you."

Winning a battle with a computer system is getting to be more fun than sneaking into the subway through an exit gate used to be. Let's give a great big hand to latest winner Jerome T. Parker. Mr. Parker, for reasons unknown to him, received a bill from an oil company for several consecutive months for $0.00. He laughingly showed the bills to friends and waited for the bills to stop coming. When he got one marked "Final Notice," however, plus a threat to turn the account over to a notoriously tough collection agency, he wrote out a check for no dollar and no cents, signed his name thereto, and mailed it to the oil company with a note saying, "This pays my account in full." Darned if he didn't get a form letter in return, thanking him for his patronage. —Bennett Cerf

The big difference between man and computers is that computers can't think . . . but they know it.

Have you experienced the frustration of trying to rectify incorrect billing that was sent you automatically by a computer? Then you might identify with this correspondence:

August 17
Dear Madam:
Our records show an outstanding balance of $2.98 on your account. If you have already remitted this amount, kindly disregard this letter.
THIS IS A MACHINE CARD.
PLEASE DO NOT SPINDLE OR MUTILATE.

August 19
Gentlemen:
I do not have an outstanding balance. I attached a note with my payment advising you that I had been billed twice for the same amount: once under my first name, middle initial, and last name; and then under my two first initials and my last name. (The former is correct.) Please check your records.

September 17
Dear Madam:
Our records show a delinquent balance of $2.98 on your account. Please remit $3.40. This includes a handling charge.
THIS IS A MACHINE CARD.
PLEASE DO NOT SPINDLE OR MUTILATE.

September 19
Dear Machine:
You're not paying attention! I am *not* delinquent. I do *not* owe this. I was billed TWICE for the same purchase. *Please* look into this.

October 17

Dear Madam:

Our records show you to be delinquent for three months. Please remit the new charges of $13.46, plus $4.10. (This includes a handling charge.) May we have your immediate attention in this matter.

THIS IS A MACHINE CARD.

PLEASE DO NOT SPINDLE OR MUTILATE.

October 19

Dear Machine:

My attention! You want *my* attention! Listen here, *you are wrong!!!* I *don't* owe you $4.10. CAN YOU UNDERSTAND THAT? I also *don't* owe you the new charge of $13.46. You billed ME for my MOTHER'S purchase. Please correct this statement at ONCE!

November 17

Dear Madam:

Our records now show you to be delinquent for four months in the total amount of $17.56, plus $1.87 handling charges.

Please remit in full in ten days, or your account with be turned over to our Auditing Department for collection.

THIS IS A MACHINE CARD.

PLEASE DO NOT SPINDLE OR MUTILATE.

November 19

Dear Human Machine Programmer—

Dear ANYONE Human:

WILL YOU PLEASE TAKE YOUR HEAD OUT OF THE COMPUTER LONG ENOUGH TO READ THIS? I DON'T OWE YOU THIS!!! I DON'T OWE YOU ANYTHING. NONE!

December 17

Dear Madam:

Is there some question about your statement? Our records show no payments on your account since August. Please call DI 7-9601 and ask for Miss Gilbert at your earliest convenience.

THIS IS A MACHINE CARD.

PLEASE DO NOT SPINDLE OR MUTILATE.

December 18

. . . *Deck the halls with boughs of holly. . .* "Good afternoon. Carver's hopes you've enjoyed its recorded program of carols. May I help you?"

"Hello. Yes. . . . My bill is . . . should I wait for a beep before I talk?"

"About your bill?"

"Yes. Yes, it's my bill. There's a mistake—"

"One moment, please. I'll connect you with Adjustments!"

"Good afternoon and merry Christmas. This is a recorded message. All our lines are in service now. If you will please be patient, one of our adjusters will be with you soon. Meanwhile, Carver's hopes you enjoy its program of Christmas carols." . . . *the halls with boughs of holly . . .*

December 26th

Dear Machine:

I tried to call you on December 18. Also the 19th, 20th, 21st, 22nd, 23rd, and the 24th. But all I got was a recorded message and those Christmas carols. Please, oh, please, won't you turn me over to a human? Any human?

January 17

Dear Madam:

Our Credit Department has turned your delinquent account over to us for collection. Won't you please remit this amount now? We wish to cooperate with you in every way possible, but this is considerably past due. May we have your check at this time?

Very truly yours,
Henry J. Hooper, Auditor

January 19

Dear Mr. Hooper:

You DOLL! You gorgeous *human* doll! I refer you to letters I sent to your department, dated the 19th of September, October, November, and December, which should clarify the fact that I owe you nothing.

February 17

Dear Madam:

According to our microfilm records, our billing was in error. Your account is clear; you have no balance. We hope there will be no further inconvenience to you. This was our fault.

Very truly yours,
Henry J. Hooper, Auditor

February 19
Dear Mr. Hooper:
Thank you! Oh, thank you, thank you, thank you!

March 17
Dear Madam:
Our records show you to be delinquent in the amount of $2.98, erroneously posted last August to a nonexistent account. May we have your remittance at this time?

THIS IS A MACHINE CARD.
PLEASE DO NOT SPINDLE OR MUTILATE.

March 19
Dear Machine:
I give up. You win. Here's a check for $2.98. Enjoy yourself.

April 17
Dear Madam:
Our records show an overpayment on your part of $2.98. We are crediting this amount to your account.

THIS IS A MACHINE CARD.
PLEASE DO NOT SPINDLE OR MUTILATE.

There are about thirty thousand students at the University of Illinois, so the College of Fine and Applied Arts has tried to find a way of humanizing their computerization. Early in the semester the administration sends out a card to check the student's program. It begins, "Dear 344-28-0430: We have a personal interest in you."

"This computer system," said the salesperson, "will do half your job for you."

After looking over the machine, the senior VP said, "I'll take two!"

Computer wizards never quit—they just lose their byte.

A large computer-oriented Dallas corporation has the following entry in one of its ledgers: "This correcting entry is to correct an incorrect correction made incorrectly in January."

One unemployed man to another: "What hurts was that I wasn't replaced."

Bill Gates dies and appears at the portal to heaven, where he is greeted by St. Peter.

St. Peter offers Gates a choice. He says, "Look around here for a while and then pop down to hell and see what the devil has to offer. Check out both places and then let us know where you want to spend eternity."

Gates looks around heaven. He finds lots of somber people singing hymns. He goes down to hell, where he finds lots of beautiful beaches, sun, sand, surf, and attractive women. He has twenty or thirty long, cool drinks, but he never gets drunk.

Gates loves it. He goes back to St. Peter and says, "Look, I know you're really doing good things here, but hell seems more with it. More my kind of scene, you know what I mean? No hard feelings, but I pick hell."

St. Peter says, "No problem. You've got it."

Instantly Gates finds himself back in hell, neck deep in fire and brimstone, suffering eternal torment. He cries out to St. Peter across the eternal void: "Hey, St. Peter! Where are the beautiful girls and beaches and cool drinks?"

St. Peter. replies, "I'm sorry if you got confused. That was just the demo version!"

My brother joined a cult. We haven't seen him in two years. That's so scary 'cause they brainwash people, they all dress alike, talk alike, think alike. You might have heard of it—it's called IBM.

—Mike Dugan

Immunity to boredom gives computers the edge.

Doonesbury: Excuse me, sir. Do you have any user-friendly sales reps?

Store Manager: You mean, the consumer compatible liveware? No, he's off today.   —Garry Trudeau, *Doonesbury* cartoon, 1983

Making duplicate copies and computer printouts of things no one wanted even one of in the first place is giving America a new sense of purpose.   —Andy Rooney

A man and his wife met at the commuter train for the trip home. He looked haggard, and she asked, "Did you have a tough day, dear?"

"You bet I did," he answered. "The computer was down, and we had to think all day long."

In the computer world, hardware is anything you can hit with a hammer. Software is what you can only curse at.

Computers make it easy to do a lot of things, but most of the things they make it easier to do don't need to be done.   —Andy Rooney

Computers will never be perfected until they can compute how much more than the estimate the job will cost.   —Laurence J. Peter

THE VERMONTER'S GUIDE TO COMPUTER LINGO

Modem: What you did to the hayfields.

Windows: What to shut when it's 30 below.

Log On: Making the wood stove hotter.

Hard Drive: Getting home during mud season.

Microchips: What are left in the bag when the big chips are gone.

Download: Getting the firewood off the pickup.

Megahertz: What you get when you're not careful downloading.

—Quoted in *Fax Daily*

I think there is a world market for maybe five computers.

—Thomas Watson, chairman of IBM, 1943

When shopping for a new computer, I asked the clerk if the store honored credit cards. "Honor them?" he said. "We worship them!"

Computers in the future may weigh no more than 1.5 tons.

—*Popular Mechanics*, 1949

Q: What is the difference between IBM and Jurassic Park?
A: One is a theme park full of ancient mechanical monsters that scare its customers; the other is a movie.   —*Enterprise Systems Journal*

Further Reading:
Computer Memories, Meg Abight
Cheaper than IBM, P. C. Clone

■ Computer Technical Support

Austin, Texas—The exasperated help-line caller said she couldn't get her new Dell computer to turn on. Jay Ablinger, a Dell Computer Corporation technician, had the woman verify that the computer was plugged in. He then asked the woman what happened when she pushed the power button.

"I've pushed and pushed on this foot pedal and nothing happens," the woman replied.

"Foot pedal?" the technician asked.

"Yes," the woman said, "this little white pedal with the on switch."

The "foot pedal," it turned out, was the computer's mouse.

Compaq's help center in Houston, Texas, is inundated by some eight thousand consumer calls a day, with inquiries like this one related by technician John Wolf:

A frustrated customer called, who said her brand new Contura would not work. She said she had unpacked the unit, plugged it in, opened it up, and sat there for twenty minutes waiting for something to happen. When asked what happened when she pressed the power switch, she asked, "What power switch?"

Seemingly simple computer features baffle some users. So many people have called to ask where the "any" key is when "Press Any Key" flashes on the screen that Compaq is considering changing the command to "Press Return Key."

Some people can't figure out the mouse. Tamra Eagle, an AST technical support supervisor, says one customer complained that her mouse was hard to control with the "dust cover" on. The cover turned out to be the plastic bag the mouse was packaged in.

Dell technician Wayne Zieschang says one of his customers held the mouse in mid-air and pointed it at the screen, all the while clicking madly.

Disk drives are another bugaboo. Compaq technician Brent Sullivan says a customer was having trouble reading word-processing files from his old diskettes. After troubleshooting for magnets and heat failed to diagnose the problem, Mr. Sullivan asked what else was being done with the diskette. The customer's response: "I put a label on the diskette, roll it into the typewriter . . ."

At AST, another customer dutifully complied with a technician's request that she send in a copy of a defective floppy disk. A letter from the customer arrived days later, along with a photocopy of the floppy.

And at Dell, a technician advised his customer to put his troubled floppy back in the drive and "close the door." Asking the technician to "hold on," the customer put the phone down and was heard walking over to shut the door to his room.

The software inside the computer can be equally befuddling. A Dell customer called to say he couldn't get his computer to fax anything. After forty minutes of troubleshooting, the technician discovered the man was trying to fax a piece of paper by holding it in front of the monitor screen and hitting the "send" key.

Not realizing how fragile computers can be, some people end up damaging parts beyond repair. A Dell customer called to complain that his keyboard no longer worked. He had cleaned it, he said, filling up his tub with soap and water and soaking his keyboard for a day, and then removing all the keys and washing them individually.

Computers make some people paranoid. Dell technician Morgan Vergara says he once calmed a man who became enraged because "his computer had told him he was bad and an invalid." Mr. Vergara patiently explained that the computer's "bad command" and "invalid" responses shouldn't be taken personally.

These days PC-help technicians increasingly find themselves taking on the role of amateur psychologists. Mr. Shuler, the Dell technician who once worked as a psychiatric nurse, says he defused a potential domestic fight by soothingly talking a man through a computer problem after the man had screamed threats at his wife and children in the background.

—Jim Carlton

Tech Rep: Okay, now double-click on "My Computer."
Customer: Huh? How am I supposed to click on your computer?

An actual transcript of a conversation between a technician and an end user:
Caller: Hello, is this tech support?
Tech Rep: Yes, how may I help you?
Caller: The cup holder on my PC is broken, and I am within my warranty period. How do I go about getting it fixed?
Tech Rep: I'm sorry, but did you say cup holder?
Caller: Yes, it's attached to the front of my computer.
Tech Rep: Please excuse me if I seem a bit stumped, it's because I am. Did you receive this as a part of a promotion, like at a trade show? How did you get this cup holder? Does it have a trademark on it?
Caller: No I didn't get it from a tradeshow, but it does have a trademark on it: 4X.

At this point the tech rep had to mute the caller because he couldn't keep from laughing. The caller had been using the load drawer of his CD-ROM as a cup holder, and snapped it off!

A woman called the Canon help desk with a problem with her printer. The tech asked her if she was "running it under Windows". The woman then responded "No, my desk is next to the door. But that is a good point. The man sitting in the cubicle next to me is under a window and his is working fine."

I used to work technical support, in mobiles division. I had a call one day where a customer's laptop beeped every hour, on the hour, whether he had it on or off. He got so frustrated he unplugged the battery and the power cord, and it *still* beeped every hour. After a few futile troubleshooting tips, I told him I'd call him back after researching it a bit more. When I called back, he said he had found the problem. His watch was on the desk near the computer, and it was the watch that was beeping the whole time—not the computer.

What if customers purchased automobiles the way they purchase computers—without knowing much about them? Can you imagine a General Motors helpline for people who don't know how to drive? Just imagine:

Helpline: General Motors Helpline, how can I help you?
Customer: I got in my car, closed the door, and nothing happened!
Helpline: Did you put the key in the ignition slot and turn it?
Customer: What's an ignition?
Helpline: It's a starter motor that draws current from your battery and turns over the engine.
Customer: Ignition? Motor? Battery? Engine? How come I have to know all of these technical terms just to use my car?

Helpline: General Motors Helpline, how can I help you?
Customer: My car ran fine for a week, and now it won't go!
Helpline: Is the gas tank empty?
Customer: Huh? How do I know!?
Helpline: There's a little gauge on the front panel, with a needle, and markings from *E* to *F*. Where is the needle pointing?
Customer: It's pointing to *E*. What does that mean?

Helpline: It means that you have to purchase more gasoline. You can install it yourself or pay a gas vendor to install it for you.

Customer: What!? I paid $22,000 for this car! Now you tell me that I have to keep buying more components? I want a car that comes with everything built in!

Helpline: General Motors Helpline, how can I help you?

Customer: Your cars stink!

Helpline: What's wrong?

Customer: It crashed, that's what went wrong!

Helpline: What were you doing?

Customer: I wanted to drive faster, so I pushed the accelerator pedal all the way to the floor. It worked for a while, and then it crashed—and now it won't start!

Helpline: It's your responsibility if you misuse the product. What do you expect us to do about it?

Customer: I want you to send me one of the latest versions that doesn't crash anymore!

Helpline: General Motors Helpline, how can I help you?

Customer: Hi! I just bought my first car, and I chose yours because it has automatic transmission, cruise control, power steering, power brakes, and power door locks.

Helpline: Thanks for buying our car. How can I help you?

Customer: How do I work it?

Helpline: Do you know how to drive?

Customer: Do I know how to what?

Helpline: Do you know how to drive?

Customer: I'm not a technical person! I just want to go places!

Years ago, I was vice president of Microtech Computer Services in Burlingame, California. Microtech provided computer products and service for individuals and small businesses. One customer, an author, bought an expensive new system and repeatedly phoned, reporting disasters and demanding help. He kept losing all his data. We walked him through all the usual tips and tricks but found no lasting solution, so one of our technicians made a house call.

There in a room adjacent to his kitchen was a neatly arranged and well-equipped home office. The technician tested all of the customer's components and found nothing amiss. Then he asked to see the computer files in which the author kept his working drafts. The customer explained that he did not use his hard disk for this purpose, but preferred to put each chapter on a separate floppy disk.

"OK," said the tech. "May I see the disks?"

"Sure," answered the author. "They're right in the kitchen."

And sure enough, there they were, all neatly arranged in alphabetical order and held fast to the family refrigerator with decorative magnets.

Further Reading:

It Won't Work!, Mel Function

Fixing Computer Programs, Dee Bugger

■ Congress

If ignorance is bliss, Congress must be paradise.

People watch these Congressional investigations and are divided. Ten percent think the accused is a villain. Ten percent think the accused is a hero. And the other eighty percent are just mad at the accused because he's making them miss their soap opera.

—Gene and Linda Perret

In the sage words of longtime lobbyist Tom Korologos: "The things Congress does best are nothing and overreacting."

Bumper sticker: Invest in America . . . Buy a Congressman

Congress is so strange. A man gets up to speak and says nothing, nobody listens, and then they all disagree.   —Will Rogers

Think of what would happen to us in America if there were no humorists; life would be one long Congressional Record.

—Tom Masson

Take it all in all, I believe [Congress] ought to have their raise. We are a rich nation, and our officials should be the best paid in the world. The principal bad feature is that it will make more men want to hold office, and once a man wants to hold a public office he is absolutely no good for honest work.　　　　　—Will Rogers

True bipartisanship really works. It's the backbone of democracy and the inspiration of all free nations. Unfortunately, it's usually used only when the House votes itself a pay raise.

—Gene and Linda Perret

An old bishop in Virginia once urged a newly elected Congressman to go out into the pouring rain and look heavenward. "It will bring you a revelation," he predicted. The Congressman did as bidden, and came back soaked to the skin. "Look at me," he wailed. "I didn't get any revelation. I only felt like a blithering idiot."

"Not bad," chuckled the bishop. "Don't you think that was quite a revelation for a first try?"　　　　　—Bennett Cerf

Many years ago, when Edward Everett Hale, chaplain of the United States Senate, was asked, "Do you pray for the senators?" he replied, "No, I look at the senators and pray for the country."

Congressional hearings are fun to watch on TV. They look like *The People's Court* with an all-star cast.　　　　—Gene and Linda Perret

■ Conscience

Conscience is the inner voice that warns us that someone may be looking.
                                                              —H. L. Mencken

A guilty conscience is the mother of invention.   —Carolyn Wells

Conscience is the one thing that hurts when everything else feels great.
                                                              —H. Aaron Cohl

■ Cooking

I remember one year we were invited to Grandma's house for dinner. Grandpa said, "This turkey tastes funny. What did you stuff it with?"

Grandma said, "I didn't have to stuff it. It wasn't hollow."
                                                              —Ron Dentinger

Reader Sylvia Bursztyn's sister Harriet and nephew Michael, age eight, were making potato latkes for Hanukkah. While his mother grated the spuds, Michael read the recipe and gathered the other ingredients and necessary utensils. Rummaging through a drawer, the boy looked up and said, "Mom, I can't find the pinch spoon."

Eating her cooking is like playing Russian roulette. I never know which meal is going to kill me.
                                                              —Harvey Stone

An American soldier, billeted in England during World War II, didn't like the way the food was cooked at a local inn. He barely touched the food that was set down before him. The waiter was indignant. "Aren't you ashamed to be wasting food that way?" he chided. "Don't you know that food will win the war?"

"Could be," allowed the American. "But who's going to get the enemy to eat here?"
                                                              —Bennett Cerf

I idolized my mother. I didn't realize she was a lousy cook until I went into the Army.

—Jackie Gayle

The best way to cook any part of a rangy ol' longhorn is to toss it in a pot with a horseshoe, and when the horseshoe is soft and tender, you can eat the beef.

—Texas Bix Bender

One woman to another: "I have a marvelous meat loaf recipe. All I do is mention it to my husband and he says, 'Let's eat out.'"

Note on a Greenwich Village bulletin board: Dear John, Come home. Forgive and forget. I have destroyed that cherry-pie recipe. Helen.

Further Reading:

The World's Best Recipes, Gus Tatorial
What's for Dinner?, Chuck Roast
How to Cook a Steak, Porter House
After the Corned Beef and Cabbage, Kay O'Pectate
How to Make Cornmeal Flapjacks, Johnny Cake
Outdoor Cookery, Barbie Cue
Outdoor Dining, Alf Resco
The Good Breakfast, Hammond Deggs
The Proper Texture of Spaghetti, Al Dente
Southern California Waffles, Sandy Eggo
The French Chef, Sue Flay
Indian/Italian Cuisine, Ravi Oley
Mexican/Italian Cuisine, Pepe Roney
Italian Delicacies, Liz Onya
Things to Cook Meat In, Stu Potts

■ Cowboys

A huge, menacing-looking cowboy rode into town and stopped at the saloon for a drink. When he finished, he found his horse had been stolen. He came back into the bar, handily flipped his gun into the air, caught it above his head without even looking and fired a shot into the ceiling. "WHICH ONE OF YOU SIDEWINDERS STOLE MY HOSS?" he boomed.

No one answered.

"All right," he growled. "I'm gonna have another beer. And if my hoss ain't back outside by the time I finish," he threatened, his anger growing, *"I'm gonna do what I dun in Texas!* AND I DON'T *LIKE* TO HAVE TO DO WHAT I *DUUUUN IN TEXAS!"*

Some of the locals shifted restlessly. He had another beer, walked outside, and his horse had been returned. In stern silence, he mounted and started to ride out of town.

The bartender wandered out of the bar and asked, "Say partner, what happened in Texas?"

The cowboy turned back and, looking hurt, said, "I had to walk home!"

A tall weather-worn cowboy walked into the saloon and ordered a beer. The regulars quietly observed the drifter through half-closed eyelids. No one spoke, but they all noticed that the stranger's hat was made of brown wrapping paper. His shirt and vest were also made of paper, as were his chaps, pants, and even his boots, including paper spurs. Even the saddle, blanket and bridle on his horse were made entirely of paper. He was soon arrested for rustling.

A kid visiting his grandparents in Texas gets to meet a real cowboy who is sitting on a real horse. The following conversation takes place:

"Why do you guys wear those big hats?"

"To keep the sun out of our eyes when we're out on the trail."

"Why do you guys wear those handkerchiefs around your necks?"

"When it's dusty, we pull 'em up over our noses to keep the dust out."

"Why do you wear that leather stuff over your pants?"

"The chaps protect our legs from the thorns when we're riding in the brush."

"How come you wear tennis shoes?"

"So people can tell us apart from truck drivers."

—Ron Dentinger, *Down Time*

The original point and click interface was a Smith & Wesson.

DON'T SQUAT WITH YER SPURS ON: A COWBOY'S GUIDE TO LIFE

- Never kick a fresh cow chip on a hot day.
- There's two theories to arguin' with a woman. Neither one works.
- Don't worry about bitin' off more than you can chew. Your mouth is probably a whole lot bigger'n you think.
- If you get to thinkin' you're a person of some influence, try orderin' somebody else's dog around.
- Never ask a man the size of his spread.
- After eating an entire bull, a mountain lion felt so good he started roaring. He kept it up until a hunter came along and shot him. The moral: When you're full of bull, keep your mouth shut.
- If you find yourself in a hole the first thing to do is stop diggin'.
- Never smack a man who's chewin' tobacco.
- It don't take a genius to spot a goat in a flock of sheep.
- Never ask a barber if he thinks you need a haircut.
- Good judgment comes from experience, and a lot of that comes from bad judgment.
- Always drink upstream from the herd.
- Never drop your gun to hug a grizzly.
- If you're ridin' ahead of the herd, take a look back every now and then to make sure it's still there.
- When you give a lesson in meanness to a critter or a person, don't be surprised if they learn their lesson.
- When you're throwin' your weight around, be ready to have it thrown around by somebody else.

- Lettin' the cat outta the bag is a whole lot easier 'n puttin' it back.
- Always take a good look at what you're about to eat. It's not so important to know what it is, but it's critical to know what it was.
- The quickest way to double your money is to fold it over and put it back in your pocket. —Texas Bix Bender

Further Reading:
Bad Cow Jokes, Terry Bull
Fastest Gun in the West, Everett DeReady
Battle Axes of Native Americans, Tom A. Hawk
The Last Roundup, Brandon Irons
That Ride Was Too Long and Too Rough, Soren Redd
Gunslingers with Gas, Wyatt Urp
Preparing Leather, Tanya Hyde

■ Critics and Criticism

Any critic can establish a wonderful batting average by just rejecting every new idea. —J. D. Williams

No one appreciates the value of constructive criticism more thoroughly than the one who's giving it. —Hal Chadwick

Those who criticize others should keep in mind Franklin P. Jones' words, "Honest criticism is hard to take, particularly from a relative, a friend, an acquaintance, or a stranger."

When ye build yer triumphant arch to yer conquerin' hero, build it out of brick—so the people will have somethin' convenient to throw at him as he passes through. —Peter Finley Dunn

George Kaufman, after viewing a play that he thoroughly detested, gave his immortal opinion: "I saw it under adverse conditions—the curtain was up."

If you can't be kind, at least be vague. —Judith Martin

Journalist Bide Dudley about a disdained play: "It was so terrible that the audience even hissed the ushers."

Hobe Morrison, *Variety*'s great historian of the legitimate theater, once attended the out-of-town opening of a play called *Hollywood Be Thy Name*. Early in the first act, it became apparent that the show was a total turkey—witless and jumbled. Chaos came to a climax when one character pointed a gun at another and fired—without sound. The actor clicked the gun a second time while his victim waited hopefully to drop dead—but still no sound. There was a third, then a fourth click of the gun, but still no surcease from agony. Finally the desperate stage manager dropped the curtain. Immediately after, there was a sharp gun report from the stage. Hobe Morrison rose from his seat and sighed, "Well, at least he got the author!" —Art Linkletter

The acerbic H. L. Mencken used a happy formula for answering all controversial letters. He simply replied, "Dear Sir (or Madam): You may be right!"

She weighs her friends' faults with her thumbs on the scale.

Critic Walter Kerr, reviewing one particularly horrendous Broadway opening this spring: "This was the sort of play that gives failures a bad name."

◼ Cynicism

Men have a much better time of it than women; for one thing, they marry later; for another thing, they die earlier.   —H. L. Mencken

Progress is what people who are planning to do something really terrible almost always justify themselves on the grounds of.

—Russell Baker

A cynic is a man who, when he smells flowers, looks around for a coffin.   —H. L. Mencken (attributed)

Pessimist: A person who has had to listen to too many optimists.

—Don Marquis

It is a sin to believe evil of others, but it is seldom a mistake.

—H. L. Mencken

Further Reading:
Greek Unbeliever!, Hera Tick

■ Dating

Steve Allen encountered a hopeful suitor who dropped into a computer dating center and registered his qualifications. He wanted someone who enjoyed water sports, liked company, favored formal attire, and was very small. The computer operated faultlessly. It sent him a penguin.
—Bennett Cerf

I went to a computer dating service—and they gave me the number of Dial-a-Prayer.
—Joey Bishop

Q: What do you think of computer dating?
A: It's terrific if you're a computer.
—Rita Mae Brown

Bachelor: A man who leans toward women, but not far enough to altar his stance.

A little woman falls in love with a man ninety years old—until she makes a date with him. She goes out with him that night, and a friend asks the next morning, "How did you like him?"
    She says, "I had to slap his face three times!"
    The friend says, "Why, did he get fresh?"
    She said, "No, I thought he was dead."
—Mickey Katz

Why are women wearing perfumes that smell like flowers? Men don't like flowers. I've been wearing a great scent. It's called New Car Interior.

—Rita Rudner

As I welcomed my daughter Susan's first date, I said to him, "She'll be right down. How about a couple of games of chess?"

I asked this guy if he had the time. He said he'd love to give it to me, but he wasn't sure he could make a commitment.

—Carol Siskind

Woman to man at a singles bar: "Why, yes, I'd love to go back to your place. But do you think both of us could fit under a rock?"

—Vic Lee, King Features

I have such poor vision I can date anybody.   —Garry Shandling

Whoever called it necking was a poor judge of anatomy.

—Groucho Marx

I think; therefore, I'm single.   —Lizz Winstead

I've been on so many blind dates I should get a free dog.

—Wendy Liebman

Dear Abby: I've been going with a girl for two years and can't get her to say "yes." What should I do? Signed, Joe
Dear Joe: What's the question?

■ Death

I am ready to meet my Maker. Whether my Maker is prepared for the great ordeal of meeting me is another matter.

—Winston Churchill

If Shaw and Einstein couldn't beat death, what chance have I got? Practically none.

—Mel Brooks

There's an undertaker in Washington who signs all his letters "Eventually yours."

—Bennett Cerf

Epitaph: A belated advertisement for a line of goods that has been permanently discontinued.

—Irving S. Cobb

DEAD MEN READ NO MAIL

Scott Hanson, news reporter and anchor with WESH in Orlando, recalls:

My father died on January 2, 1995. He left no forwarding address. Therefore, it fell to me to collect his mail. I didn't expect much of it, since my sisters and I had been careful to notify his bank, insurance agent, and a host of other businesses that one of their customers was no more.

You would think a death notice would cut down on the amount of correspondence from those firms. Quite the contrary. Instead—for months, mind you—my deceased father continued to receive mail from companies that had been told of his passing but pressed on, determined to contact him anyway.

The first to hope for a reply from beyond the grave was my father's bank.

Dear Mr. Hanson,
Our records indicate payment is due for overdraft protection on your checking account. Efforts to contact you have proven unsuccessful. Therefore, we are automatically withdrawing your monthly

$28.00 service charge from you account. Please adjust your records accordingly.

Sincerely,
The Phoenix Branch

Dear Phoenix Branch,
This is to notify you once again that Mr. Hanson died January 2, 1995. It is, therefore, unlikely he will be overdrawing his account. Please close his account, and adjust your books accordingly.

Sincerely,
Scott Hanson

Later that same week, I receive this note from Dad's insurance company. Again, this is a firm that had been told in no uncertain terms of his death.

Dear Mr. Hanson,
It's time to renew your auto insurance policy! To continue your coverage, you must send $54.17 to this office immediately. Failure to do so will result in the cancellation of your policy and interruption of your coverage.

Sincerely,
Your Insurance Agent

Dear Insurance Agent,
This is to remind you that Mr. Hanson has been dead since January. As such, the odds he'll be involved in a collision are quite minimal. Please cancel the policy, and adjust your books accordingly.

Sincerely,
Scott Hanson.

The next day, I went to my mailbox to find this:

Dear Mr. Hanson,
Let me introduce myself. I am a psychic reader, and it is very important that you contact me immediately. I sense that you are about to enter a time of unprecedented financial prosperity. Please call the

enclosed 900-number immediately, so I can tell you how best to take full advantage of the opportunities that are coming your way.

Sincerely,
Your Psychic Reader

Dear Psychic Reader,
My father regrets he will be unable to call your 900-number. As a psychic reader, I'm sure you already know that my father is dead, and had been for more than three weeks when you mailed your letter to him. I sense my father would be more than happy to take you up on your offer of a psychic reading, should you care to meet with him personally.

Sincerely,
Scott Hanson

PS: Should you be in contact with my father in the future, please ask him if he'd like to renew his car insurance.

A few months of calm passed, and then these arrived:

Dear Mr. Hanson,
Our records indicate a balance of $112 has accrued for overdraft protection on your checking account. Efforts to contact you have proven unsuccessful. Please pay the minimum amount due, or contact this office to make other arrangements.

We appreciate your business and look forward to serving all of your future borrowing needs.

Sincerely,
Your Bank's San Diego District Office

Dear San Diego District Office,
I am writing to you for the third time now to tell you that my father died in January. Since then, the number of checks he's written has dropped dramatically. Being dead, he has no plans to use his overdraft protection or pay even the minimum amount due for a service he no longer needs. As for future borrowing needs, well, don't hold your breath.

Sincerely,
Scott Hanson

Dear Mr. Hanson,

Records show you owe a balance of $54.17 to your insurance agent. Efforts to contact you have proven unsuccessful. Therefore, the matter has been turned over to us for collection. Please remit the amount to our office, or we will be forced to take legal action.

Sincerely,
Your Insurance Agent's Collection Agency

Dear Collection Agency,

I told your client. Now I'm telling you. Dad's dead. He doesn't need insurance. He's dead. Dead, dead, dead. I doubt even your lawyers can change that. Please adjust your books accordingly.

Sincerely,
Scott Hanson

A few more months, and:

Dear Mr. Hanson,

Our records show an unpaid balance of $224 has accrued for over-draft protection on your checking account. Our efforts to contact you have proven unsuccessful. Please remit the amount in full to this office, or the matter will be turned over to a collection agency. Such action will adversely affect your credit history.

Sincerely,
Your Bank's Los Angeles Regional Office

Dear Los Angeles Regional Office,

I am writing for the fourth time to the fourth person at the fourth address to tell your bank that my father passed away in January. Since that time, I've watched with a mixture of amazement and amusement as your bank continues to transact business with him. Now, you are even threatening his credit history. It should come as no surprise that you have received little response from my deceased father. It should also be small news that his credit history is of minor importance to him now.

For the fourth time, please adjust your books accordingly.

Sincerely,
Scott Hanson

Dear Mr. Hanson,

This is your final notice of payment due to your insurance agent. If our firm does not receive payment of $54.17, we will commence legal action on the matter.

Please contact us at once.

Sincerely,
Your Insurance Agent's Collection Agency

Dear Insurance Agent's Collection Agency,

You may contact my father via the enclosed 900-number.

Sincerely,
Scott Hanson

It has now been a couple of months since I've heard from these firms. Either the people writing these letters finally believe my father is dead, or they themselves have died and are now receiving similar correspondence.

Actually, there has been a lesson in these letters. Any one of them would be cause for great worry, if sent to a living person. The dead are immune from corporate bullying. There's nothing like dying to put business correspondence in its proper perspective.

The son was sitting at the bedside of his elderly father, who was dying. "Where do you want to be buried?" asked the son. "Forest Lawn or New York City?"

The old man got up on his elbow and said, "Surprise me!"

—Joey Adams

Of the two basic certainties, death and taxes, death is preferable. At least you're not called in six months for an audit.

—Bill Vaughan

Here lies the body of Harry Hershfield. If not, notify Ginsberg and Co., undertakers, at once.

—Harry Hershfield's suggestion for his own epitaph

The humorist Dorothy Parker had a sarcastic reaction when informed of ex-President Coolidge's death in January 1933. Said Parker, "How could they tell?"

FAMOUS LAST WORDS

- "Ha! They couldn't hit an elephant at this dist—"

  —Union General John B. Sedgwick at the Battle of Spotsylvania (1864)
- "Don't unplug it, it will just take a moment to fix."
- "Let's take the shortcut, he can't see us from there."
- "What happens if you touch these two wires tog—"
- "We won't need reservations."
- "It's always sunny there this time of the year."
- "They'd never be stupid enough to make him a manager."
- "Gimme a match. I think my gas tank is empty."
- "Wife, these biscuits are tough."
- "Step on her, boy, we're only going seventy-five."
- "Just watch me dive from that bridge."
- "If you knew anything, you wouldn't be a traffic cop."
- "Lemme have that bottle; I'll try it."
- "What? Your mother is going to stay another month?"
- "Say, who's boss of this joint, anyhow?"
- "Luke, I lied. Bill Shatner is your real father."   —Darth Vader
- "Don't worry about the Rover. That's no cliff."   —NASA techie
- "And now that I'm running my life support equipment through Windows 95, I'll never have to worry about—" *beeeeeeeep* . . .
- "How's he gonna read a magazine rolled up like that?"   —insect
- "No, dude, this stuff is completely natural and safe, man. That's why it's called 'herbal.'"

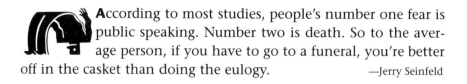 According to most studies, people's number one fear is public speaking. Number two is death. So to the average person, if you have to go to a funeral, you're better off in the casket than doing the eulogy.   —Jerry Seinfeld

■ Dental

Years ago, my then eighty-year-old grandmother went to the dentist to have her false teeth adjusted for the fifth time. She said they still didn't fit.

"Well," said the dentist, "I'll do it again this time, but no more. There's no reason why these shouldn't fit your mouth easily."

"Who said anything about my mouth?" Grandma replied. "They don't fit in the glass!"

If you get dental floss caught in your teeth, what do you use to get it out? Popcorn?
                                                                    —Brad Stine

During a routine checkup, a dentist asked his patient if he had been eating any different foods lately. The man replied that, yes, his wife had learned to make a wonderful hollandaise sauce, and that he'd been eating it on just about everything.

"Well," the dentist said, "I think the acidity in the sauce's lemon juice is eroding your denture plate. I'll make you a new one, but this time I'll make it out of chrome."

"Chrome?" the patient asked. "Why chrome?"

"Because," the dentist replied, "everyone knows there is no plate like chrome for the hollandaise."

Our dentist, Ed Brown, was upset because one of his patients never seemed to pay attention to the bills his office sent. So Ed resolved to go up to the skinflint's house and collect in person. An hour later he was back at his office, looking very glum. "I can see by your face that he didn't pay you," said his receptionist.

"He not only didn't pay me," said the dentist ruefully, "but he bit me with my own teeth."

In an ancient chateau, an American reporter found an old Frenchman who was quite hale and hearty though his baptismal certificate proved that he was 105. "Good eating and good drinking is what has preserved me," he told the reporter. "Wine is the only beverage for a sensible human being. Why am I in such perfect health? Because not a drop of water has ever passed my lips."

"I can't quite believe that," laughed the reporter. "Don't you ever brush your teeth in the morning?"

"For that," replied the old gentleman gravely, "I use a light sauterne."

One morning at breakfast my Cousin Bobby Lee was jubilant. "I've finally cured my husband Earl of biting his nails," she declared.

"For goodness sakes," I said. "How?"

Her answer was simple: "I hid his teeth."

Further Reading:

Irish Dentistry, Perry O'Dontal

■ Diets

Diet: A short period of starvation preceding a gain of five pounds.

Spot reducing doesn't work. If it did, people who chew gum would have skinny faces.   —Covert Bailey, Fitness and Nutrition expert

I have to lose weight. My doctor said the best way to lose weight is to drink warm water an hour before every meal. Well, I just can't do it. I'm okay at first, but after about ten minutes of drinking I feel bloated and sick."   —Ron Dentinger

Overweight: Just desserts.

"I heard your wife is on an onion diet. Did she lose anything?"

"Yes. Five pounds and all of her friends."

I have a great diet. You're allowed to eat anything you want, but you have to eat it with naked fat people.
                                                      —Ed Bluestone

It's time to go on a diet when:
• the man from Prudential offers you group insurance.
• you take a shower, and you have to let out the shower curtain.
• you stand next to your car and get a ticket for double parking.
                                                      —Totie Fields

"Your cholesterol level is unbelievably high," a doctor told his patient during a physical examination.
    "How bad is it?"
    The doctor pointed out the window. "See that field of oats?"
    "Yes?"
    "Bon appetit!"   —Parker and Hart, North America Syndicate

Further Reading:
The All-Sweets Diet, Pepper Mintz

■ Doctors

Never go to a doctor whose office plants have died.   —Erma Bombeck

Patient: I told the pharmacist about my symptoms.
Doctor: Ha! What foolish advice did he give you?
Patient: He told me to see you.   —Ron Dentinger

Several doctors were consulting one another on what to do with a patient, while he eavesdropped. Later, his wife asked him what the doctors had decided. "I don't know," the man replied. "They used medical terms I didn't understand. They said something about finding out for sure at the autopsy, whatever that means."
                                                      —*The Ohio Motorist*

Labor dispute: Difference of opinion between two obstetricians.

Representative Pete Stark (D–CA) has introduced a bill in Congress that would make it illegal for doctors to discuss payment options with patients while conducting embarrassing examinations.

Minor operation: One performed on somebody else.

My son was apprehensive about a long wait when we visited a hospital for tests. Looking around, he commented, "Most waiting rooms have magazines, but this one has novels. Is that a bad sign?"

I called for an appointment with the doctor. I was told that they couldn't fit me in for at least two weeks. I said, "I could be dead by then."

They said, "That's no problem. Just have your wife let us know, and we will cancel the appointment." —Ron Dentinger

Once I was sick, and I had to go to an ear, nose, and throat man to get well. There are ear doctors, nose doctors, throat doctors, gynecologists, proctologists—any place you've got a hole, there's a guy who specializes in your hole. They make an entire career out of that hole. And if the ear doctor, nose doctor, throat doctor, gynecologist, or proctologist can't help you, he sends you to a surgeon. Why? So he can make a new hole! —Alan Prophet

"I think you ought to stop taking sleeping pills every night," the Beverly Hills physician told a famous Hollywood actor. "They're habit forming."

"Habit forming!" repeated the star. "Don't be absurd. I've been taking them for twenty years."

The hospital patient was worried. "Are you sure it's pneumonia, doctor?" he asked. "I've heard of cases where a doctor treated a patient for pneumonia, and he ended up dying of something else."

"Don't worry," said the doctor. "When I treat a patient for pneumonia, he dies of pneumonia."

—Winston K. Pendleton, *Funny Stories, Jokes and Anecdotes*

The operation was about to begin,
A five-dollar bet was the surgeon's to win,
If he would just make the initial incision,
But where to begin was the crucial decision.
A little to the left or a little to the right,
and he'd be repairing his mistake the rest of the night.
Tools in hand, he was about to begin.
But knowing he'd blow it, and that was a sin.
His assistant had lost all her patience by now,
and was bound and determined that she'd show him how.
His fingers were shaking, and his hands were jerky,
So she grabbed the knife and just butchered the turkey!

How many doctors does it take to screw in a light bulb?
It depends. How much insurance does the light bulb have?

—*Journal on Nursing Jocularity*

The best doctors in the world are Dr. Diet, Dr. Quiet, and Dr. Merryman.

—Jonathan Swift

Dr. Abernathy, a famous London diagnostician, was approached at a social function by a dowager who tried to wangle free medical advice. "Oh, Dr. Abernathy," she said, "if a patient came to you with such and such a symptom, what would you recommend?"

"Why, I would recommend Dr. Abernathy," he replied.

Casey came home from seeing the doctor looking very worried. His wife said, "What's the problem?"

Casey answered, "The doctor told me I have to take a pill every day for the rest of my life."

She said, "So what? Lots of people have to take a pill every day for the rest of their lives."

He said, "I know, but he only gave me four." 　　—Hal Roach

A sick man went to a doctor he hadn't visited before. As he entered the office, he noticed a sign: "$60 first visit, $30 subsequent visits." To save a few bucks, he greeted the doctor by saying, "Nice to see you again."

The doctor nodded his hello, then began the exam, his expression turning grave as he poked and prodded the ill man.

"Doc, what is it?" the patient asked. "What should I do?"

"Well," the doctor said, setting his stethoscope down, "just keep doing the same thing I told you to do last time you were here."

　　—*Executive Speechwriter Newsletter*

"Doc, my child just swallowed a dozen aspirins. What should I do?"

"Give him a headache. Next." 　　—Paul Dickson

"Doc, thanks so much for making this house call to see my husband."

"Think nothing of it. There's another man sick in the neighborhood, and I thought I could kill two birds with one stone. Next."

　　—Paul Dickson

The man told his doctor that he wasn't able to do all the things around the house that he used to do. When the examination was complete, he said, "Now, Doc, I can take it. Tell me in plain English what is wrong with me."

"Well, in plain English," the doctor replied, "you're just lazy."

"Okay," said the man. "Now give me the medical term so I can tell my wife." 　　—Herschel H. Hobbs in *Open Windows*

After recent minor surgery, my eighty-three-year-old dad protested: "When I got the bill for my operation, I found out why they wear masks in the operating room."

He added: "They call these the 'golden years.' Yeah, right! I have the years, and the doctors have all my gold!"

 A doctor came into a hospital room and told the patient's husband to wait outside while he examined his wife. A few minutes later the doctor came out and asked a nurse's aide if she could get him a pair of pliers. She did, and he went back into the patient's room. Five minutes later he came out and asked for a screwdriver. When he came out a third time and asked for a hammer, the anxious husband demanded to know what was wrong with his wife. "I don't know yet," the doctor said. "I can't get my bag open."

—*Executive Speechwriter Newsletter*

A CODE OF ETHICAL BEHAVIOR FOR PATIENTS

- Do not expect your doctor to share your discomfort. Involvement with the patient's suffering might cause him to lose valuable scientific objectivity.
- Be cheerful at all times. Your doctor leads a busy and trying life and requires all the gentleness and reassurance he can get.
- Try to suffer from the disease for which you are being treated. Remember that your doctor has a professional reputation to uphold.
- Do not complain if the treatment fails to bring relief. You must believe that your doctor has achieved a deep insight into the true nature of your illness, which transcends any mere permanent disability you may have experienced.
- Never ask your doctor to explain what he is doing or why he is doing it. It is presumptuous to assume that such profound matters could be explained in terms that you would understand.
- Pay your medical bills promptly and willingly. You should consider it a privilege to contribute, however modestly, to the well-being of physicians, health care managers, and other humanitarians.

- Do not suffer from ailments not covered by your health care plan. It is a waste of resources to contract illnesses that are beyond your means.
- Never reveal any of the shortcomings that have come to light in the course of treatment by your doctor. The patient-doctor relationship is a privileged one, and you have a sacred duty to protect him from exposure.
- Never die while in your doctor's presence or under his direct care. This will only cause him needless inconvenience and embarrassment.

Doctor to patient: "Good news, Mr. Figby! The insurance company says you're well!"   —Fred Wagner and Ralph Dunagin, North America Syndicate

The thing I like about speaking before doctors is that you generate as many anecdotes as do politicians . . . Like the one about the fellow who went to the hospital for a complete checkup. He was very depressed, and said to the doctor, 'I look in the mirror—I'm a mess. My jowls are sagging. I have blotches all over my face. My hair has fallen out. I feel ugly. What is it?' And the doctor said, 'I don't know what it is, but your eyesight is perfect.'"   —Ronald Reagan

Uncle Sid went to his doctor. "Hey, Doc," he said. "Remember two years ago you cured me of rheumatism?"
    "Yes, I remember," answered the doctor.
    "You told me to stay away from dampness too, remember?"
    "Yes," said the doctor.
    "Is it OK to take a bath now?"   —Joe Laurie Jr. (adapted)

My dad had a friend at Rotary who was a respected physician. But the poor fellow was addicted to gambling. He squandered every cent he owned playing the horses. Then, to make up for the lost money, he tried to rob a bank. But none of the tellers could read his handwriting on the demand note.

Further Reading:
The Telltale Heart, Stefi Scope
Foot Problems of Big Lumberjacks, Paul Bunion
The Irish Heart Surgeon, Angie O'Plasty
Brane Surjery Maid Simpel, Sarah Bellum

■ Dogs

A nursery school teacher was delivering a station wagon full of kids home one day when a fire truck zoomed past. Sitting in the front seat of the fire truck was a Dalmatian dog. The children fell to discussing the dog's duties.

"They use him to keep crowds back," said one youngster.

"No," said another, "he's just for good luck."

A third child brought the argument to a close. "They use the dogs," she said firmly, "to find the fire hydrant."

Outside of a dog, a book is man's best friend. Inside of a dog, it's too dark to read.
—Groucho Marx

My dog is worried about the economy because Alpo is up to ninety-nine cents a can. That's almost seven dollars in dog.
—Joe Weinstein in *Bonkers Magazine*

My wife fell in love with a puppy she saw cavorting in a pet shop window and entered the shop to ask about the dog's pedigree. "The mother," the proprietor told her earnestly, "is a purebred Golden Retriever. As for the father—well, the father comes from a very good neighborhood."

Sign seen near the highway: George Jones, Veterinarian/Taxidermist. Either way, you get your dog back.

Jones, seated in a movie house, could not help being aware that the man immediately in front of him had his arm around the neck of a large dog which occupied the seat next to him. The dog clearly understood the picture, for he snarled softly when the villain spoke, yelped joyously at the funny remarks, and so on.

Jones leaned forward and tapped the man in front of him on the shoulder. He said, "Pardon me, sir, but I can't get over your dog's behavior."

The man turned around and said, "Frankly, it surprises me, too. He hated the book."

Bumper sticker: My dog can lick anyone

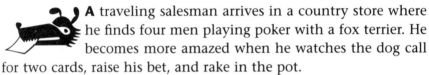

A traveling salesman arrives in a country store where he finds four men playing poker with a fox terrier. He becomes more amazed when he watches the dog call for two cards, raise his bet, and rake in the pot.

Finally he says, "That's amazing. I've never seen such a smart dog."

"He ain't that smart," says one of the men at the table. "Whenever he gets a real good hand he wags his tail." —Paul Dickson

My uncle Joe once walked into a bar in which there were only the bartender, a dog, and a cat.

As Uncle Joe ordered his drink, the dog rose, yawned, and said, "Well, so long, Joe," then walked out.

Joe's jaw dropped. He said to the bartender, "Did you hear that? The dog talked."

"Don't be ridiculous," said the bartender. "A dog can't talk."

"But I heard him," protested Joe.

"You just think you heard him. It's that smart aleck cat over there. He's a ventriloquist."

A dog teaches a boy fidelity, perseverance, and to turn around three times before lying down. —Robert Benchley

When the farmer arrived at the obedience school to pick up his newly trained bird dog, he asked the instructor for a demonstration. The two men and the dog went to a nearby field, where the dog immediately pointed to a clump of brush, then rolled over twice. "There are two birds in there," the instructor said, and sure enough, two birds were flushed. A minute later the dog pointed to another bunch of bushes, and then rolled over five times. "There are five birds in there," the instructor noted, and indeed five birds were driven from the brush. Then the dog pointed to a third clump. He began to whine and run in circles until he found a stick, which he shook mightily and dropped at the men's feet. "And in that clump of brush there," the proud instructor concluded, "there are more birds than you can shake a stick at!"

—Country

Milton Fells, a potato farmer, runs into veterinarian Doc Hyde's office carrying a dog, screaming for help. Doc rushes Milt back to an examination room and has him put his dog down on the table. Doc examines the pet's eyes, feels for a pulse, and listens with his stethoscope to the animal's chest. After a few moments Doc tells Milt that his dog, regrettably, is dead.

Milt, clearly agitated and not willing to accept this, demands a second opinion.

Doc goes into the back room and comes out with a cat and puts the cat down next to the dog's body. The cat sniffs the body, walks from head to tail poking and sniffing the dog's body, and finally looks at Doc and meows.

Doc looks at Milt and says, "I'm sorry, but the cat thinks that your dog is dead, too."

Milt is still unwilling to accept that his dog is dead and demands another test.

Doc brings in a black Labrador. The lab sniffs the body, walks from head to tail, and finally looks at Doc and barks. Doc looks at Milt and says, "I'm sorry, but this Labrador thinks your dog is dead, too."

Milt, finally resigned to the diagnosis, thanks Doc and asks how much he owes.

Doc answers, "$650."

"$650 to tell me my dog is dead?" exclaimed Milt.

"Well," Doc replies, "I would only have charged you $50 for my initial diagnosis. The additional $600 was for the CAT scan and Lab tests."

DOG PROPERTY LAWS

- If I like it, it's mine.
- If it's in my mouth, it's mine.
- If I can take it from you, it's mine.
- If I had it a little while ago, it's mine.
- If it's mine, it must never appear to be yours in any way.
- If I'm chewing something up, all the pieces are mine.
- If it just looks like mine, it's mine.
- If I saw it first, it's mine.
- If you are playing with something and you put it down, it automatically becomes mine.
- If it's broken, it's yours.

LESSONS LEARNED FROM A DOG

- If you stare at someone long enough, eventually you'll get what you want.
- Don't go out without ID.
- Be direct with people; let them know exactly how you feel by piddling on their shoes.
- Be aware of when to hold your tongue and when to use it.
- Leave room in your schedule for a good nap.
- Always give people a friendly greeting. A cold nose in the crotch is effective.
- When you do something wrong, always take responsibility (as soon as you're dragged out from under the bed).
- If it's not wet and sloppy, it's not a real kiss.

HOW MANY DOGS DOES IT TAKE TO CHANGE A LIGHT BULB?

Golden Retriever: The sun is shining, the day is young, we've got our whole lives ahead of us, and you're inside worrying about a stupid burned-out light bulb?

Border Collie: Just one. And I'll replace any wiring that's not up to code.

Dachshund: I can't reach the stupid lamp!

Toy Poodle: I'll just blow in the Border collie's ear, and he'll do it. By the time he finishes rewiring the house, my nails will be dry.

Rottweiler: Go ahead! Make me!

Shi-tzu: Puh-leeze, dah-ling. Let the servants.

Labrador: Oh, me, me! *Pleeeeeze* let me change the light bulb! Can I? Can I? Huh? Can I?

Malamute: Let the Border collie do it. You can feed me while he's busy.

Cocker Spaniel: Why change it? I can still pee on the carpet in the dark.

Doberman Pinscher: While it's dark, I'm going to sleep on the couch.

Mastiff: Mastiffs are NOT afraid of the dark.

Hound Dog: ZZZZZZZZ

Chihuahua: Yo quiero Taco Bulb.

Pointer: I see it, there it is, right there!

Greyhound: It isn't moving, so who cares?

Australian Shepherd: Put all the light bulbs in a little circle. . . .

Old English Sheep Dog: Light bulb? You mean that thing I just ate?

You can say any foolish thing to a dog, and the dog will give you this look that says, "My gosh, you're right! I never would've thought of that!"

—Dave Barry

My son has just moved to Manhattan. He recently spotted a woman walking down Park Avenue with a rather peculiar greyhound dog. It had a bus painted on its side.

My dad once went to a flea circus where a dog stole the whole show.

Dogs feel very strongly that they should always go with you in the car, in case the need should arise for them to bark violently at nothing right in your ear.

—Dave Barry

I was walking the other morning. During my stroll, I passed a pair of fellows and overheard the pair discussing a cute little cocker spaniel one of them was taking for its morning walk.

"Oh, what a cute little pup," commented one.

"I got it for my wife," beamed the other.

"How'd you ever make a trade like that?"　　　　　　—Myron Cohen

TOP TEN REASONS WHY A DOG IS BETTER THAN A WOMAN

10. A dog's parents will never visit you.
 9. A dog loves you when you leave your clothes on the floor.
 8. A dog limits its time in the bathroom to a quick drink.
 7. A dog never expects you to telephone.
 6. A dog will not get mad at you if you forget its birthday.
 5. A dog does not care about the previous dogs in your life.
 4. A dog does not get mad at you if you pet another dog.
 3. A dog never expects flowers on Valentine's Day.
 2. The later you are, the happier a dog is to see you.
 1. A dog does not shop.

TOP TEN WAYS MEN AND DOGS ARE ALIKE

10. Both take up too much space on the bed.
 9. Both have irrational fears about vacuum cleaning.
 8. Both mark their territory.
 7. Neither tells you what's bothering them.
 6. The smaller ones tend to be more nervous.
 5. Neither does any dishes.
 4. Both pass gas shamelessly.
 3. Neither of them notice when you get your hair cut.
 2. Both like dominance games.
 1. Neither understands what women see in cats.

The Heimlich maneuver works on house pets. My pit bull was choking on his dinner. I squeezed his stomach, and the neighbor's cat shot right out.

　　　　　　—Scott Wood

Did you ever walk in a room and forget why you walked in? I think that's how dogs spend their lives.

—Sue Murphy

 Dachshunds are ideal dogs for small children, as they are already stretched and pulled to such a length that the child cannot do much harm one way or the other.

—Robert Benchley

My then five-year-old daughter Susie was overheard explaining things to her brand-new puppy. "You mustn't chew me," she was saying. "Bones are for chewing, silly. People are for lapping."

From the very beginning dogs set out to please their masters, not the other way around. . . . They were put to work to perform a wide variety of chores. And so today's canine community is broken up into such groups as hunting dogs, shepherd dogs, military dogs, racing dogs, watchdogs. . . . Not so with cats. All go under the banner of "pet," a word the dictionary defines as "any loved and cherished creature," an excellent choice of words from the cat's point of view. . . . Dogs travel hundreds of miles during their lifetime responding to such commands as "come" and "fetch." Cats approach people only when there is a reason, and not always even then.

—Stephen Baker

Chihuahua. There's a waste of dog food. Looks like a dog that is still far away.

—Billiam Coronell

My Labrador retriever had a nervous breakdown. I kept throwing him a boomerang.

—Nick Arnette

I went to a ritzy kennel club. It was very exclusive. There was a sign out front: "No Dogs Allowed."

—Phil Foster

Two dachshunds were chatting. "I can't figure it out," said the first dog. "I'm in perfect physical shape, but I'm constantly anxious."

"Why don't you go to a psychiatrist?" said the second.

"How can I? I'm not allowed on the couch."   —Paul Dickson

A dog does not want much and is happy to get it. A cat does not know what it wants and wants more of it.   —Richard Hexem

I'm used to dogs. When you leave them in the morning, they stick their noses in the door crack and stand there like a portrait until you return eight hours later. A cat would never put up with that kind of rejection. When you returned, she'd stalk you until you dozed off and then suck the air out of your body.   —Erma Bombeck

Dogs come when they're called. Cats take a message and get back to you.   —Missy Dizick

Further Reading:
Those Funny Dogs, Joe Kur

■ Drinking

My aunt Betty narrowly escaped with her life one night when her house exploded due to a gas leak. Miraculously, she herself was uninjured. A physician who rushed to the scene told her that one of the few things that had not been destroyed in her home was a bottle of brandy, and he suggested that she take a nip of it to steady her nerve. "Nothing doing," said Aunt Betty. "I'm saving that for an emergency!"

Rehab is for quitters.

A hangover is the wrath of grapes.

Dear Abby: My boyfriend took me out for my twenty-first birthday and wanted to show me a very special good time. I usually don't go in much for drinking, but since it was an occasion to celebrate, I had three martinis. During the dinner we split a bottle of champagne. After dinner we had two brandies. Did I do wrong? Blondie
     Dear Blondie: Probably.

Buck, a rancher in Montana, hated to wear a seat belt, but one day he spotted a state policeman behind him and decided to quickly put it on. "Here, take the wheel," he told his wife. She did, but it was too late, and the trooper pulled them over.

"I noticed you weren't wearing your seat belt," the officer said.

"Yes, I was," the rancher said. "But don't take my word for it. Ask my wife."

"So how about it, ma'am?" the state policeman asked.

"Officer, I've been married to Buck for twenty years," she replied. "And one thing I've learned in all that time is, never argue with him when he's drunk." —Garrison Keillor on *A Prairie Home Companion*

Further Reading:
Soda Pop History, Ginger Aile
I Like Liquor, Ethyl Alcohol

■ Driving
Traffic Light: A trick to get pedestrians halfway across the street safely.

If you must give your child lessons, send him to driving school. He is far more likely to end up owning a Datsun than he is a Stradivarius.
—Fran Lebowitz

Woman driver: A person who, when obeying every rule, is blamed for slowing down some man who isn't.

"**H**oney, I can't get the car started. I think it's flooded."
  "Let me try it. Where is it?"
  "In the river."

A local radio announcer commenting on hazardous driving conditions: "Please don't do any unnecessary driving unless it's absolutely necessary."

Before you only had to roll down your window to curse a passing motorist; now you can call him on your car phone.

Everything is drive-through. In California they even have a burial service called Jump-in-the-Box.
                                                    —Wil Shriner

A couple of morons pooled their bankrolls and bought a little second-hand car. They went driving up the mountains, going around corners and dangerous curves at sixty miles an hour. Finally one moron couldn't stand it any longer. "Every time you go around one of those hairpin bends so fast, I get frightened," he confessed.
  "If you get frightened," advised the other, "why don't you do like I do? I keep my eyes closed!"
                                                    —Harry Hershfield

I said, "Officer, I'm speeding because I'm taking my mom to the hospital. She OD'd on reducing pills."
  He said, "I don't see any woman in the car with you."
  I said, "I'm too late!"
                                                    —Emo Philips

Pedestrian: Man who thought there were still a couple of gallons of gas left in the tank.

My cousin Walt has multiple personality disorder. Can he use the carpool lane?

Pulling over a car full of nuns because they were traveling so slowly, a police officer asked the driver why she couldn't go faster. "But, officer," the nun replied, "all the signs read 15."

"Sister," the cop replied, "that's the route number, not the speed limit."

"Gee, I guess that explains why the others were screaming earlier," the nun realized.

"What are you talking about?"

"Well," the nun answered, "we just got off Route 128."

Further Reading:
Long Walk, Miss D. Bus
The Hitchhiker, Juan Nalift

■ Ecology

Cutler Daily Scoop, on the Ukraine agreeing to shut down the Chernobyl nuclear reactor by the year 2000: "All local residents in favor, raise your right hands. Both of them."

Earth Day was held recently. In honor of that event, I decided that I am just going to use only recycled jokes.　　　—David Letterman

Remember when you were considered an environmentalist if you didn't throw junk out of the car window? I sure do miss that happier, simpler time.　　　—Paula Poundstone

Our water doesn't look good. If he were alive today, Washington could have rolled the dollar across the Potomac!

A new report from the government says raw eggs may have salmonella and may be unsafe. In fact, the latest government theory says it wasn't the fall that killed Humpty Dumpty—he was dead before he hit the ground.　　　—Jay Leno

Pollution is so bad that when I put air in my tires two of them died.　　　—Lee Tully

Mop and Glow: Floor wax used by Three Mile Island cleanup team.

What about all those detergents that are going out into our rivers and the ocean? If this keeps up, it's going to leave a ring around the country.
—John Byner

Further Reading:
Falling Trees, Tim Burr
Wind in the Maple Trees, Russell Ingleaves
Rangers in the Night, Forrest Fyar
The Bog, Pete Maas

■ Economics

Circular Economics 101: The city of Charleston has pledged to contribute at least $5.5 million to help fund the proposed Center for the Arts and Sciences downtown. Where does the city plan to get the money? About one million of it is expected to come from building permit fees charged to the construction contractors who will put up the building.

A little boy said to his father, "Papa, will you please explain the difference between capital and labor?"

His father replied, "If you lend, it's capital. When you try to get it back, it's labor!"
—"Senator" Ed Ford

When the May Day parade was still a big deal in Moscow, a Westerner noted a phalanx of Soviet economists marching between military units.

"Why are the economists marching in ranks with the army?" the Westerner asked then-president Leonid I. Brezhnev.

"You'd be surprised at the damage they do," said the president.
—Paul Dickson

A friend of mine was asked to a costume ball a short time ago. He slapped some egg on his face and went as a liberal economist.

—Ronald Reagan, February 11, 1988

Further Reading:
The Economy Is Recovering, Knott Quite
Fortune Telling, Crystal Ball
The Shrinking Society, Les Ismoor

■ Education

There is nothing so stupid as the educated man if you get off the thing he was educated in.

—Will Rogers

A man that has never gone to school may steal from a freight car, but if he has a university education, he may steal the whole railroad.

—Teddy Roosevelt

"President Clinton said that the country's educational system has to be fixed," says Conan O'Brien. "This came right after a poll revealed that 83 percent of Americans agree, which I'm pretty sure is almost half."

—*Late Night with Conan O'Brien*, NBC

Botany is not a science; it is the art of insulting flowers in Greek and Latin.

—Alphonse Karr

When ignorance gets started it knows no boundaries.   —Will Rogers

If you're truly serious about preparing your child for the future, don't teach him to subtract—teach him to deduct.   —Fran Lebowitz

Addressing the winners of the Bicentennial of the Constitution National Essay Contest on September 10, 1987, President Reagan declared, "History's no easy subject. Even in my day it wasn't, and we had so much less of it to learn then."

Do you know the difference between education and experience? Education is when you read the fine print; experience is what you get when you don't.

—Pete Seeger

Further Reading:
Columbus, Vespucci, and Me, Enzo DiUrth
The Industrial Revolution, Otto Mattick
Teach Me!, I. Wanda Know

■ Enemies

In all matters of opinion, our adversaries are insane. —Mark Twain

James Thurber used to delight in reminiscing about his grandfather, who was one of the most renowned Indian fighters of his day. When the doughty old man was on his deathbed, the preacher asked him if he had made peace with his enemies.

"Don't have any," he replied.

"Amazing," said the preacher. "Pray, tell me how you've managed to live so long without making enemies?"

"I shot 'em."

—Art Linkletter

He hasn't an enemy in the world—but all his friends hate him.

—Eddie Cantor

When my enemies stop hissing, I shall know I'm slipping.

—Maria Callas

▪ Families

One day a man came home from work to find total mayhem at home. The kids were outside still in their pajamas playing in the mud. There were empty food boxes and wrappers all around. Entering the house, he found an even bigger mess. Dishes on the counter, dog food spilled on the floor, a broken glass under the table, and a small pile of sand by the back door. The family room was strewn with toys and various items of clothing, and a lamp had been knocked over. He headed up the stairs, stepping over toys, to look for his wife. He was becoming worried that she may be ill, or that something had happened to her.

He found her in the bedroom, still in bed with her pajamas on, reading a book. She looked up at him, smiled, and asked how his day went. He looked at her bewildered and asked "What happened here today?"

She again smiled and answered, "You know every day when you come home from work and ask me what I did today?"

"Yes," he replied."

She answered, "Well, today I didn't do it!"

I come from a typical American family. You know, me, my mother, her third husband, his daughter from a second marriage. My step-sister. Her illegitimate son.
—Carol Henry

I come from a middle-class family in Brooklyn. Radio City Hall is slightly less ornate than my parents' dining room.   —Elayne Boosler

Doctors will tell you that if you eat slowly you will eat less. Anyone raised in a large family will tell you the same thing.

—Sam Levenson

A family is a unit composed not only of children but of men, women, an occasional animal, and the common cold.

—Ogden Nash

After all, what is a pedestrian? He is a man who has two cars—one being driven by his wife, the other by one of his children.

—Robert Bradbury

During a business trip to Memphis, I visited my cousin Roberta, who goes by the nickname, Bobby Lee. "Cousin Lowell," boasted Bobby Lee, "my husband Earl and ah has fo' fine sons! Eenie, Meenie, Minie, and Elvis."
"Why Elvis?" I asked. "After Presley?"
"Partly," said Bobby Lee. "But princip'ly 'cause we don' want no Mo'!"

My friend Helen has twelve children, and she dresses all of them alike. "When we had only four," she explains, "I dressed them alike so we wouldn't lose any. Now that we have twelve, I dress them alike so we won't pick up any that don't belong to us."

My cousin Esther firmly refused to take "the pill"—even after the birth of her fifth child. So her husband, a local sheriff's deputy, arrested her for practicing license without a medicine.

My wife wanted to call our daughter Sue, but I felt that in our family that was usually a verb.

—Dennis Wolfberg

The family that plays together gets on each other's nerves.

—Erma Bombeck

I came from a big family. As a matter of fact, I never got to sleep alone until I was married.

—Lewis Grizzard

Years ago, my happy married life almost went on the rocks because of the presence in the household of old uncle Buddy. For twelve long years he lived with my wife and me, always crotchety, always demanding, always the first one at the table at mealtimes. Finally, the old man caught double pneumonia and died. On the way back from the cemetery, my wife told me that she had a confession to make. "Darling" she said, "if I didn't love you so much, I don't think I ever could have stood having your uncle Buddy in the house all that time."

I stared at her aghast. "My uncle Buddy!" I exclaimed. "I thought he was your uncle Buddy!"

■ Farmers

Up in my town, a farmer owns a boarding house. One summer, a boarder showed unusual interest in everything rural and asked how long cows should be milked. "The same as short ones," informed the farmer.

—"Senator" Ed Ford

Late one night in 1945, a farmer noticed a light in his barn, so he went to see what it was all about. He discovered a farmhand with a lantern. "What's the idea of carrying around a lighted lantern when we can use the oil for the war effort?" he asked.

"I'm going to call on a girl for the first time," the farmhand explained. "I've got to go through the woods and it's dark."

"When I was your age calling on my wife for the first time," said the farmer, "I went through the woods without a lantern."

"Yeah," reminded the farmhand, "but look what you got!"

—Harry Hershfield

I grew up on a big farm. Last time I was home visiting my folks, I delivered a calf. I tell ya, I feel so much thinner now.

—Henriette Mantel

The farmer is the only man in our economy who buys everything at retail, sells everything he produces at wholesale, and pays the freight both ways.

—John F. Kennedy

It's so cold. . . .Father can't milk the cows by hand because he has to wear his wool mittens. This tickles the cows. They get hysterical, and nothing comes out but cottage cheese.

—Charley Weaver (Cliff Arquette)

Farmer Jones got out of his car and while heading for his friend's door, noticed a pig with a wooden leg. His curiosity roused, he asked, "Fred, how'd that pig get him a wooden leg?"

"Well, Michael, that's a mighty special pig! A while back a wild boar attacked me in the woods. That pig there came a runnin', went after that boar, and chased him away. Saved my life!"

"And the boar tore up his leg?"

"No, he was fine after that. But a bit later we had that fire. Started in the shed up against the barn. Well, that ol' pig started squealin' like he was stuck, woke us up, and 'fore we got out here, the dern thing had herded the other animals out of the barn and saved 'em all!"

"So that's when he hurt his leg, huh, Fred?"

"No, Michael. He was a might winded, though. When my tractor hit a rock and rolled down the hill into the pond, I was knocked clean out. When I came to, that pig had dove into the pond and dragged me out 'fore I drownded. Sure did save my life."

"And that was when he hurt his leg?"

"Oh no, he was fine. Cleaned him up, too."

"OK, Fred. So just tell me. How did he get the wooden leg?"

"Well," the farmer tells him, "a pig like that, you don't want to eat all at once."

We will ask you now to turn your attention to the Ozarks where, according to Mr. Otto Ernest Rayburn, in Eureka Springs, Arkansas, a thrifty farmer fell into the well. He announced his mishap in rather strong language, and his wife came running. She said she'd call the hired man from the field. "Don't bother," he replied after mentally computing time and wages. "It's eleven-thirty now. I'll just paddle around down here until he comes in at noon."

My cousin Bobby Lee's then boyfriend Earl, an unspoiled farm boy, was drafted during the Vietnamese war. Home on his first furlough, he was asked what he thought of army life. "It's fine," he declared enthusiastically. "The food's good, the work's easy, and best of all, they let you sleep real late in the mornings."

When speaking in farm states, President Reagan liked to tell about a farmer who owned some dry, rocky land. Over the years, though, the farmer worked very hard on the land. In time he turned it into dark, rich soil.

One day the local minister came to visit. The minister admired the land. He said, "It is remarkable what you have accomplished with the Lord's help."

The farmer scratched his head. "Reverend, I wish you could have seen this place when the Lord was doing it alone."

A succinct letter received by our Congressman from a farmer in our district: "I beg you not to improve my lot any further. I can't afford it."

Further Reading:
Shoes for Farm and Ranch, Claude Hopper
Mystery in the Barnyard, Hu Flung Dung

■ Fashion

Fashion plate: Where a catcher wearing a tuxedo stands.

You have to remember one thing about the will of the people—a few years ago we were swept away by the Macarena.

Said about CBS announcer John Madden: "He is one man who doesn't let success go to his clothes." —*Sports Illustrated*

A shoulder strap is "a little piece of ribbon designed to keep an attraction from becoming a sensation."
—Myron Cohen, quoting Jack Silverman

Fashion is what you adopt when you don't know who you are.
—Quentin Crisp

Life is tough on women in Arizona prisons now that they have to work on chain gangs. And what's worse, all their stripes are horizontal.
—Rosie O'Donnell

I base my fashion taste on what doesn't itch. —Gilda Radner

Where lipstick is concerned, the important thing is not color, but to accept God's final word on where your lips end. —Jerry Seinfeld

I like to wear clip-on bow ties because they are easy to put on and take off, but my daughter frowns on them as utterly gauche and demands four-in-hands. Furthermore, I like a dash of color here and there, while Robyn prefers a more funereal style of dress—for me, not for herself.

One time, taking my courage in both hands, I prepared for an outing by putting on a large bow tie covered with bright orange stripes. I walked into the living room defiantly and said, "How do I look?"

Robyn looked at me calmly and replied, "You look great, Dad. Now all you have to do is paint your cheeks white and your nose red."

—Isaac Asimov

Further Reading:
Tailoring, Serge Soote
Scottish Kilt Patterns, Glen Pladd

■ Fathers

I was raised by just my mom. See, my father died when I was eight years old. At least, that's what he told us in the letter.   —Drew Carey

Father to adolescent son: "I won't be able to attend your final ballgame. I'm giving a speech on family values."

—Roy Delgado in *Saturday Evening Post*

A father, Princeton alumnus, was quite a grouch. His son had finished his first term and said that his grades were next to the top of his class. "Next to the top?" the father exclaimed. "I'm not sending you to college to be NEXT! Why aren't you the top?"

The son was crestfallen. He studied harder, and the next semester he announced to his father that he was indeed the top of his class.

The father looked at him for a moment and shrugged. "At the head of your class, eh? Well, that's a fine commentary on Princeton University!"

—Alan Young

My father's a strange guy. He's allergic to cotton. He has pills he can take, but he can't get them out of the bottle.   —Brian Killed

When I meet a man I ask myself, "Is this the man I want my children to spend their weekends with?"   —Rita Rudner

I'll never forget the day my father and I hosted the Father-Son Breakfast at church. He never will either because just before he was to speak, I spilled my cup of coffee in his lap.

—Stephen Douglas Williford

"When I was in high school, I got in trouble with my girlfriend's dad," says comedian Steven Wright. "He said, 'I want my daughter back by 8:15.'"

"Cool," I replied, "the middle of August."

Artemus Ward was bragging about his father. "My father was a great artist," he said. "Everything my father made was true to life. Once he made a scarecrow. And gentlemen, that scarecrow was so scary the crows brought back the corn they had stolen two years before."

—Beatrice Schenk de Regniers

A father is a man who expects his children to be as good as he meant to be.

—Carolyn Coats, *Things Your Dad Always Told You But You Didn't Want to Hear*

There are three stages of a man's life:
1. He believes in Santa Claus.
2. He doesn't believe in Santa Claus.
3. He is Santa Claus.

What is it about American fathers as they grow older that makes them dress like flags from other countries? —Cary Odes

Getting tired of those predictable letters from your kids at summer camp? Why not send them this one?

Hi! I am fine. Our home is fine. The food is okay, and I like my wife. Yesterday we went on a trip to the golf course. The pro is nice, and let me ride in a golf cart. I fed it some gasoline. Can I have a golf cart when you get home? Today we had a competition at work to see who could make the fastest voice mail message. I came in last. But your mother won the spending contest. Please send me a CARE package. Love, Dad

We modern, sensitive husbands realize that it's very unfair to place the entire child-care burden on our wives, so many of us are starting to assume maybe 3 percent of it. —Dave Barry

Why are men reluctant to become fathers? They aren't through being children. —Cindy Garner

Boy to father reading the financial news: "Here's a leading economic indicator, Dad. It's only Tuesday, and my weekly allowance is shot." —Abbott in *The Wall Street Journal*

■ Fear

I suppose all this portrays me as a classic xenophobe. Actually, I'm not afraid of xenos. It's foreigners who frighten me. —Lewis Grizzard

I have six locks on my door all in a row. When I go out, I lock every other one. I figure no matter how long somebody stands there picking the locks, they are always locking three. —Elayne Boosler

A lot of people are afraid of heights. Not me, I'm afraid of widths.

—Steven Wright

Don't worry about the world coming to an end today. It's already tomorrow in Australia.   —Charles Schultz

Further Reading:
I'm Scared!, Emma Fraid
Surprised!, Omar Gosh
Acrophobia Explained, Alfredo Heights
Joys of Cowardice, Lily Livard

■ First Ladies

In 1990, First Lady Barbara Bush addressed the graduating class of Wellesley College and declared, "Somewhere out in this audience may even be someone who will one day follow in my footsteps and preside over the White House as the president's spouse. I wish him well."

At a National Prayer Luncheon several years back, Hillary Clinton stated, "In the Bible it says they asked Jesus how many times you should forgive, and he said seventy times seven. Well, I want you all to know that I'm keeping a chart."

Eleanor Roosevelt's witty but wise instructions: "Campaign behavior for wives: Always be on time. Do as little talking as humanly possible. Lean back in the parade car so everybody can see the president."

During Ronald Reagan's second term, the media often reported that there was tension between the First Lady and the White House Chief of Staff Donald Regan. Reagan defused the issue by informing the press: "Nancy and Don at one point tried to patch things up. They met privately over lunch. Just the two of them and their food tasters."

Further Reading:
Gardening with the First Lady, Rose Bush

■ Fitness

They always give you a personal trainer at these fitness centers. Mine looked like one of the American Gladiators; a huge, steroid-looking monster. I think her name was Kelly. —Scott Wood

I joined a health club last year, spent four hundred bucks. Haven't lost a pound. Apparently you have to show up. —Rich Ceisler

I signed up for an exercise class, and the instructor told us to wear tennis shoes and loose-fitting clothing. If I had any loose-fitting clothing, I wouldn't have signed up in the first place.
—*Current Comedy*

I don't do drugs anymore 'cause I find I get the same effect just by standing up really fast. —Johnathan Katz

The best form of exercise is picnics. You can use up two thousand calories trying to keep the ants and flies away from the potato salad.
—Jack E. Leonard

I don't exercise. What's in it for me? You've got to offer me more than my life to get me on a Stairmaster, grunting for two hours. I view my body as a way of getting my head from one place to another.
—Dave Thomas

Sign on a fitness club in Spencer, NC: Live long and perspire.

The doctor decided to put his overweight patient on a diet. "I want you to eat regularly for two days," the physician directed. "Then skip a day, and repeat this procedure for two weeks. The next time I see you, you should have lost at least five pounds."

When the man returned, he had lost twenty pounds. "You did this just by following my instructions?" the doctor asked.

The fellow nodded. "I'll tell you, though, I thought I was going to drop dead that third day."

"From hunger?"

"No, from skipping!"

—Jeff Rovin, *1001 Great Jokes*

Classified ad spotted in the Great Falls, Montana, *Tribune:* "Uninspired fat guy wants to sell intimidating exercise machine. You can reach me in the evenings on the couch."

Actual headline from a small suburban newspaper: Open House! Body Shapers Toning Salon—Free Coffee and Donuts

I tried Flintstones vitamins. I didn't feel any better, but I could stop the car with my feet.

—Joan Onge

Further Reading:
The Beach Bully, Harry Ayp
Exercise on Wheels, Cy Kling
The Scent of a Man, Jim Nasium

■ Food

An hors d'oeuvre is an unfamiliar creature curled up on a cracker and stabbed with a toothpick to make sure it's dead.   —Pat Buttram

Luther Burbank crossed a potato with a sponge. He got something that tastes awful, but it holds a lot of gravy. —Doodles Weaver

Cookbook definition of eternity: Two people and a ham.

Joe Adams says, "It's fun to eat in America, the melting pot. Yesterday I had a Mexican omelet for breakfast, egg foo young for lunch, ravioli for dinner, and sukiyaki for a snack. Late at night I ate the only American thing—a Rolaids."

Ever wonder if illiterate people get the full effect of alphabet soup?
—John Mendoza

I visited an American supermarket. They have so many amazing products here. Like powdered milk: you add water and you get milk. And powdered orange juice: you add water and you get orange juice. Then I saw baby powder. And I said to myself, what a country! I'm making my family tonight! —Yakov Smirnoff

They have this stuff in the supermarket—imitation crabmeat. You know there aren't fish at the bottom of the ocean going, "Wait—I do a great crab!" —Rick Corso

According to statistics, a man eats a prune every twenty seconds. I don't know who this fella is, but I know where to find him.
—Morey Amsterdam

Bananas are a waste of time. After you skin them and throw the bone away, there's nothing left to eat. —Charley Weaver (Cliff Arquette)

We've got a name for sushi in Georgia . . . "bait."   —Blake Clark

Said one friend to another in an upscale coffee bar: "I wish you wouldn't embarrass me by ordering plain coffee."

—S. Harris in *The Wall Street Journal*

Today, we are urged to eat cereals with names like Nutri-Grain. Isn't that something they feed to cows out in Nebraska? And Fiber One. Sounds like a classification of racing cars. Then there's Product 19. And what happened to Products 1 through 18? Inquiring minds want to know.   —Lewis Grizzard

Dinner guest: "We hate to eat and run, but we're still hungry."

—Ron Dentinger

I was in a convenience store. Somebody had blown a hole through every one of the Cheerios. It wasn't hard to figure who it was—a cereal killer.   —Tommy Sledge

My husband thinks that health food is anything he eats before the expiration date.   —Rita Rudner

Further Reading:
Overweight Vegetables, O. Beets
Hot Dog!, Frank Furter
Some Like It Sweet, Sugar Kane
You're So Sweet, Mable Syrup
Classic Groceries, Chopin Liszt
Small Vegetables, ̶ ̶ ̶l Sprout
Tyrant of the Po ̶ ̶ ̶ ̶ ̶ *)ick* Tater
Meat Eaters Rule!, Carney Vore
Oh What a Relief It Is, Al Kaseltzer

■ Football

Famed Oklahoma University football coach Bud Wilkinson was once asked what he thought was the contribution of football to physical fitness. "Absolutely nothing," Wilkinson immediately replied.

"Absolutely nothing?" the startled interviewer asked. "Would you elaborate?"

"Certainly," said Wilkinson. "I define football as twenty-two men on the field desperately in need of rest, and forty thousand in the stands desperately in need of exercise."

—Quoted by Dale E. Turner in *The Hope Health Letter*

A football player and his girl were standing on the sidelines watching the rest of the team scrimmage. It was obvious that a tall end was the star of the team.

"Next year," said the fellow to his girl, "Jim is going to be our best man."

"Oh darling," the girl trilled, giving him a quick kiss on the cheek. "What a nice way to ask me!"   —Myron Cohen

Floyd Little was an All-American running back at Syracuse University who went on to play professionally for the Denver Broncos. He told me the following story:

Dick Butkus of the Chicago Bears was one of the hardest hitting linebackers in football history. As a running back, you could never let the opposing team know they hurt you with a hard hit. One time I got hit harder by Mr. Butkus than I can ever remember. He hit me so hard I don't think there was any fluid left in my body.

I didn't want to let him know how bad he shook me up, so I got up and said, "Is that all you got? Was that your best hit?"

Butkus just looked at me and said, "You all right, Little?"

I answered, "I thought you were a hard hitter, man."

Again he asked me if I was OK.

So I said, "Why do you keep asking me that, man?"

Butkus looked at me with a smirk and said, "Because you're in the wrong huddle, Floyd."   —David Naster

I give the same half-time speech over and over. It works best when my players are better than the other coach's players.   —Chuck Mills

Football is not a contact sport. It's a collision sport. Dancing is a good example of a contact sport.   —Duffy Daugherty

In Mississippi, the ACLU is attempting to stop the practice of a public address prayer before high school football games. The ACLU is also trying to change the name of the Hail Mary pass to the Secular Desperation Heave.   —Dennis Miller

If a man watches three football games in a row, he should be declared legally dead.   —Erma Bombeck

■ Foreign Languages

When an American destroyer laid over for a weekend in Swedish waters, two praiseworthy gobs aboard decided to go to church. Unable to understand one word of Swedish, they resolved to play it safe by sitting behind a solid-looking citizen and doing whatever he did. In the course of the service, the pastor paused to make some special announcement, whereupon the citizen leaped to his feet. The two sailors promptly did likewise, whereupon the entire congregation dissolved into a gale of laughter.

Later the sailors learned the cause of the merriment. The pastor had announced a baptism and requested the father of the baby to rise.

    —Bennett Cerf

A Chinese student at the University of Michigan who memorized phrases from an etiquette book had his first opportunity to try them out at a reception given by President Ruthven. When a cup of tea was handed to him, he solemnly responded, "Thank you, sir or madam, as the case may be."

Red Smith, the sports columnist, was an honored guest one evening at a banquet tendered by the Don Q Rum Company in Puerto Rico. Smith delivered his speech nobly, but for one detail—he persisted in referring to his hosts as the "makers of that wonderful Bacardi rum." Every time he mentioned the competing name "Bacardi," a mortified Don Q official would jump up and correct him with, "Don Q, señor, Don Q." And every time Red Smith answered graciously, "You're welcome."

A firm in Singapore was surprised to receive an inquiry from Saigon for twelve million trombones. Even though orders are pouring into Singapore from the American services in Vietnam, this did seem rather excessive.

The French commercial attaché solved the problem—"trombone" is the French word for paper clip.

A Pasadena girl took a job as a supervisor in a shop employing several Mexican women. The first morning she addressed each of them cordially in her high school Spanish. The women shrank from her. When the same thing happened the next day, the mystified girl told the boss. He asked her what she had said to them. "Just good morning," she replied.

"But how did you say it?"

"I said, 'Buenos Dios, Buenos Dios!'"

The boss howled. "If you wanted to say good morning you should have said 'Buenas dias.' You've looked at each of these women first thing in the morning and said, 'Good God, Good God!'"

Mr. Goldberg, returning from Europe, was assigned by the head steward to a table for two. He was presently joined by a polite Frenchman who, before sitting, bowed, smiled, and said, "Bon appetit."

Not to be outdone, Mr. Goldberg rose, bowed, and said, "Goldberg."

This little ceremony was repeated at each meal for three days. On the fourth day, Mr. Goldberg confided his perplexity to a man in the smoking lounge: "It was like this, you see. This Frenchman tells me his name—Bon Appetit—and I tell him my name—Goldberg. So we are introduced. That is good. But why keep it up day after day?"

"Oh—but you don't understand, Mr. Goldberg," replied the other. "Bon appetit isn't his name. It means 'I hope you have a pleasant meal.'"

"Ah!" exclaimed Goldberg. "Thanks."

That evening it was Mr. Goldberg who arrived late for dinner. Before sitting down he bowed ceremoniously, and said, "Bon appetit."

And the Frenchman rose, smiled, and murmured, "Goldberg."

Two American women stopping at the Hotel Tivoli in Lisbon wanted another chair in their room. The steward who answered their ring could not understand English. One of the women pointed to the only chair in the room, then tried pantomime, seating herself in an imaginary chair. With a knowing smile, the steward bowed and motioned for her to follow him.

At the end of the corridor, he stopped, smiled, and bowed again, and pointed triumphantly to the door of the Ladies' Room.

When I first visited London some thirty-five years ago, I had a terrible time with my pronunciation. It was bad enough to learn that Worcester was pronounced "Wooster," and that Chumley was spelled out as "Cholmondeley." Then I saw a headline in the *London Times*: "A Revival of *Cavalcade* Pronounced Success."

"That settles it," I told my wife. "I'm going home."

President Ronald Reagan gave a speech in Mexico City after which he received very little applause. The next speaker, who spoke in Spanish, was cheered loudly. President Reagan applauded heartily —until the American Ambassador whispered to him, "I wouldn't do that if I were you. She just translated your speech."

It's one thing, for a foreigner to learn the rudiments of English in school, and another to master our peculiar and puzzling idioms, spellings, and pronunciations. One European student, understandably baffled, presented this poetic protest to his professor:

> The wind was rough and cold and blough;
> She kept her hands inside her mough.
> It chilled her through, her nose turned blough,
> And still the squall the faster flough.
> And yet although there was no snough,
> The weather was a cruel fough.
> It made her cough. (Please do not scough);
> She coughed until her hat blough ough.

> —Bennett Cerf

 One humorist has suggested that there should be an annual Chevy Nova Award for the worst in translating American advertising into foreign languages. This award is given out in honor of General Motor's fiasco in trying to market the Nova in Latin American without realizing that in Spanish "No va" means "it doesn't go."

The Dairy Association's huge success with the campaign "Got Milk?" prompted them to expand advertising to Mexico. It was soon brought to their attention that the Spanish translation read "Are you lactating?"

Coors put its slogan, "Turn It Loose," into Spanish, where it was read as "Suffer from Diarrhea."

Clairol introduced the "Mist Stick," a curling iron, into Germany only to find out that "mist" is slang for manure.

When Gerber started selling baby food in Africa, they used the same packaging as in the U.S., with the smiling baby on the label. Later they learned that in Africa, companies routinely put pictures on the labels of what's inside, since many people can't read.

An American T-shirt maker in Miami printed shirts for the Spanish market which promoted the Pope's visit. Instead of "I Saw the Pope" (*el Papa*), the shirts read "I Saw the Potato" (*la papa*).

Pepsi's "Come Alive with the Pepsi Generation" translated into Chinese reads as "Pepsi Brings Your Ancestors Back From the Grave."

The Coca-Cola name in China was first read as *Kekoukela,* meaning "bite the wax tadpole" or "female horse stuffed with wax," depending on the dialect. Coke then researched forty thousand characters to find a phonetic equivalent: *kokoukole,* translating to "happiness in the mouth."

When I was at the Austrian/German conference of Smith's Friends (an evangelical church movement) at Hessenhøfe, Germany, I attempted to deliver a full-fledged sermon with the aid of a translator. I had prepared notes on my laptop computer, which I placed on the lectern in front of me. Everything was going well when suddenly my computer froze. "Just a minute," I said, "my computer is acting up. So just sit quietly and love one another." As I corrected the problem, I could hear the translator but was unable to pay attention to what he was saying. As he finished his remarks, the audience erupted in pandemonious laughter. It was a year later that a friend in Austria explained to me that the translator had directed the group "to sit quietly and make love to one another."

In a Tokyo hotel: Is forbidden to steal hotel towels please. If you are not a person to do such thing is please not to read notis.

In a Bucharest hotel lobby: The lift is being fixed for the next day. During that time we regret that you will be unbearable.

In a Leipzig elevator: Do not enter the lift backwards, and only when lit up.

In a Belgrade hotel elevator: To move the cabin, push button for wishing floor. If the cabin should enter more persons, each one should press a number of wishing floor. Driving is then going alphabetically by national order.

In a Paris hotel elevator: Please leave your values at the front desk.

In a hotel in Athens: Visitors are expected to complain at the office between the hours of 9:00 and 11:00 A.M. daily.

In the lobby of a Moscow hotel across from a Russian Orthodox monastery: You are welcome to visit the cemetery where famous Russian and Soviet composers, artists, and writers are buried daily except Thursday.

In an Austrian hotel that caters to skiers: Not to perambulate the corridors in the hours of repose in the boots of ascension.

On the menu of a Swiss restaurant: Our wines leave you nothing to hope for.

On the menu of a Polish hotel: Salad, a firm's own make; limpid red beet soup with cheesy dumplings in the form of a finger; roasted duck let loose; beef rashers beaten up in the country people's fashion.

Outside a Hong Kong tailor shop: Ladies may have a fit upstairs.

In a Bangkok dry cleaners: Drop your trousers here for best results.

Outside a Paris dress shop: Dresses for street walking.

From the *Soviet Weekly*: There will be a Moscow Exhibition of Arts by 15,000 Soviet Republic painters and sculptors. These were executed over the past two years.

A sign posted in Germany's Black Forest: It is strictly forbidden on our Black Forest camping site that people of different sex, for instance, men and women, live together in one tent unless they are married with each other for that purpose.

In an advertisement by a Hong Kong dentist: Teeth extracted by the latest Methodists.

In a Copenhagen airline ticket office: We take your bags and send them in all directions.

On the door of a Moscow hotel room: If this is your first visit to the USSR, you are welcome to it.

In a Norwegian cocktail lounge: Ladies are requested not to have children in the bar.

In a Budapest zoo: Please do not feed the animals. If you have any suitable food, give it to the guard on duty.

In a doctor's office in Rome: Specialist in women and other diseases.

In a Tokyo shop: Our nylons cost more than common, but you'll find they are best in the long run.

From a Japanese information booklet about using a hotel air conditioner: Cools and Heats: If you want just condition of warm in your room, please control yourself.

From a brochure of a car rental firm in Tokyo: When passenger of foot heave in sight, tootle the horn. Trumpet him melodiously at first, but if he still obstacles your passage then tootle him with vigor.

Two signs from a Majorcan shop entrance: English well talking. Here speeching American.

The following are actual English subtitles used in films originally from Hong Kong:

- Fatty, you with your thick face have hurt my instep.
- Gun wounds again?
- Same old rules: no eyes, no groin.
- A normal person wouldn't steal pituitaries.
- How can you use my intestines as a gift?
- Who gave you the nerve to get killed here?
- Quiet or I'll blow your throat up.
- You always use violence. I should've ordered glutinous rice chicken.
- I'll fire aimlessly if you don't come out!
- You daring lousy guy.
- Beat him out of recognizable shape!
- Take my advice, or I'll spank you without pants.
- I got knife scars more than the number of your leg's hair!
- Beware! Your bones are going to be disconnected.
- The bullets inside are very hot. Why do I feel so cold?

PHONY FRENCH TRANSLATIONS

Aperitif: a set of dentures.

Coup de grace: Lawn mower.

Chateaubriand: Your hat is on fire.

Pas de tout: Father of twins.

Entrechat: Let the cat in.

Marseillaise: Ma says OK.

—F. S. Pearson II

An ad appears in the paper asking for an individual who can type, take dictation, program a computer, and speak more than one language. The first applicant for the job is a dog. The dog is able to type 145 words per minute, takes perfect dictation, and not only can program a computer but has written several programming manuals. The prospective employer has the dog demonstrate all of these skills, and then turns to him and says, "I'm dazzled by your qualifications. I only have one final question: What about the language requirement?"

The dog looks at him and says, "Meow!" —Paul Dickson

■ Friends

Some friends are a habit; others are a luxury.

When it comes to helping a friend, some people will stop at nothing.

A friend in need is the only kind of friend a person has nowadays.

Ambrose Bierce tartly observed, "Acquaintance is a degree of friendship called slight when its object is poor or obscure and intimate when he is rich or famous."

My dad's face lit up as he recognized the man who was walking ahead of him at the supermarket. He clapped the man so heartily on the back that the man nearly collapsed, and exclaimed, "Hank Mandelbaum, my old college roommate! I hardly recognized you. Why, you've gained a hundred pounds since I saw you last, and you've had your nose fixed, and I swear you are about two feet taller."

The man looked at him angrily. "I beg your pardon," he said in icy tones, "but I am not Hank Mandelbaum. My name is Phil Goldberg."

"Aha," said Dad. "You've even changed your name!"

A true friend is someone who knows all about you and loves you just the same.

Be kind to your friends. Without them you'd be a complete stranger.

A true friend walks in when the rest of the world walks out.

Bubba brags to his boss one day, "I know everyone there is to know. Just name someone, anyone, and I know them."

Tired of his boasting, his boss called his bluff. "OK, Bubba, how about Tom Cruise?"

"Sure! Yes, Tom and I are old friends, and I can prove it." So Bubba and his boss fly out to Hollywood and knock on Tom Cruise's door, and sure enough, Tom Cruise shouts, "Bubba! Great to see you! You and your friend come right in and join me for lunch!"

Although impressed, Bubba's boss is still skeptical. After they leave Cruise's house, he tells Bubba that he thinks Bubba's knowing Cruise was just lucky.

"No, no, just name anyone else," Bubba says.

"President Clinton," his boss quickly retorts.

"Sure!" Bubba says. "I know him! Let's fly out to Washington." And off they go.

At the White House, Clinton spots Bubba on the tour and motions him and his boss over, saying, "Bubba, what a surprise! I was just on my way to a meeting, but you and your friend come on in, and let's have a cup of coffee first and catch up."

Well, the boss is very shaken, but still not totally convinced. After they leave the White House grounds, he expresses his doubts to Bubba, who again implores him to name anyone else. "The Pope," his boss replies.

"Sure!" says Bubba. "My folks are from Poland, and I've known the Pope a long time." So off they fly to Rome.

Bubba and his boss are assembled with the masses in Vatican Square when Bubba says, "This will never work. I can't catch the

Pope's eye among all these people. Tell you what, I know all the guards, so let me just go upstairs, and I'll come out on the balcony with the Pope." And he disappears into the crowd headed toward the Vatican.

Sure enough, half an hour later Bubba emerges with the Pope on the balcony. But by the time Bubba returns, he finds that his boss has had a heart attack and is flat out on the ground, surrounded by paramedics. Working his way to his boss' side, Bubba asks him, "What happened?"

His boss looks up and says, "I was doing fine until you and the Pope came out on the balcony, and the man next to me said, 'Who's that on the balcony with Bubba?'"

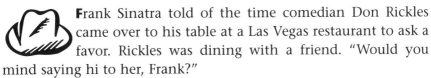

Frank Sinatra told of the time comedian Don Rickles came over to his table at a Las Vegas restaurant to ask a favor. Rickles was dining with a friend. "Would you mind saying hi to her, Frank?"

"Of course not," the singer replied. "Bring her over."

Then Rickles said that his friend would be even more impressed if Sinatra would come over to their table. So a short time later, Sinatra good-naturedly walked across the restaurant, slapped Rickles on the back, and said how delighted he was to see him. Whereupon Rickles said, "Beat it, Frank. This is personal."

—Larry King

Further Reading:
Hiya Fella, Gladys Eeya
Come on In!, Doris Open
I Love Crowds, Morris Merrier

■ Funerals

I'm not afraid of death. It's the make-over at the undertaker's that scares me. . . .They try to make you look as lifelike as possible, which defeats the whole purpose. It's hard to feel bad for somebody who looks better than you do.
—Anita Wise

A funeral eulogy is a belated plea for the defense delivered after the evidence is all in.

—Irving S. Cobb

Martin Levine has passed away at the age of seventy-five. Mr. Levine owned a movie theater chain here in New York. The funeral will be held on Thursday, at 2:15, 4:20, 6:30, 8:40, and 10:50.

—David Letterman

My uncle's funeral cost five thousand dollars so far. We buried him in a rented tuxedo.

—Dave Madden

They say such nice things about people at their funeral that it makes me sad to realize that I'm going to miss mine by just a few days.

—Garrison Keillor

Three aged men arrive at the Pearly Gates at the same time. As part of their orientation to heaven, St. Peter asks what kind of remarks they would most like to hear from their family and friends at their funerals.

"I would like to hear them say I was a great doctor and a good family man," said the first.

"I would like to hear that I was a wonderful husband and that, during my career as a schoolteacher, I made a difference in many lives," chimed in the second fellow.

"Those both sound terrific," replied the third, "but I'd like to hear them say, 'Look! He's moving!'"

Further Reading:
Grave Matters, Paul Bearer
Life Six Feet Under, Doug Graves

■ Gambling

Gambling is a way of getting nothing for something.

—Wilson Mizner

When entering the hotel where she and her husband were staying, Gladys, a devout Baptist, noticed a shabbily dressed man lounging idly in front of the newspaper stand in the lobby. She noticed that several men stopped to talk to him and gave him a little money. He seemed so cheered by these encounters that she impulsively put ten dollars in an envelope, wrote "God bless" on the outside, and handed it to him.

The next day the man stopped her on the street. "Here's your $250," he said cheerily. "God Bless won at 28 to 1."

Celebrated author Isaac Asimov confessed that he had gambled only once in his life. Here is his true story:

Shortly after I had married, my wife left town to visit her folks. I was at loose ends, and I was lured into a poker game with the boys. When it was all over, my conscience smote me, for I had been brought up by a puritanical father to eschew gambling in all its forms (and I had never rebelled). All I could do was confess.

On my next trip home, I said with all the casualness I could manage, "I played a game of poker with the boys, Papa. For money."

My father stared at me in astonishment and said, "How did you make out?"

I said, "I lost fifteen cents."

He said, "Thank goodness. You might have won fifteen cents."

He was probably right. Winning the first time out might have hooked me. As it was, I never played again.

> They head the list of bad to bet on,
> But I insist they're worse to get on.
>
> —Richard Armour

Although horse racing is allegedly the sport of kings, Sir Gordon Richards is the first jockey to have been knighted by the British Crown. When five-foot Sir Gordon, who was scarcely obliged to kneel to receive the Queen's sword on his shoulder, first heard of the honor, he quipped, "I never realized that I'd end up being the shortest knight of the year." —Art Linkletter

You know horses are smarter than people. You never heard of a horse going broke betting on people. —Will Rogers

■ Gardens

Last year, I planted my very first vegetable garden. It was such an enormous success that my neighbor's chickens won first prize at the poultry show.

Whoever said "What you see is what you get" never ordered from a spring seed catalog.

You know those seed catalogs? I think the pictures are posed by professional flowers getting fifty dollars an hour. I don't consider gardening so much growing flowers as burying seeds. —H. Aaron Cohl

Every year about Easter, I begin to feel the urge to get out the old hoe, buy some peat moss, and carefully select some tomato plants. I faithfully water these tomato plants, watch them grow, and am subsequently always disappointed by the meager, puny, embarrassing results. Yet, like Linus who faithfully awaits the Great Pumpkin year after year, I hold the Great Tomato Hope. I do all the right things. I watch *Victory Garden*. I build a raised garden bed. I read *Square Foot Gardening*. I buy a tomato cage. I get a drip-drop hose. I make a compost cage. I get a tiller. I get manure. I get *The Tomato Book* at the hardware store. This year, I'm pulling out all of the stops. I'm going to enroll in a gardening class. I'm going to attend a Tomato Support Group. Hello, my name is Steve, and I killed my tomatoes. I'm installing a cyclone fence with razor wire around my garden. I'm going to buy an electronic timer which waters the plants at precisely the moment they become thirsty. At this rate, my tomatoes should be worth about fifty-seven dollars a pound. And if all that doesn't work, I'll buy some tomatoes from the grocery and glue them on.
                                        —Stephen Douglas Williford

A San Diego store attaches this label to every package of seeds: Warning—After planting, step back quickly!

I've killed so many plants my photo has been posted on nursery walls.
                                        —Rita Rudner

A minister illustrated a point in his sermon by saying that a beneficent wisdom knows which of us grows best in sunlight and which of us must have shade. "You know you plant roses in the sunlight," he said. "But if you want your fuchsias to grow, they must be kept in a shady nook."

Afterward a woman came up to him, her face radiant. "Dr. Smith," she said clasping his hand. "I'm so grateful for your splendid sermon." His heart glowed for a moment. But then she went on fervently, "I never knew before just what was the matter with my fuchsias!"

179

Further Reading:
Bad Gardeners, Wilt Plant
In Farmer MacGregor's Garden, Peter Abbott
A Bestiary of Plant Eaters, Herb Avore
The Excitement of Trees, I. M. Board
The Squeaking Gate, Rusty Hinges
Cab Calloway's Garden, Heidi Ho
The Garden State, Ida Hoe
I Like Weeding, Manuel Labour
Cut the Grass!, Moses Lawn
How to Cut Grass, Lon Moore
Lawn Care, Ray King
Harvesting Wild Plants, Dudley Nightshade
Exotic Irish Plants, Phil O'Dendron
The Fall of a Watermelon, S. Platt
House Plants, Clay Potts
Nordic Groundskeepers, Leif Raker
May Flowers, April Showers
Red Vegetables, B. Troot

■ God

If God seems so far away—who moved?   —Sam Levenson

God is a great humorist. He just has a slow audience to work with.
                                                —Garrison Keillor

"God Speaks" billboards are catching the eyes of highway commuters in Dallas. The billboards feature simple white text on a black background. No fine print or sponsoring organization is included. A list of all that have appeared to date:

* Let's meet at my house Sunday before the game. —God
* C'mon over and bring the kids. —God
* What part of "Thou shalt not" didn't you understand? —God
* We need to talk. —God

- Keep using my name in vain, I'll make rush hour longer. —God
- Loved the wedding, invite me to the marriage. —God
- That "Love thy neighbor" thing? I meant it. —God
- Will the road you're on get you to my place? —God
- Big bang theory, you've got to be kidding! —God
- My way is the highway. —God
- Need directions? —God
- You think it's hot here? —God
- Have you read my No. 1 best seller? There will be a test. —God
- Do you have any idea where you're going? —God
- Don't make me come down there. —God

You say you don't go to services because "the place is full of hypocrites"? Don't let that bother you. There's always room for one more.

—Sam Levenson

Why God never received tenure at any university:

- He had only one major publication, and it had no references.
- Some people doubted that he wrote it himself.
- He never applied to the ethics board for permission to use human subjects.
- He expelled his first two students—for learning.
- When one particular experiment went awry, he tried to cover it up by drowning the subjects.
- He rarely appeared in class, usually just telling students to read the book.
- His office hours were infrequent and usually held on a mountain top.
- Although there were only ten requirements, the great majority of students could never pass his tests.

—B. Kliban

Further Reading:
Prepare to Meet Your Maker, Eva de Struction

■ Golf

Men don't give birth. They don't have to. They get all the pain they need from golf.

A hole in one, scored by pure accident, can keep a complete duffer playing golf for the rest of his life. —Tony Lema

Give me my golf clubs, the fresh air, and a beautiful girl for a partner, and you can keep my golf clubs and the fresh air. —Jack Benny

Pastor Ben Thompson of Mount Pisco Holiness Church admonished one of his deacons, "I didn't see you in church on Sunday. I heard you were playing golf instead."

The deacon responded, "That's not true, Reverend. And I have the fish to prove it."

"Minister, is it a sin to play golf on Sunday?"

"Son, I've watched you play, and it's a sin for you to play any day of the week."

Some golfers are just natural cheaters. My brother-in-law cheats so much that the other day he had a hole in one, and he marked a zero on his score card. —Joey Adams

Golf is a good walk spoiled. —Mark Twain

From a prayer printed in a Reading, Ohio, church bulletin: "Lord, you are more precious than silver. Lord, you are more costly than golf."

Golf is not a game; it's a punishment for not taking up another sport.

—Gene and Linda Perret

Eric: You know what your main trouble is?
Ernie: What?
Eric: You stand too close to the ball after you've hit it.

—Eric Morecambe and Ernie Wise

Golf is a great weekend sport. It makes going back to work on Monday seem almost a relief.

Playing golf for fun is like going to the dentist because you enjoy rinsing.

The greenhorn golfer asked his seasoned chum, "When do I get to use the putter?"

His friend said, "Hopefully, sometime before sunset."

I play golf every chance I get. I think the world needs more laughter.

The old priest and his young friend went golfing, and, as usual, the game went well for the clergyman. "God must be on your side again," moaned his friend. "You sink every putt you take!"

"Look at it this way," said the priest. "One day you'll bury me, and you'll have won the most important game of all."

"Won, shmun!" said his friend. "You'll be first in the hole!"

At an Alaskan golf club, this sign was posted in the locker room: Three feet of snow on the greens will make them rather slow this weekend.

Golf is nature's way of making everyone a comedian.

I'm convinced the reason most people play golf is to wear clothes they would not be caught dead in otherwise.   —Roger Simon

If you watch a game, it's fun. If you play it, it's recreation. If you work at it, it's golf.   —Bob Hope

Sign on a municipal golf course: Please don't find golf balls until at least they've stopped rolling.

Golf, there's a thing that torments you and won't let you enjoy yourself. You've got to relax. I got out of this country's worst sand trap with just one stroke. Of course, the doctor said if I had another stroke like that it would be all over.   —Dave Astor

I play in the low 80s. If it's any hotter than that, I won't play.
          —Joe E. Lewis

Nothing increases your golf score like witnesses.   —*Bits and Pieces*

I had a wonderful experience on the golf course today. I had a hole in nothing. Missed the ball and sank the divot.   —Don Adams

■ Government
Our Supreme Court has gone so conservative. They took a group portrait the other day, and the Court had moved so far right, only four of the judges were still in the picture.   —Gene and Linda Perret

The contractor wanted to give the government official a sports car. The official objected, saying, "Sir, common decency and my basic sense of honor would never permit me to accept a gift like that."

The contractor said, "I quite understand. Suppose we do this: I'll sell you the car for ten dollars."

The official thought for a moment and said, "In that case, I'll take two."

—Joey Adams

One way to make sure crime doesn't pay would be to let the government run it.

—Ronald Reagan

President Lincoln found out that in government, as in the private sector, prize positions are often given out on the basis of who you know, not what you know. A woman once begged of Lincoln saying, "Mr. President, you must grant me a colonel's commission for my son. I demand it of you, Sir, not as a favor but as a right. My grandfather fought at Lexington, my father fought at New Orleans, and my husband was killed at Monterey."

Lincoln said, "Madam, I suppose your family has done enough for our country. It's time we give someone else a chance."

According to Ronald Reagan, the government's view of the economy may be summed up in just a few short phrases: "If it moves, tax it; if it keeps moving, regulate it; if it stops moving, subsidize it."

Too many people, especially in government, feel that the nearest thing to eternal life we will ever see on this earth is a government program.

—Ronald Reagan, May 10, 1972

The Supreme Court was so liberal for such a long time that it got so you had to commit a crime to get any rights in this country.

—Gene and Linda Perret

At the immigration office in Los Angeles, when immigrants arrive for the oath of allegiance ceremony to become citizens of the United States, they give them small American flags, made in Korea.
—Nazareth Veterans Administration

Put a federal agency in charge of the Sahara Desert, and it would run out of sand.
—Peggy Noonan

Government seems to be able to come up with solutions that are more troublesome than the problems.

When you mention common sense in Washington, you cause traumatic shock.
—Ronald Reagan

The government just put a wonderful machine in all of its buildings. It does the work of six people. Of course, it takes twelve to operate it.

Where else but in Washington could they call the department that's in charge of everything outside and out-of-doors the Department of the Interior?
—Ronald Reagan

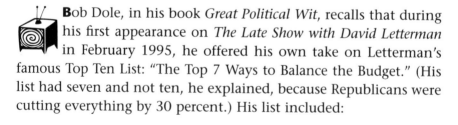 **B**ob Dole, in his book *Great Political Wit*, recalls that during his first appearance on *The Late Show with David Letterman* in February 1995, he offered his own take on Letterman's famous Top Ten List: "The Top 7 Ways to Balance the Budget." (His list had seven and not ten, he explained, because Republicans were cutting everything by 30 percent.) His list included:

- Stop paying Clinton speech writers by the word.
- Save government ink by replacing the long William Jefferson Clinton signature with 66 percent shorter Bob Dole signature.

- Make Gore and Gingrich pay for those good seats at State of the Union addresses.
- Fire the White House gardeners and require Al Gore to do something to earn his keep.
- And the No. 1 way to balance the budget? Sell Arkansas.

Thomas Jefferson said, "The best government is no government at all." Lately it seems that's what we get closer and closer to electing.

—Gene and Linda Perret

When John Gardner assumed the duties of secretary of health, education, and welfare, he was filled with optimism: "We are all faced with a series of great opportunities—brilliantly disguised as insoluble problems."

—Bob Dole

I don't make jokes; I just watch the government and report the facts.

—Will Rogers

MICROSOFT TO ACQUIRE FEDERAL GOVERNMENT

Redmond, Wash.—In direct response to accusations made by the Department of Justice, the Microsoft Corp announced today that it will be acquiring the federal government of the United States of America for an undisclosed sum.

"It's actually a logical extension of our planned growth," said Microsoft chairman Bill Gates. "It really is going to be a positive arrangement for everyone." Microsoft representatives held a briefing in the Oval Office of the White House with U.S. President Bill Clinton, and assured members of the press that changes will be "minimal." The United States will be managed as a wholly owned division of Microsoft. An IPO is planned for July of next year, and the federal government is expected to be profitable by "Q4 2003 at latest" according to Microsoft CEO Steve Ballmer.

In a related announcement, Clinton stated that he had "willingly and enthusiastically" accepted a position as a vice president with

Microsoft, and will continue to manage the United States government, reporting directly to Bill Gates. When asked how it felt to give up the mantle of executive authority to Gates, Clinton smiled and referred to it as "a relief." He went on to say that Gates has a "proven track record," and that U.S. citizens should offer Gates their "full support and confidence." In his new role at Microsoft, Clinton will reportedly be earning several times the $200,000 annually he has earned as U.S. president.

Gates dismissed a suggestion that the U.S. capitol be moved to Redmond as "silly," though he did say that he would make executive decisions for the U.S. government from his existing office at Microsoft headquarters. Gates went on to say that the House and Senate would "of course" be abolished. "Microsoft isn't a democracy," he observed, "and look how well we're doing."

When asked if the rumored attendant acquisition of Canada was proceeding, Gates said, "We don't deny that discussions are taking place." Microsoft representatives closed the conference by stating that U.S. citizens will be able to expect lower taxes, increases in government services, and discounts on all Microsoft products.

About Microsoft. Founded in 1975, Microsoft (NASDAQ "MSFT") is the worldwide leader in software for personal computers, and democratic government. The company offers a wide range of products and services for public, business, and personal use, each designed with the mission of making it easier and more enjoyable for people to take advantage of the full power of personal computing and free society every day.

About the United States. Founded in 1783, the United States of America is the most successful nation in the history of the world and has been a beacon of democracy and opportunity for over two hundred years. Headquartered in Washington, D.C., the United States is a wholly owned subsidiary of Microsoft Corporation.

■ Grandparents

A grandmother will put a sweater on you when she is cold, feed you when she is hungry, and put you to bed when she is tired.

—Erma Bombeck

A mother becomes a true grandmother the day she stops noticing the terrible things her children do because she is so enchanted with the wonderful things her grandchildren do. —Lois Wyse

When our daughter-in-law Dalacie had just given birth to a beautiful baby boy, her first child, and I was being congratulated, I apparently looked downcast. So a friend asked, "What's the matter, Lowell? Don't you like the idea of being a grandfather?"

I heaved an enormous sigh and said, "Being a grandfather is fine. That doesn't bother me much at all. It's just that it's so humiliating to have to go to bed with a grandmother," I said laughingly.

When I stopped the bus to pick up Karissa for preschool, I noticed an older woman hugging her as she left the house.

"Is that your Gramma?" I asked.

"Yes," Karissa said. "She's come to visit us for Christmas."

"How nice," I said. "And where does your Gramma live?"

"At the airport," Karissa replied. "Whenever we want her we just go out there and get her."

You feel completely comfortable entrusting your baby to [them] for long periods, which is why most grandparents flee to Florida at the earliest opportunity. —Dave Barry

No one is prouder than grandmothers. They have forgotten the wet diapers and hard work associated with bringing up a baby. All they notice is how many steps their little darlings can take, the cute words of wisdom that come from the mouths of the little angels, and how many times the sweet little things kissed Grandma on her last visit.

Last week while walking through the park, I met a neighbor who was taking her two grandsons for a walk. I waved to her and said, "You have nice looking grandchildren, Mrs. Brown. How old are they?"

Smiling proudly, she said, "The lawyer is four and the doctor is six."

—Myron Cohen

T-shirt seen on an eight-year-old: That's It! I'm Calling Grandma!

Infant undershirts were made to keep Grandma happy on those chilly ninety degree days in mid-August.   —Linda Fiterman

My children think that my mother is the most wonderful person in the world. I keep telling them, "That is not the same person I grew up with. You're looking at an old person who's trying to get into heaven."   —Bill Cosby

A retired California couple received this circular from their young married son in Denver: "Vacation Contest. Free round-trip transportation to beautiful mile-high Denver. Free golf and use of all facilities of new million-dollar country club. Unlimited use of slightly battered station wagon, color TV set, pool table, and set of bongo drums. Maid and laundry service included. To enter contest, just complete the following sentence in twenty-five words or less: 'We would like to come to Denver and take care of four healthy young children for two weeks while our son and daughter-in-law take a richly earned vacation in the Canadian Rockies because . . ."   —Bennett Cerf

Why is it that grandchildren grow faster than children?
                                            —Alex Thien in *Milwaukee Sentinel*

The simplest toy, one which even the youngest child can operate, is called a grandparent.   —Sam Levenson

■ Hair

My elderly neighbor Hetty met her cousin Sally for lunch. They had not seen one another for two years. Hetty stared at Sally for a moment and then said, "Cousin Sally, whatever have you done to your hair? It looks exactly like a wig."

"To tell you the truth," replied Sally with evident embarrassment, "It is a wig."

Hetty's tactful response: "Really? Well, you certainly can't tell."

His toupee makes him look twenty years sillier.

—Bill Dana

A new barber nicked a customer badly in giving him a shave. Hoping to restore the man's feeling of well-being, he asked solicitously, "Do you want your head wrapped in a hot towel?"

"No, thanks," said the customer. "I'll carry it home under my arm."

My wife teased her hair so much, it finally attacked her.

—Luke Files

Never say "Surprise me!" to your hairdresser or barber.

—William Rotsler

"**E**veryone talks about the effects of tobacco smoke," a husband remarked to his wife as they got ready for work. "Where are the studies on the effects of second-hand hair spray?"

—Howard & Macintosh, King Feature

A bald man took a seat in a beauty shop. "How can I help you?" asked the stylist.

"I went for a hair transplant," the guy explained. "But I couldn't stand the pain. If you can make my hair look like yours without causing me any discomfort, I'll pay you $5000."

"No problem," said the stylist. And she quickly shaved her head.

—Debbie Costet

A barber in Coventry, England, boasts, "My ancestors were official hairdressers of Lady Godiva."

Further Reading:
Trim Those Sideburns Too?, Buzz Cutt
We're All Flakes, Dan Druff
Rapunzel, Rapunzel!, Harris Long
Dull Razor, Nick Shaving

■ Headlines

Over the years, I've run into some pretty remarkable headlines. Here are some of the most outrageous.

- Three Ambulances Take Blast Victim to Hospital
- Gas Cloud Clears Out Taco Bell
- Drought Turns Coyotes to Watermelons
- Lack of Water Hurts Ice Fishing
- Death in the Ring: Most Boxers Are Not the Same Afterward. Jay Leno comments, "Yeah, I hear some of them are smarter."
- Free for Qualified Senior Citizens and Persons with Low Income, Spay/Neuter Service

- Liquor Sales Dip Blamed on Less Drinking
- Bush Gets Briefing on Drought; Says Rain Needed to End It. Jay Leno responds, "This is the kind of no-nonsense, put-your-reputation-on-the-line problem-solver we need in the White House."
- Heading on column of figures published by Census Bureau: Population of U.S. Broken Down by Age and Sex
- Researchers Call Murders a Threat to Public Health
- Searchers Find Big Ugly Child. (From a newspaper in Big Ugly, West Virginia.)
- Death Row Inmates No Longer Allowed Day Off after Execution, Official Says. Comments Jay Leno, "Boy, you thought the other warden was tough!"
- Stress Higher for Working Moms than for Childless Moms
- For Women Only—Free Confidential Pregnancy Test
- Furniture Drive for Homeless Launched
- Blind Workers Eye Better Wages
- Area Man Wins Ad for Nuclear Plant Accident
- Crime: Sheriff Asks for 13.7% Increase
- Mayor Says D.C. Is Safe Except for Murders
- Married Women Can Enter the Mrs. Arizona Pageant
- Pope to Be Arraigned for Burglarizing Clinic
- Studies Indicate Fat Intake Affects Obesity
- Helicopter Powered by Human Flies
- Pet Cooking Contest Coming to Highland
- Blow to Head Is Common Cause of Brain Injury
- Ski Areas Closed Due to Snow

When *New York Times Magazine* ran a piece about how the J. Paul Getty Museum's art collection survived the Northridge earthquake unscathed, the headline read: "Be Still, My Art."

■ Health

MEDICAL TERMS DEFINED

Benign: What you be after you be eight
Artery: The study of paintings
Bacteria: Back door to cafeteria

Barium: What doctors do when patients die
Caesarean section: A neighborhood in Rome
G. I. Series: World Series of military baseball
Hangnail: What you hang your coat on
Labor pain: Getting hurt at work
Medical staff: A doctor's cane
Nitrates: Cheaper than day rates
Recovery room: Place to do upholstery
Tablet: A small table
Terminal illness: Getting sick at the airport
Tumor: More than one
Urine: Opposite of you're out

Shortly before the outbreak of the Civil War, President Lincoln had a mild attack of smallpox to add to his troubles. Informed of the nature of his illness, Lincoln didn't lose his precious sense of humor. "It is too bad," he noted dryly, "that this one time while I have something to give everybody—no one comes near me!"

—Bennett Cerf

My poor uncle Joe. He just can't win. He gave up cigarettes and started chewing toothpicks. He now has Dutch elm disease.

This is the same uncle who tried tapering off smoking by puffing a cigarette once or twice, dropping it on the ground, then stamping it out. Unfortunately, he contracted cancer of the shoe.

Maybe all of us should band together and say, "Enough is enough. Please don't tell us what else will kill us." —Lewis Grizzard

My allergy tests suggest that I may have been intended for some other planet. —Walt Wetterberg

Eddie Cantor ran into his friend George Jessel one day and asked him, "How's your Ma?"

"Terrible," said George. "She's got chronic frontal sinusitis."

"Good Lord, where did she get that?" asked a concerned Eddie.

"From *Reader's Digest*. She read about it last month."

Further Reading:
The Miracle Drug, Penny Cillin
Irish First Aid, R. U. O'Kaye
Pain in My Body, Otis Leghurts
Pain Relief, Ann L. Gesick

■ Health Maintenance Organizations (HMOS)

Patient to HMO screening nurse: Help, I have chest pain! Call me an ambulance!

HMO Screening Nurse: Okay, you're an ambulance.

Waiter to customers: "I'm sorry, but your managed-care organization required me to substitute the fish for the prime rib."

—Dan Gallagher in *Funny Times*

The Northern County Psychiatric Associates (which has offices in Monkton and Lutherville, Maryland) maintains an Internet website (http://www.ncpamd.com/mcjokes.htm) of Managed Care Jokes. The following excerpt is reproduced with their kind permission.

Two little girls were having an argument about which of their daddies was better. "My daddy is better than yours. He's a carpenter and builds houses."

"That isn't so great," said the other girl. "My daddy writes health insurance contracts, and he makes loopholes."

Changing HMOS is like changing deck chairs on the *Titanic*.

A billing clerk for a managed care company proudly told a friend that she had just finished a jigsaw puzzle, "And it only took me five months," she beamed.

"Five months?" said her friend. "That sounds like an awfully long time to finish a jigsaw puzzle."

"Not really, " the clerk explained. "The box says six to twelve years."

Q: How many managed care reviewers does it take to change a light bulb?

A: Five. One to receive the authorization forms and put them at the bottom of a pile; the second to put the pile in a storage closet; the third to refuse to authorize the light bulb change because the authorization forms were never received; the fourth to process the resubmitted authorization forms; and the fifth to authorize a ten-watt light bulb because it uses less electricity.

GREAT MOMENTS IN PAPERWORK

Actual comments on medical review forms:

- The patient has been depressed ever since she began seeing me in 1988.
- She is tearful and crying constantly. She also appears to be depressed.
- Patient has left her white blood cells at her primary care doctor's office.
- The patient is ready to leave the hospital. She is feeling much better except for her original complaints.
- Discharge status: Alive but without permission.
- The patient will need disposition, and therefore we will get the outpatient psychiatrist to dispose of her.
- Patient has chest pains if she lies on her left side for over a year.
- By the time she was admitted to the hospital, her rapid heartbeat had stopped, and she was feeling much better.
- Patient was seen in consultation by the physician, who felt we should sit tight on the abdomen, and I agreed.
- If he squeezes the back of his neck for four or five years, it comes and goes.

■ Heaven and Hell

My friend Virgil couldn't have gotten through the Pearly Gates with a gold American Express card and written recommendations from three of the original disciples.

—Lewis Grizzard

Just before World War II, in Flushing, New York, two clergymen attended an annual interfaith luncheon. Father Robert Felts, an Episcopalian minister, in a playful mood said to his friend Rabbi Cohen, "You know, Rabbi, I dreamed of a Jewish heaven the other night. It was very lifelike, and it seemed to me to just suit the Jewish ideal. It was a crowded tenement district with Jewish people everywhere. There were clothes on lines from every window, women on every stoop, pushcart peddlers on every corner, children playing ball on every street. The noise and confusion was so great that I woke up."

The rabbi replied, "By a strange coincidence, Father Felts, I dreamed the other night of an Episcopalian heaven. It was very lifelike, and it seemed to me to just suit the ideal of Episcopalians. It was a neat suburb, with well-spaced houses in excellent condition, with beautiful lawns, each with its flower bed, with clean, wide, tree-lined streets, and all was immersed in mild sunshine."

Reverend Felts smiled. "And the people?"

"Oh," murmured the rabbi, "there were no people."

■ Honesty

Received by a teacher: "Thank you for your remarks on our young Dustin's piano-playing ability, but in your next report, we would appreciate you not giving us your honest opinion."

The louder he talked of his honor, the faster we counted our spoons.

—Ralph Waldo Emerson

Honesty is the best policy, but insanity is a better defense.

—Steve Landesberg

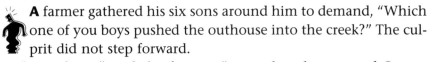

A farmer gathered his six sons around him to demand, "Which one of you boys pushed the outhouse into the creek?" The culprit did not step forward.

"Now, boys," said the farmer, "remember the story of George Washington and the cherry tree. It's true that young George chopped down that tree, but he told his father the truth, and his father was proud of him." Whereupon the farmer's youngest son stepped forward and admitted that he had pushed the outhouse into the creek. The farmer picked up a switch and whipped his son soundly.

"But Pa," protested the boy tearfully, "you told me that George Washington's father was proud of him when he confessed to chopping down the cherry tree."

"He was, son," replied the farmer. "But when George Washington chopped down that cherry tree, his father wasn't sitting in it."

—George Jessel

Watching his new employee count out the day's receipts, the boss walked over and asked the man where he got his financial training.

"Yale," he answered.

"Good. And what is your name?"

"Yackson." —Paul Dickson

Aunt Aggie was distressed when she lost her handbag in a shopping center recently. An honest young man lad found it and returned it to her.

"Funny," Aggie commented. "When I misplaced the bag there was a ten-dollar bill it. Now I find ten one-dollar bills."

"That's right lady," explained the honest lad. "The last time I found a lady's purse, she didn't have any change for a reward."

Further Reading:

To Be Honest, Frank Lee

I Say So!, Frank O. Pinion

■ Hospitals

Mr. Horntoot admitted to his wife that he was feeling much better since his operation, but couldn't account for the enormous bump on the back of his head.

"Oh, that," chuckled Mrs. Horntoot. "Just before your operation they suddenly ran out of ether!"

—Bennett Cerf

A hospital bed is a parked taxi with the meter running.

Doctor: Wow, Frank. What happened to your ear?
Frank: I was ironing my shirt, when the phone rang, and I had to iron the phone, I mean answer the iron— oh, you know what I mean.
Doctor: I think I understand. But what happened to your other ear?
Frank: I had to call the hospital, didn't I?

I was real calm about the operation—until I realized what I was doing. I'm lying there naked. On a table in front of people I don't know. And they have knives. What's wrong with this picture?

—Tom Parks

Further Reading:
Ambulance Driving, Adam Muhway

■ House and Home

One of America's most popular socialites credits three simple words for making guests at her dinner parties feel welcome and at home. When they arrive, she murmurs, "At last!" And when they depart she protests, "Already?"

Perfect timing: Being able to turn off the hot and cold shower faucets at the same time.

Family swimming pool: A small body of water completely surrounded by other people's children.

Wood: That remarkable material which burns so easily in a forest and with such difficulty in the fireplace.

Junk: Something you keep ten years and then throw away two weeks before you need it.

Time heals all things—except a leaky faucet.   —Sam Ewing

SIGNS YOU HAVE A BAD APARTMENT

- It's the same bedroom you had as a kid, but now your parents are charging you two grand a month.
- Your building's security system is a cardboard cutout of Clint Eastwood.
- Rent must be paid in small, non-sequential bills.
- Every time you pass the doorman, he's wearing another article of your clothing.
- You can't get through your bedroom door because of the yellow police tape.   —*The Late Show with David Letterman*, CBS

Further Reading:
Interior Decorating, Curt Enrod
You Drip!, Lee K. Fawcette
No More Circuit Breakers!, Ira Fuse
House Construction, Bill Jerome Holme
Green Lawn Chairs, Patty O. Furniture
Irish Flooring, Lynn O'Leum
Carpet Fitting, Walter Wall
Plumb Good, Dwayne Pipe
Keeping Old Furniture Looking Good, Ann Teak
I Can Fix It, Jerry Rigg

■ House Cleaning

Helpful hint: You can remove ink stains from a silk dress with ordinary scissors.

—Ron Dentinger

THIRTY MINUTES TO A CLEANER HOUSE

You're getting company in thirty minutes. Your house is a mess. *What will you do?*

Welcome, ladies and gentlemen, to the first session of Housekeeping Tips for Regular People. If you're a Martha Stewart type of housekeeper, this column is *not* for you. However, for the rest of you, this is your chance to learn 15 Secret Shortcuts to Good Housekeeping that your mother never told you.

SECRET TIP 1: DOOR LOCKS

If a room clearly can't be whipped into shape in thirty days—much less thirty minutes—employ the Locked Door method of cleaning. Tell anyone who tries to go in the room that the door is intentionally locked. CAUTION: It is not advisable to use this tip for the bathroom. *Time:* 2 seconds

SECRET TIP 2: DUCT TAPE

No home should be without an ample supply. Not only is it handy for plumbing repairs, but it's a great way to hem drapes, tablecloths, clothes, just about anything. No muss, no fuss. *Time:* 2–3 minutes

SECRET TIP 3: OVENS

If you think ovens are just for baking, think again. Ovens represent at least nine cubic feet of hidden storage space, which means they're a great place to shove dirty dishes, dirty clothes, or just about anything you want to get out of sight when company's coming. *Time:* 2 minutes

SECRET TIP 4: DRYERS

Like Secret Tip 3, except bigger. CAUTION: Avoid hiding flammable objects here. *Time:* 2.5 minutes

SECRET TIP 5: WASHING MACHINES AND FREEZERS

Like Secret Tip 4, except even bigger. *Time:* 3 minutes

SECRET TIP 6: DUST RUFFLES

No bed should be without one. Devotees of Martha Stewart believe dust ruffles exist to keep dust out from under a bed or to help coordinate the colorful look of a bedroom. The rest of us know a dust ruffle's highest and best use is to hide whatever you've managed to shove under the bed. (Refer to Secret Tips 3–5.) *Time:* 4 minutes

SECRET TIP 7: DUSTING

Never dust under what you can dust around. *Time:* 3 minutes

SECRET TIP 8: DISHES

Don't use them. Use plastic or paper, and you won't have to wash. *Time:* 1 minute

SECRET TIP 9: WASHING

This secret tip is brought to you by an inventive teenager. When this teen's mother went on a housekeeping strike for a month, the teen discovered you can double the life of your underwear—if you turn it inside out and, yes, rerun it. CAUTION: This tip is recommended only for teens and those who don't care if they get in a car wreck. *Time:* 3 seconds

SECRET TIP 10: IRONING

If an article of clothing doesn't require a full press and your hair does, a curling iron is the answer. In between curls, use the hot wand to iron minor wrinkles out of your clothes. Yes, it really does work, or so I'm told, by other disciples of the Thirty-Minutes-to-a-Cleaner-House philosophy. *Time:* 5 minutes (including curling your hair)

SECRET TIP 11: VACUUMING

Stick to the middle of the room, which is the only place people look. Don't bother vacuuming under furniture. It takes way too long, and no one looks there anyway. *Time:* 5 minutes, entire house; 45 seconds, living room only.

SECRET TIP 12: LIGHTING

The key here is low, low, and lower. It's not only romantic, but bad lighting can hide a multitude of dirt. Time: 10 seconds

SECRET TIP 13: BED MAKING

Get an old-fashioned waterbed. No one can tell if those things are made up or not, saving you, oh, hundreds of seconds over the course of a lifetime. *Time:* 0

SECRET TIP 14: SHOWERS, TOILETS, AND SINKS

Forget showers and toilets. Concentrate on sinks. *Time:* 1 minute

SECRET TIP 15: KEEPING YOUR GUARD UP

If you already knew at least ten of these tips, don't even think about inviting a Martha Stewart type to your home.

There's the commercial on TV where the woman is smelling her clothes. She says, "They smell as fresh as all outdoors!" Is that ridiculous? Do you realize what all outdoors smells like? If she lived in New York, she'd cough for twenty-two minutes.   —Larry Wilde

I've got a messy house. I haven't cleaned in a while. In fact, I have a milk carton with a picture of the Lindbergh baby on it. —Greg Ray

My mother loves to clean. She'll say, "Look at this. You could eat off my floor." You could eat off my floor, too. There're thousands of things down there.   —Elayne Boosler

You make the beds, you do the dishes, and six months later you have to start all over again.   —Joan Rivers

Cleaning your house while your kids are still growing is like shoveling the walk before it stops snowing.   —Phyllis Diller

Everyone who ever walked barefoot into his child's room late at night hates Legos.

—Tony Kornheiser

Give me a home where the buffalo roam, and I'll give you a messy house!

—old song parody

Further Reading:
Housework, Dustin Cook
Scuffed Floors, Mark Tupp
You Wash, I'll Dry, Terry Cloth
Good Housekeeping, Lottie Dust
Keep It Clean!, Armand Hammer
Neat Shirts, Preston Ironed

■ Human Nature

The chief obstacle to the progress of the human race is the human race.

—Don Marquis

Mayor Richard J. Daley of Chicago, asked by reporters to comment on a trucking strike, offered this comment: "What keeps people apart is their inability to get together."

There ain't no civilization where there ain't no satisfaction and that's what's the trouble now. Nobody is satisfied.

—Will Rogers

If you could kick in the pants the fellow responsible for most of your troubles, you wouldn't be able to sit down for six months.

—Bill Nye

Egotist: A man who thinks that if he hadn't been born, people would have wondered why.

—Dan Post

Immorality: The morality of those who are having a better time.
—H. L. Mencken

A man seldom makes the same mistake twice. Generally it's three times or more.
—Perry Giswold

Perfectionist: A person who cannot enjoy Tchaikovsky's music without knowing how to spell his name.
—Jim Reed, *A Treasury of Ozark Country Humor*

Optimist: The guy who mails a postcard marked "Personal."

An optimist is a parent who'll let his kid borrow the new car for a date. A pessimist is one who won't. A cynic is one who did.
—H. Aaron Cohl

Hope is the feeling you have that the feeling you have isn't permanent.
—Jean Kerr

By trying, we can easily learn to endure adversity—another man's, I mean.
—Mark Twain

Will power: The ability, after you have used three-fourths of a can of paint and finished the job, to close the can and clean the brush, instead of painting something else that doesn't really need it.

A fanatic is one who can't change his mind and won't change the subject.
—Winston Churchill, July 5, 1954

Tragedy is if I cut my finger. Comedy is if you walk into an open sewer and die.

—Mel Brooks

Opportunist: Any man who goes ahead and does what you always intended to do.

Ostentation: That showy quality deplored in anything we can't afford.

■ Humor, Sense of

Even when he first arrived in the hospital, unsure of how serious his condition was, President Ronald Reagan maintained a sense of humor. He quipped to doctors as he was taken to surgery: "Please tell me you're a Republican."

—*The Uncommon Wisdom of Ronald Reagan*

You are never so slow as when you are the only one in the room who doesn't get the joke.

—Wise & Aldrich

Everything is funny as long as it is happening to somebody else.

—Will Rogers

> Some anecdotes are dull and old,
> But some, I think, are swell.
> The former are the ones I'm told,
> The latter, those I tell.

—Richard Armour

Further Reading:
You're Kidding!, Shirley U. Jest

■ Husbands and Wives

There is a vast difference between the savage and the civilized man, but it is never apparent to their wives until after breakfast.

—Helen Rowland

Dear Abby: My husband has always been very close to his mother, and she has never cared much for me. I asked my husband if I was drowning and his mother was drowning which one would he save? He said, "My mother, because I owe her more." I am so terribly hurt, Abby. What shall I do? Arlene

Dear Arlene: Learn to swim.

He can recall the score of the Army-Navy game of '54, the electoral votes the Republicans won in the last election, and the gas mileage of the first car he ever owned. But he can't remember what size socks he wears, the ages of his children, or the name of that old Cole Porter number that his wife refers to as "our" song.

—Jane Goodsell

Bumper sticker seen in San Jose, California: My wife keeps saying I never listen to her . . .or something like that.

Smith goes to see his supervisor in the front office. "Boss," he says, "we're doing some heavy housecleaning at home tomorrow, and my wife needs me to help with the attic and the garage, moving and hauling stuff."

"We're short-handed, Smith," the boss replies. "I can't give you the day off."

"Thanks, boss," says Smith. "I knew I could count on you!"

—Jay Trachman in *One to One*

My wife thinks that I'm too nosy. At least that's what she keeps scribbling in her diary.

—Drake Sather

Q: How many men does it take to put on a roll of toilet paper?
A: We don't know. It has never been done.   —Cindy Troutwine

Husband: We haven't agreed on anything in six months.
Wife: It's been seven months, dear.

A wife and husband both talked in their sleep. She loved auctions; his hobby was golf. The other night, the golfer yelled, "Fore!" His wife yelled back, "Four and a quarter!"   —Herbert V. Prochnow

A woman was carrying several bags of purchases as she stood at the entrance to a downtown department store and asked a mounted officer: "Did you by any chance notice a very angry man in a blue sedan drive by here nine or ten times?"

One night at 3:00 A.M., Dr. Roland was awakened by a frantic call from an old friend who beseeched him to rush to the aid of his wife. "She's having an acute case of appendicitis."

"Nonsense," said Dr. Roland. "I took your wife's appendix out five years ago. Nobody can have another case of appendicitis."

"Maybe so," yelled the man. "But a guy can have another wife, can't he?"

One night Fred Allen went to see a preview of a movie at one of those small projection rooms in the producing company's office building. After the showing everyone tried to squeeze into the single elevator. Fred found himself wedged in next to a plump lady who began to get hysterical as the operator tried to shut the door. "My husband's left behind!" she cried. "You can't go without my husband!"

"Courage, madam," said Fred. "This elevator may be going down, but it's not the *Titanic*."   —Art Linkletter

It is reliably reported that Mrs. Paul Revere was overheard to say, "I don't care *who* is coming. I'm using the horse tonight!"

While talking with her husband, a woman explains that she is tired of having to handle everything for their family.

"Really?" the husband replies. "You think we depend on you too much?"

"Look around!" the woman exclaims. "Not only do I do all the cooking, cleaning, and organizing, but I'm also the main problem solver. If there's a disaster, call Mom. If there's an errand that needs to be run, call Mom. If there's a decision, an appointment, or a mess, call Mom!"

"Hmm," the man says, "what do you think we ought to do about this?"
—Kirkman/Scott, King Features

The minister reproved the husband for spending so much time tinkering with his new car.

"If I were you," asserted the clergyman, "I'd put my wife before my car."

"I'd sure like to," he sighed, "but I'm afraid someone might catch me at it."
—Red Skelton

My wife and I have been together so long, I know we'll never break up. Yes, there's love and commitment, but the main reason we'll always be together is that neither one of us can imagine having to retrain somebody new.
—Robert G. Lee

A woman was waiting for a diagnosis of her husband's illness. The doctor came to her with a dour expression and said, "I don't like the look of him." The man's wife said, "I don't either, but he's good to the children."
—Milton Berle's Private Joke File

Every year my wife throws a big party on our anniversary, but she never tells me where.

—Ron Dentinger

A newly married man asked his wife, "Would you have married me if my father hadn't left me a fortune?"

"Honey," the woman replied sweetly, "I'd have married you no matter who left you a fortune."

—Jack Delf, *Come Laugh with Me*

My aunt Lou is a wonderful hostess. She has discovered over the years that at a party, there are two kinds of people—those who want to go home early and those who want to be the last ones in the place. Unfortunately, she relates, they're always married to each other.

When a husband opens the car door for his wife, either the car is new or the wife is new.

—Carol Rumsey

A crystal ball gazer informed my uncle Sid, "I see a buried treasure."

"I know," Sid exclaimed. "My wife's first husband."

Whenever I risk a verbal encounter with my wife, words flail me.

ACTUAL CLASSIFIED ADS

- From Minnesota: "Adolph, please come back home. The children miss you, the lawn hasn't been mowed in three weeks, and the garden needs a worm like you. Your loving wife, Gretchen."
- From North Dakota: "Wanted: Husband for beautiful eighteen-year-old blonde. Must have income to support her in style she believes she was born to—including minks, caviar, and diamonds. Applicant please write 'Desperate Father, Box 44.'"

210

i

■ Insults

Gertrude Stein once got off this adroit insult: "She was the kind you liked better the more you saw her less."

During one of his mock-serious duels with Jack Benny, Fred Allen was ridiculing Benny's dependence on a large stable of gag writers. In an inspired moment, Fred delivered this wholly spontaneous and absolutely un-toppable coup de grace: "Jack Benny couldn't ad-lib a belch after a Hungarian dinner!" —Art Linkletter

Career diplomat Cordell Hull's advice: Never insult an alligator till after you've crossed the river.

A British noblewoman, whom we shall call "Lady None-such," once sent George Bernard Shaw a message reading, "Lady None-such will be at home from 4:30 to 6:30 on Thursday next."
He quickly jotted down his reply: "So will Mr. Shaw."

He was the nearest thing I'd seen to a human being without actually being one. —Spike Milligan

You are excess baggage in the airport of life.

—Judy Tenuta

Comedian Don Rickles is known as the king of put-downs. In Las Vegas, people flock to his show, not only to see him, but to become part of his routine.

This particular evening Don was thirty minutes into his act when a man and woman were escorted to the front row. Rickles stopped and acknowledged the couple's entrance with, "Hey Mr. and Mrs. Hockey Puck, you're thirty minutes late."

The man shot back, "No, we're early. You're still on."

Don literally dropped to his knees laughing. The man received a standing ovation for his comeback while Mr. Put-down laughed so hard he was crying.

—David Naster

Don't let your mind wander. It's too little to be out alone.

An old tramp sidled up to the back door of a little English tavern called the George and Dragon and beckoned to the landlady. "I ain't had nuthin' to eat for three days," he wheedled. "Would you spare an old man a bite of dinner?"

"I should say not, you good-for-nothing loafer," said the landlady, and slammed the door in his face.

The tramp's face reappeared at the kitchen window. "I was just wonderin'," he said, "if I could 'ave a word or two with George."

—Bennett Cerf

Dorothy Parker's legion of admirers like to recall the day she slapped down one of the most arrogant, self-satisfied celebrities of our day. Said celebrity announced, "I make it a point always to be especially gracious to my inferiors."

"How wonderful," gurgled Miss Parker. "But tell me—where do you find them?"

—Bennett Cerf

Someone sent me a postcard picture of the entire Earth. On the back it said, "Wish you were here." —Steven Wright

Columnist Earl Wilson asked the husky-voiced actress Tallulah Bankhead, "Have you ever been mistaken for a man?"
Her reply: "No, dahling. Have you?"

From a rural district of England comes the story of a driver of a small sedan braking hastily as the tweedy mistress of the largest estate nearby came hurtling around a sharp bend in the narrow road in her large Rolls. Before he could say a word, she shouted "Pig!" and drove on.
"Fat old cow," he cried after her in retaliation. Then he drove round the bend himself—and crashed head-on into the biggest pig he had ever seen. —Bennett Cerf

Repartee is something we think of twenty-four hours too late.
—Mark Twain

Further Reading:
Stop Arguing, Xavier Breath
Parting Shots, Sid Semper Tyrannis

■ Intellect

Intelligence: A sterling quality possessed by anybody who will listen attentively to what you have to say and nod in agreement.

Sometimes I think the surest sign that intelligent life exists elsewhere in the universe is that none of it has tried to contact us.
—Woody Allen

My seventy-year-old cousin Judi had spent her life in a very small town in Tennessee. She was a lover of country and saved up for years, so she could attend a performance of the Grand Old Opry.

When she arrived in Nashville for the first time, she checked into her hotel, and the bellhop took her bags. She followed the man, and as the door closed, she looked around and shook her fist at him, exclaiming, "Young man—I may be old, straight from the hills, but that don't mean I'm stupid! I paid good, and this room won't do at all! It's too small, no ventilation, no TV—there's not even a *bed!*"

Said the bellman: "But, Ma'am, this is the elevator."

Comedian Rich Purpura was working on a cruise ship that docked in Key West, Florida. He hurried off the ship so he could call his pregnant wife, Pam, at home in Youngstown, Ohio. He had no more than said "hello," when Pam said, "Call me back in fifteen minutes. I'm expecting a call from the doctor."

Rich's fifteen-minute wait seemed like an eternity. When he called back, Pam told him there was nothing to worry about. I'll let Rich continue the story:

"My adorable pregnant wife was getting ready to take her pre-natal pills. At the same time, she was about to give our dog, Elroy, his heart worm pills. Somehow, she ended up taking Elroy's heart worm pills instead of her prenatal pills. She called the doctor to see if she or the baby was in any danger. The doctor told her they would both be fine.

"Then I asked her if she gave Elroy the prenatal pills.

"Pam answered, 'What do you think I am, stupid?'"

—David Naster

When you go to a mind reader, do you get half price?

—Ben Creed

Bumper sticker: Artificial Intelligence is no match against Real Stupidity.

Intelligence is like underwear. We all should have it, but we shouldn't show it off.

Informed by his academic fans that he enjoyed "the support of all thinking Americans," Adlai Stevenson joked, "That's not enough. I'm going to need a majority."

Real warning labels:
- On a Superman costume: Parent—cape does not enable wearer to fly.
- On a hair dryer: Warning— Do not use in shower. Never use while sleeping.
- On a fire log: Caution: Risk of fire.

I came from a very intellectual neighborhood. When we played cowboys and Indians, I had to be Gandhi.   —Robert G. Lee

If you make people think they're thinking, they'll love you. If you really make them think, they'll hate you.   —Don Marquis

■ International Humor

If one could only teach the English how to talk and the Irish how to listen, society in London would be more civilized.   —Oscar Wilde

Lord Halifax amused a banquet audience gathered to honor him in Washington with the story of a tramp ship with a heterogeneous passenger list that was stranded on an idyllic Polynesian islet. Soon the little spot was a beehive of activity. The Germans were drilling the natives into an army. The Americans opened a general store and auto agency. The Australians started a racetrack; the French a restaurant. Two Scots were financing the whole show, and a couple of Englishmen were still standing around waiting to be introduced.

—Bennett Cerf

Each country in the NATO force has its own rules of engagement. For the U.S and Britain, it's fire when fired upon. For the French, it's white wine with fish, red wine with steak.
                                                                —Argus Hamilton

The Swiss have an interesting army. Five hundred years without a war. Pretty impressive. Also pretty lucky for them. Ever see that little Swiss Army knife they have to fight with? Not much of a weapon there—corkscrews, bottle openers. "Come on, buddy, let's go. You get past me, the guy in back of me, he's got a spoon. Back off. I've got the toe clippers right here."
                                                                —Jerry Seinfeld

Further Reading:
Held Hostage by Italian Terrorists!, Aldo Anything
French Overpopulation, Francis Crowded
Events in the Soviet Union, Perry Stroika
Star Spangled Barrio, Jose Canusee

■ Internet
One day a lady called me and told me that she had a problem with her modem. She said she couldn't connect with the Internet. I asked her, "Is your modem external or internal?"

She replied, "Of course it's internal. It's inside my house!"

Customer: OH!! You mean I need a modem *and* a computer to get on the Internet?

Seen on a T-shirt worn by a middle-aged man: www.clueless.com.

The computer now brings a world of information into the workplace. Remember when that task was handled by the office gossip?

Father reading fairy tale to daughter: So the prince, determined to find the owner of the glass slipper, launched a home page on the World Wide Web.
—David Teitelbaum, Tribune Media Services

A study shows that Internet use can be addictive. So now there's a 12-step program for Net junkies. The first step is to acknowledge that there is a higher power, and his name is Bill Gates.
—Gary Easley, quoted in the *Los Angeles Times*

Woman to man in coffee room at work: I won't go out with you, Jonathan, but please feel free to visit my Web site.
—Roy Delgado in *Medical Economics*

Not tonight, dear. I have a modem.

Little girl to her friend: I'm never having kids. I hear they take nine months to download.
—Bunny Hoest and John Reiner in *Parade*

Bumper sticker seen in San Jose, California: Feeling like roadkill on the Information Superhighway?

■ Jesus

I had a dream in which Jesus walked into a bar right here in the county where I live. He approached three sad-faced gentlemen at a table and greeted the first one. "What's troubling you, brother?" he asked.

The first man replied, "My eyes. I keep getting stronger and stronger glasses, and I still can't see."

Jesus touched the man, who ran outside to tell the world about his now 20/20 vision.

The next gentleman couldn't hear Jesus' question, so Jesus touched his ears, restoring his hearing to perfection. This man, too, ran out the door, probably on his way to the audiologist to get a hearing-aid refund.

The third man leapt from his chair and backed up against the wall, even before Jesus could greet him. "Don't you come near me, man! Don't touch me!" he bellowed. "I'm on disability!"

Jesus was walking in the rain one day, and he passed the shop of Samson, who made clothes. Samson called out to Jesus and gave him a cloak he had just made. Jesus' cloak was admired by everyone. Everywhere he preached, people asked about the workmanship of the cloak.

When Samson met Jesus six months from the day that he had given him the cloak, he said, "Jesus, we've got a great thing going here. Since people have seen you wearing your cloak, I have had so many orders for others like it. I think we should go into business together. The only problem I'm having is trying to decide what to call the business. Should it be called 'Samson and Jesus' or 'Jesus and Samson'?"

Jesus suggested, "How about Lord and Taylor?"   —H. Aaron Cohl

■ Jewish Humor

When my wife and I were trying to find a shop in Tel Aviv, we stopped an old Jewish peddler carrying two large watermelons and asked, "Sir, could you tell us how to find Ben Yehuda Street?"

The peddler answered, "Please hold these two watermelons."

I somehow managed to gather them in my arms, whereupon the peddler shrugged, made an expansive gesture with his hands, and exclaimed, "How should I know?"

A ship drops anchor off a small island that doesn't even seem to be on the charts, and the captain goes ashore to investigate. He walks inland a little way and is astonished to come upon a little town. There are houses and shops, flower gardens, and vegetable gardens, even a fountain, but the place seems to be deserted. Then a short, bearded man walks out of one of the houses. "Who are you?" the captain asks. "How did you get here?"

"My name is Irving Schwartz," replies the man. "I was shipwrecked twenty, maybe twenty-five years ago, and I've lived here all this time."

"And you built this town, all these buildings, by yourself?"

"Sure. What else did I have to do?"

"It's amazing," says the captain. "But Mr. Schwartz, I see that you've built two synagogues. Why is that?"

"Every Jew," replies Mr. Schwartz, "has the right to have one synagogue he wouldn't set foot into."   —Arthur Hale

I'm from a very liberal Jewish family. My parents believe in the Ten Commandments, but they believe you can pick five.   —Bill Scheft

Probably the worst thing about being Jewish at Christmas time is shopping in stores, because the lines are so long. They should have a Jewish express line: "Look, I'm a Jew, it's not a gift. It's just paper towels!"

—Sue Kolinsky

On a certain holiday in which special prayers are said, a House of Worship sold tickets. Strict instructions were given that no one was permitted to enter the sacred portals without one, and an usher was stationed at the door to enforce this order.

A man approached and tried to enter. "I'm very sorry," he apologized. "I haven't got a ticket, but my brother is inside and I need to talk to him."

"Sorry," the doorman said, "but you have to have a ticket."

"But my brother is inside," insisted the man, "and it's very important that I talk to him."

"All right," said the doorman, weakening. "Go inside and talk to your brother. But," he warned, "don't let me catch you praying!"

—Harry Hershfield

Q: How many Orthodox rabbis does it take to change a light bulb?
A: Change?
Q: How many Conservative rabbis does it take to change a light bulb?
A: None. Call a committee meeting.
Q: How many Reform rabbis does it take to change a light bulb?
A: None. Anyone can change it whenever they want to.
Q: How many Jewish Renewal rabbis does it take to change a light bulb?
A: It depends. One if it's an eco-kosher bulb that isn't going to be lit from electricity, but from nuclear power. Two, as long as a man and a woman rabbi have equal turns putting in the bulb. Three, one to change it, one to do a Buddhist mindfulness practice during the change, and one to document the paradigm shift in a best selling book called *The Jew in the Light Bulb*. Four, same as above and an additional rabbi to study the psycho-halachic implications of such a change and then lead a retreat weekend on the experience.

Q: How many Shlomo Hassidim does it take to change a light bulb?

A: Gevaldt, it's mamash such a great opportunity to do teshuvah. So it takes everyone there to get real close, sing a niggun, listen to an Ishbitzer teaching, tell a Levi Yitchak story, and change the bulb at two in the morning.

Q: How many Reconstructionist rabbis does it take to change a light bulb?

A: Four. One to wish they were doing what the Orthodox rabbi does, one to wish they were doing what the Reform rabbi does, one to wish they were doing what the Renewal rabbi does, and one to eventually change the stupid bulb.

Q: How many Jews does it take to change a light bulb?

A: Thirty. One to change the bulb and twenty-nine to discuss it and give contradictory advice to the person changing the bulb.

Q. How many Lubavitchers does it take to change a light bulb?

A. None. It never died.

Q: How many Bratzlaver Chassidim does it take to change a light bulb?

A: None. We will never find one that burned as brightly as the first one.

Q: How many congregants does it take to change a light bulb in a synagogue?

A: You want we should change the light bulb? My grandmother donated that light bulb!

Jacob Weingasser, a Jewish philanthropist, is waiting in line to be knighted by her royal majesty, Elizabeth II, Queen of England. He knows he's supposed to kneel and recite a sentence in Latin. When his turn comes, he kneels, the Queen taps him on the shoulders with the sword, and in the panic of excitement he forgets the Latin line. Thinking quickly, he recites the only other line he knows in a foreign language, which he remembers from the Passover Seder: "Mah nishtana halailoh hazeh mikol-halailoh."

The puzzled Queen turns to her advisor and asks, "Why is this knight different from all other knights?"

A rabbi on the West Coast was very discouraged. Half of his congregation had turned Quaker. Or as he put it, "Some of my best Jews are Friends."

—Mark Russell

One of my favorite Jewish stories involves Benjamin Moskowitz's parrot. Here is Isaac Asimov's telling of this classic tale:

Moskowitz had bought a parrot, and one morning found the bird at the eastern side of the cage, with a small prayer shawl over its head, rocking to and fro, and mumbling. Moskowitz was thunderstruck to hear the parrot intoning prayers in the finest Hebrew.

"You're Jewish?" asked Moskowitz.

"Not only Jewish," said the parrot, "but Orthodox. So will you take me to the synagogue on Rosh Hashanah?"

Rosh Hashanah, the Jewish New Year, was indeed only two days off, and it would as always usher in the high-holiday season which would end with Yom Kippur, the Day of Atonement, ten days later. Moskowitz said, "Of course, I'll take you, but can I tell my friends about you? It isn't a secret, I hope?"

"No secret at all. Tell anyone you want to." And the parrot returned to his praying.

Moskowitz went to all his friends, full of the story of his Jewish parrot. Of course no one believed him, and in no time at all Moskowitz was taking bets. By Rosh Hashanah, he had a hundred dollars, all told, riding on the parrot.

Grinning, Moskowitz brought the parrot to the synagogue in its cage. He put him in a prominent place, and everyone turned to watch as they mumbled their prayers. Even the rabbi watched, for he had seven dollars that said the parrot could not pray.

Moskowitz waited. Everyone waited. And the parrot did nothing. Moskowitz carefully arranged the prayer shawl over the bird's head, but the parrot ducked, and the shawl fell off.

After the services, Moskowitz's friends, with much mockery, collected their money. Even the rabbi snickered as he took his profit of seven dollars.

Utterly humiliated, Moskowitz returned home, turned viciously on the parrot and said, "Prepare to die, you little monster, for I'm going to wring your neck. If you can pray, now's the time."

Whereupon the parrot's voice rang out clearly: "Hold it, you dumb jerk. In ten days it's Yom Kippur, when all Jews will sing the Kol Nidre. Tell everybody that I can sing the Kol Nidre."

"Why? You didn't do anything today."

"Exactly! So for Yom Kippur, just think of the odds you'll get."

A Jewish couple dined out one evening in the neighborhood kosher delicatessen. They were amazed when a Chinese waiter approached them to take their order. But their surprise turned to shock when he addressed them in perfect Yiddish.

As soon as he had gone into the kitchen, they motioned to the proprietor. "A Chinese waiter in a Jewish delicatessen!" exclaimed the man. "And not only that, but he talks Yiddish. How come?"

The proprietor looked around quickly and put his finger to his lips. "Shhh," he whispered, "he thinks I'm teaching him English!"

—Myron Cohen

I come from a wealthy family. I was bar mitzvahed in the Vatican.

—London Lee

I was visiting a local farmer when I swear I heard one pig say to another: "If I had my way, *everybody* would be an Orthodox Jew!"

Further Reading:
Jewish Mysticism, Lev Itation
Jewish Holidays, Hannah Kuhh

K

■ Kids

When my kids become wild and unruly, I use a nice, safe playpen.
When they're finished, I climb out. —Erma Bombeck

A kid kept sniffing, which annoyed a woman who was standing
next to him. "Listen, young man," she said, "have you got a hand-
kerchief?"

"Yeah," answered the kid, "but my mother won't let me loan it
to anybody." —Joe Laurie Jr.

I've got two wonderful children—and two out of five isn't too bad.
—Henny Youngman

A child is someone who stands halfway between an adult and a TV set.

No matter what the critics say, it's hard to believe that a television
program which keeps four children quiet for an hour can be all bad.
—Beryl Pfizer

Children behave best when their stomachs are full and their blad-
ders are empty. —Vicki Lansky

What is a home without children? Quiet. —Henny Youngman

At my lemonade stand I used to give the first glass away free and charge five dollars for the second glass. The refill contained the antidote. —Emo Phillips

Once you survive growing up, the next step is to have your own kid. . . . It's a major point. I think you are at a certain level when everyone you know pretty much has caught on to you. You need to create a new person, someone who doesn't know anything about you. . . . You have a kid, the relationship is off to a great start. You give the kid food and toys, and immediately, they are very impressed with you. —Jerry Seinfeld

There's no such thing as a tough child—if you parboil them first for seven hours, they always come out tender. —W. C. Fields

A child enters your home and for the next twenty years makes so much noise you can hardly stand it. The child departs, leaving the house so silent you think you are going mad. —John Andrew Holmes

I'm beginning to wonder if it was such a good idea to give our son one of those rockets that blasts off for his ninth birthday. As of today we've got the only cat in Bedford who knows what our house looks like from three hundred feet up! —Bennett Cerf

The owner of a big electronics firm called in his personnel director: "My son will be graduating from college soon and needing a job. He's going to be your new assistant, but he's not to be shown any favoritism. Treat him just as you would any other son of mine."

Children are natural mimics—they act like their parents in spite of our efforts to teach them good manners.

TRANSLATIONS FROM CHILDSPEAK

"I didn't hit him. I just sort of pushed him." (He hit his brother.)
"He just hit me for no reason!" (He hit his brother.)
"I didn't do anything." (He hit his brother.)
"Mo-m-m-my!" (His brother hit him.)   —Robert Paul Smith

A three-year-old was saying the Lord's Prayer. She carefully enunciated each word, right up to the end of the prayer. "Lead us not into temptation," she prayed, "but deliver us some e-mail. Amen."

A child develops individuality long before he develops taste. I have seen my kid straggle into the kitchen in the morning with outfits that need only one accessory—an empty gin bottle.

—Erma Bombeck

A tiny boy of four was warned by his older sister that he couldn't talk in church. "They won't let you say anything," she said.

"Who won't?" the boy asked.

"The hushers," she replied.

Heredity is what a man believes in until his son begins to behave like a delinquent.

Ten-year-old: Give me a shovel, quick. My brother is stuck in the snow up to his boot tops.
Neighbor: Why doesn't he walk out?
Ten-year-old: He's in head first.

This classic story was recently turned into a hit country song and recorded by Kenny Rogers:

"Watch me," said six-year-old Neal to his father. "I'm the greatest hitter in the world." He tossed the ball up and took a roundhouse swing and missed. "Strike one," he called with no decrease in his enthusiasm. "Watch me connect with this one." He missed again. "Strrrrike two," he chanted. "Well, Daddy, you always tell me it only takes one swing to hit it. This is it." A third time he took a swipe at the ball, and a third time he missed. "Three strikes and yer out," he announced. "I'm the greatest pitcher in the world!"

My uncle Al says he's tired of arguing with his kids about borrowing the family car. So next time he wants it, he's just going to take it.

It costs more now to amuse a child than it cost to educate his father.

Why take your kids to Disneyland when for the same amount of money you can put them through college?   —Bruce Lansky

You know you've lost control when you're the one who goes to your room.   —Babs Bell Hajdusiewicz

By the time you talk your child into writing a thank-you note for a birthday gift, it's already broken.   —Bruce Lansky

Before I had kids, I went home after work to rest. Now I go to work to rest.   —Simon Ruddell

Humans are the only animals that have children on purpose, with the exception of guppies, who eat theirs.   —P. J. O'Rourke

Always end the name of your child with a vowel, so that when you yell, the name will carry.
—Bill Cosby

Twenty-something: The cost of a sitter for Saturday night.
—Merrill Furman, *The Parent's Dictionary*

KIDS AND FOOD

The secret to feeding your child is learning how to disguise a vegetable as a french fry.
—Jan Blaustone

Toddlers are more likely to eat healthy food if they find it on the floor.
—Fran Blaustone

Ask your child what he wants for dinner only if he is buying.
—Fran Lebowitz

As a child, my family's menu consisted of two choices: take it or leave it.
—Buddy Hackett

In general, my children refused to eat anything that hadn't danced on TV.
—Erma Bombeck

Further Reading:
The Paper Route, Avery Daye
Songs for Children, Barbara Blacksheep
Children's Songbook, Skip Tumalu

■ Kissing

A kiss is an operation, cunningly devised, for the mutual stoppage of speech at a moment when words are utterly superfluous.
—Oliver Herford

229

My neighbor told me his girlfriend is a twin. I asked him if he ever kissed the wrong twin. He said, "No, her brother won't even come near me."

—Ron Dentinger

Kissing is a custom in France. We kiss a man we haven't seen in five years—or a woman we haven't seen in five minutes.

—Maurice Chevalier

■ Laughter

President John F. Kennedy once stated, "There are three real things in life: God, human folly, and laughter. We can't understand the first two, so we'll just have to make the best of the third."

He who laughs last
Thinks slowest.

Sense of humor: What makes you laugh at something which would make you mad if it happened to you.

Among those whom I like or admire, I can find no common denominator, but among those whom I love, I can: all of them make me laugh. —W. H. Auden, *The Dyer's Hand*

Laughter feels good all over, but it only shows in one place.
—George Burns

If you can't laugh at yourself, you may be missing the colossal joke of the century. —Dame Edna

It takes a big man to cry, but it takes a bigger man to laugh at that man.
—Jack Handey, *Saturday Night Live* writer

"Laughter is God's gift to mankind," proclaimed the preacher ponderously.

"And mankind," responded the cynic, "is the proof that God has a sense of humor." —H. Aaron Cohl

The man who laughs has not yet heard the news. —Bertolt Brecht

Further Reading:
You're a Bundle of Laughs, Vera Funny

■ Law and Disorder
To save the state the expense of a trial, your honor, my client has escaped. —Chon Day

The rowdy, drunken behavior of some Eagles fans has resulted in a crackdown by Philadelphia authorities. The city has set up a special municipal court manned by two judges right in Veteran's Stadium; miscreants will go directly to trial when caught, and from there, directly to jail.

Police in Vero Beach, Florida, raided the home of a suspected drug dealer after he took the wrong bag to the cleaners. David Snyder, thirty-seven, delivered what he thought was a sack of dirty clothes to a local laundry, but a worker there found three pounds of marijuana in the bag instead.

Locomotive: An insane reason to commit a crime. —Johnny Hart

My friend Larry's in jail now. He got twenty-five years for something he didn't do. He didn't run fast enough. —Damon Wayans

Judge to convict: "The prisons are all full, so I'm sentencing you to five years in the waiting room at the department of motor vehicles." —Baloo in the *Wall Street Journal*

A convict serving a life sentence in a Wyoming jail writes a weekly column for the prison newspaper. He calls it "Here Today, Here Tomorrow." —Bennett Cerf

ROBBERY SUSPECT MUGGED

A man stole $2,100 from a Brooklyn savings bank on Friday but was mugged as he made his getaway. He immediately reported the crime to the nearest police station house; the officers promptly arrested the man.

WOULD-BE ROBBER ENTERS WRONG DOOR

Ceredo, West Virginia—An attempt to rob the state liquor store in the Ceredo Plaza shopping center this morning ended when the gunman realized he had walked into the YMCA branch instead, police said.

The judge orders the plaintiff, "Explain what happened."

The plaintiff says, "I was in a phone booth talking to my girlfriend when the defendant opened the door and dragged me out."

The defendant responds, "The only reason I dragged him out is because he refused to get out, and I needed to make a phone call."

The judge asks, "How long were you talking to your girlfriend?"

The plaintiff says, "I don't know, your honor, but I want to add that he dragged my girlfriend out, too." —Ron Dentinger

Everything I needed to know, I learned in prison.

Further Reading:
Crackdown, Lauren Order
Breaking the Law, Kermit A. Krime
Armed Heists, Rob Banks
The Great Escape, Freida Convict
How to Beat a Murder Rap, Scott Free
Chicago Gangs of the '30's, Tommy Gunn
How to Break In, Jimmy De Lock
Assault with Battery, Eva Ready
How Bailjumpers Disappear, Otto Sight
How to Tour the Prison, Robin Steele
Theft and Robbery, Andy Tover

■ Lawyers

Actual bumper sticker:

Stop Animal Experiments
Use Lawyers

Lawyers are writing to the Unabomber. They want to represent him on book and movie deals, and officials are trying to put a stop to it. I say if lawyers are giving the Unabomber their return addresses, don't ruin a good thing. Here's a problem that will take care of itself.

—Jay Leno

There has been a great proliferation of lawyers in the past twenty years, just as there has been a proliferation of computers. But unlike computers, lawyers do not get twice as intelligent and half as expensive every two years.   —E. Burns in *San Francisco Bay Guardian*

An attorney's secretary, billing a client with whom her boss had had many long conferences, issued this invoice: "Bull rendered—$50."

A lawyer shows up at the Pearly Gates. St. Peter says, "Normally we don't let you people in here, but you're in luck—we have a special this week. You go to hell for the length of time you were alive, then you get to come back up here for eternity."

The lawyer says, "I'll take the deal."

St. Peter says, "Good, I'll put you down for 212 years in hell."

The lawyer says, "What are you talking about? I'm sixty-five years old!"

St. Peter says, "Up here we go by billing hours." —Orson Bean

Further Reading:

Trial Law, Tess Temoni

Lawyers of Suffering, Grin and Barrett

I Love Wills, Benny Fishery

■ Laziness

Hard work will pay off later. Laziness pays off now!

Everything comes to he who hustles while he waits.

—Thomas A. Edison

To stir is human; to stay in bed, divine.

—Joe Greene in the *National Enquirer*

Your husband is lazy if:

• When he leaves the house, he finds out which way the wind is blowing and goes in that direction.

• His idea of dressing for dinner is wearing a necktie over his pajamas.

• Coffee doesn't keep him awake—even when it's hot and being spilled on him. —Phyllis Diller

A minister, anxious to please a new parishioner, enthused, "What a lovely place you've fixed up here, Mrs. Cooper! And in such a few days, too! But what is that I see in that stunning vase atop the TV set?"

"My husband's ashes," explained Mrs. Cooper.

Overcome with embarrassment, the minister stammered, "But nobody told me Mr. Cooper had passed away."

"He hasn't," said Mrs. Cooper grimly. "He's just too lazy to look for an ashtray."
                                                        —Bennett Cerf

Further Reading:
Lazy Employees, Hans Doolittle
Get Moving!, Sheik Aleg
Take a Break!, Colin Sick
I Want to Help, Abel N. Willin

■ Life

Life is trial and error, unless you're an incompetent crook, in which case life is error and trial.
                                        —Los Angeles Times Syndicate

I thought I had a handle on life, but then it fell off.
                                                      —Barbara Johnson

The only disability in life is a bad attitude.
                                                        —Scott Hamilton

Life is what happens to you while you're making other plans.
                                                        —Robert Balzer

The best things in life are free. And the cheesiest things in life are free with a paid subscription to *Sports Illustrated.*   —Johnny Carson

Experience: A comb life gives you after you lose your hair.

—Judith Stern

Look at life through the windshield, not the rear-view mirror.

—Byrd Baggett, *The Book of Excellence*

TIPS FOR LIFE

- Give people more than they expect, and do so cheerfully.
- Don't believe all you hear, spend all you have, and sleep all you'd like.
- Don't say I love you unless you really mean it.
- When you say I'm sorry, look the person in the eye.
- Be engaged at least six months before you get married.
- Love deeply and passionately. You might get hurt, but it's the only way to live life completely.
- In disagreements, fight fair. No name calling.
- Don't judge people by their relatives.
- When someone asks you a question you don't want to answer, smile and ask, "Why do you want to know?"
- Call your mom.
- Say "Bless you" when you hear someone sneeze.
- Don't let a little squabble damage a good friendship.
- When you realize you've made a mistake, take immediate steps to correct it.
- Smile when picking up the phone. The caller will hear it in your voice.
- Marry someone you love to talk to. As you get older, good conversation will be one of the principal elements of an enduring relationship.
- Remember that silence is sometimes the best answer.
- Read more books, and watch less TV.
- In disagreements with loved ones, deal with the current situation. Don't bring up the past.
- Never interrupt when you are being flattered.
- Mind your own business.
- Trust in God, but lock your car.

If you want my final opinion on the mystery of life and all that, I can give it to you in a nutshell. The universe is like a safe to which there is a combination. But the combination is locked up in the safe.

—Peter De Vries

Life's a tough proposition, and the first hundred years are the hardest.

Life is a cement trampoline.

—Howard Nordberg

■ Losers

When I was a girl, I only had two friends, and they were imaginary. And they would only play with each other.

—Rita Rudner

He is so unlucky that he runs into accidents which started out to happen to somebody else.

—Don Marquis

I have no luck. I have a ten-dollar check and the only guy who would cash it for me was a guy I owed nine dollars to.

—Gene Baylos

In high school my parents told me I ran with the wrong crowd. I was a loner.

—Jeff Shaw

I was classified "4P" by the draft board. In the event of a war, I become a hostage.

—Woody Allen

Did you ever feel like the whole world was a tuxedo, and you were a pair of a brown shoes?

—George Gobel

No problem is so big or so complicated that it can't be run away from.

—Linus (Charles Schulz)

I'd quit the job of being me, but I have accumulated so much seniority.

—*Ziggy* (Tom Wilson)

Further Reading:
All Alone, Saul E. Terry
My Lost Causes, Noah Veil
Wish I'd Never Been Born, Rudy Daye
It's Unfair!, Y. Me

■ Love

Bumper sticker: Do you believe in love at first sight or shall I drive by again?

Teenagers don't know what love is. They have mixed-up ideas. They go for a drive, and the boy runs out of gas, and they smooch a little, and the girl says she loves him. That isn't love. Love is when you're married twenty-five years, smooching in your living room, and he runs out of gas, and she still says she loves him. That's love!

—Norm Crosby

Infatuation is when you think that he's as sexy as Robert Redford, as smart as Henry Kissinger, as noble as Ralph Nader, as funny as Woody Allen, and as athletic as Jimmy Connors. Love is when you realize that he's as sexy as Woody Allen, as smart as Jimmy Connors, as funny as Ralph Nader, as athletic as Henry Kissinger, and nothing like Robert Redford—but you'll take him anyway.

—Judith Viorst

If it is your time, love will track you down like a cruise missile. If you say, "No, I don't want it right now," that's when you'll get it for sure. Love will make a way out of no way. Love is an exploding cigar which we willingly smoke.

—Lynda Barry

If love is blind, why is lingerie so popular?

Love is an ocean of emotions, entirely surrounded by expenses.
—James Dewar

Love is like an hourglass, with the heart filling up as the brain empties.
—Jules Renard

Further Reading:
Feelings, Cara Lott
I Love You!, Alma Hart

■ Luck

When asked by a lady admirer if he believed in luck, Mark Twain responded, "Certainly! How else can you explain the success of those you detest?"

For every set of horseshoes that human beings use for luck, somewhere in this world there's a barefoot horse. —Allan Sherman

Don't believe in superstition—it brings bad luck. —H. Aaron Cohl

Rivals for the hard luck championship of Minnesota: 1) Mr. A. received a bottle of irresistible "Come and Get Me" cologne from his best girl on Monday and was drafted into the Army on Tuesday; 2) Mr. B. moved to a suburb of St. Paul and was promptly run over by a Welcome Wagon. —Bennett Cerf

Further Reading:
Wouldn't You Know It, Murphy Slaw
Lotsa Luck, Bess Twishes

■ Lying

Ann Landers challenged her readers to come up with the world's third-biggest lie—right after "The check is in the mail" and "I'm from the government, and I'm here to help you." Here is a sampling from the thousands she received:

- "It's a good thing you came in today. We only have two more in stock."
- "Five pounds is nothing on a person of your height."
- "It's delicious, but I can't eat another bite."
- "The puppy won't be any trouble, Mom. I'll take care of it myself."
- "Your hair looks just fine."
- "You don't need it in writing. You have my personal guarantee."

Lincoln liked to tell about the time Artemus Ward, a famous comedian of the day, was invited to a party. Mr. Ward was wearing his old country clothes. But he wanted to show that he felt at home, so he stepped right up to a very proud-looking lady and said, "Jeepers creepers! You sure are handsome!"

The woman was angry. "I wish I could say the same thing about you," she said.

"You could, Madam," answered Artemus Ward, "if you were as big a liar as I am."

—Beatrice Schenk de Regniers

Three elderly matrons were rocking gently one hot summer evening on the veranda of a modest Miami Beach hotel. "You should have seen the jewelry I had last year," said the first. "My diamonds alone were worth more than a million dollars. Unfortunately we had to sell them all, since my Park Avenue doctor discovered I am allergic to jewelry."

"I assure you, ladies, I wouldn't be here at all," said the second, "if I too didn't have an allergy. My husband and I owned a ten-acre estate at Newport, but we had to sell it when I found I was allergic to salt water."

At this point the third lady fainted dead away. When she came to, the others asked her what had happened. She explained, "Well, it seems that I am allergic also—to hot air!"

Although Abraham Lincoln is remembered as Honest Abe, his political opponents sometimes accused him of being two-faced. Lincoln's succinct response to his critics: "If I had another face, do you think I would use this one?"

The late John Connally like to tell a story about his Texas roots. In boasting of his background, Big John included George Washington in the Lone Star State's pantheon of heroes. As he told the story, young George one day went out into the backyard with a hatchet in hand and chopped down the family's mesquite tree. In due course he was summoned inside by a very angry parent.

"Did you chop down my mesquite tree?" demanded George's father.

"I cannot tell a lie, Father," said George. "I did chop down your mesquite tree."

On hearing this, the elder Washington ordered his son to start packing his bags. "We're moving to Virginia," he announced.

"Why, Father? Is it because I chopped down your mesquite tree?"

"No, George," came the reply. "Because if you can't tell a lie, you'll never amount to anything in Texas."

—Bob Dole

A man with an interest in show business is walking down a country road and walks by a horse, which says, "Hello, sir, remember me? I won the Kentucky Derby five years back."

A bona fide talking horse! the man thinks as he runs to find its owner.

"That horse is no good," says the owner, "but if you really want him, you can have him for twenty dollars."

"Twenty?" the man retorts. "I'll give you two thousand!"

"Fine with me, but has that old haybag been giving you that malarkey about winning the Derby? I happen to know it was the Preakness, and he didn't even win."

—Paul Dickson

Old lie: The check is in the mail.
New lie: I didn't check the e-mail.

A distinguished San Francisco attorney named Nat Schmulowitz dug back into ancient Greek sources to prove that some of the jokes newspaper columnists claim to have "originated" are often more than two thousand years old. Here's one:

A professor met a friend and exclaimed, "I heard you had died."

"But you see I'm alive," smiled the friend.

"Impossible," decided the professor. "The man who told me is much more reliable than you are."

A man gets on a train with his little boy, and gives the conductor only one ticket.

"How old's your kid?" the conductor says.

The father answers, "He's four years old."

"He looks at least twelve to me," says the suspicious conductor.

And the father asks, "Can I help it if he worries?"

—Robert Benchley

Further Reading:

I Didn't Do It!, Ivan Alibi

Cry Wolf, Al Armist

The Fortuneteller, I. Reid Palms

M

■ Madness

Six guys walk into a restaurant and are seated at a table. The leader goes over to the manager and says, "These people are patients from the Walker County Institution. This is our weekly outing. They will probably try to pay you with bottle caps. This is okay. Accept the bottle caps. It's part of the recovery program. When they go back to the bus, I will settle up with you."

The manager agrees to go along with this, so they all order and eat. They pay for their dinner with bottle caps and get back onto their bus.

As the leader walks over to the cash register, the manager tells him, "The bill comes to $96.42."

The leader says, "Do you have change for a hubcap?"

HOW TO DRIVE OTHER PEOPLE CRAZY

- When driving colleagues around, insist on keeping your car's windshield wipers running during all weather conditions to keep 'em tuned up.
- Put your garbage can on your desk and label it "IN."
- Practice making fax and modem noises.
- Every time someone asks you to do something, ask if they want fries with that.
- Develop an unnatural fear of staplers.
- Page yourself over the office intercom. Make no effort to disguise your voice.

- As often as possible, skip rather than walk.
- Stomp on plastic ketchup packets.
- Sing along at the opera.
- Go to a poetry recital, and ask why the poems don't rhyme.

—*Bee Metro* Staff

When trouble arises and things look bad, there is always one individual who perceives a solution and is willing to take command. Very often, that person is crazy.

—Dave Barry

Isn't sanity just a one-trick pony anyway? I mean, all you get is that one trick, rational thinking, but when you're good and crazy, well, the sky's the limit!

—The Tick

■ Manners

Etiquette means behaving yourself a little better than is absolutely essential.

—Will Cuppy

Oscar Levant and wife Joan were among a group of show-business guests at a White House dinner during the Truman administration. It was one of those half-social, half-command performance soirees and, after cordials, Oscar obliged with a twenty-minute piano recital. After shaking hands with the President while waiting for his rented limousine to whisk them away from the White House portico, Oscar was overhead grumbling to his wife, "Now I guess we owe the Trumans a dinner."

—Art Linkletter

A good listener is generally thinking about something else.

—Kin Hubbard

Perfect guest: One who makes his host feel at home.

There is a chronic shortage of dependable servants in Hollywood, and Hedy Lamarr considered herself a lucky lady when she snared an impeccable English butler into her service. He had only one minor fault. He would insist on walking into her boudoir without knocking.

Miss Lamarr finally lost her patience. "Grosvenor," she declared. "I am telling you for the last time that I will not have you enter my dressing room without knocking."

"Control yourself, madam," said the imperturbable Grosvenor. "I always peek through the keyhole first, and if you have nothing on, I don't enter."   —Bennett Cerf

Apology: Politeness too late.

Amy Vanderbilt, whose book on etiquette has made even Emily Post take a back seat, found herself sitting next to a man she never had seen before at a dinner party one evening. Along about time for the main course, he turned to her and said, "The lady on my right says you're Amy Vanderbilt. She's kidding, isn't she?"

"No, I'm Amy Vanderbilt all right," laughed Ms. V.

"In that case," said the man sharply, "what are you doing eating my salad?"   —Bennett Cerf

Judith Martin: People who declare that true intimacy means you don't have to worry about being polite will quickly run out of people who want to be intimate with them.   —Miss Manners

Further Reading:
If I Invited Him, Woody Kum
No!, Kurt Reply
Allegiance to the King, Neil Downe

■ Marriage

All marriages are happy. It's the living together afterward that causes all the trouble.
—Bessie & Beulah

That married couples can live together day after day is a miracle the Vatican has overlooked.
—Bill Cosby

Kissing: A means of getting two people so close together that they can't see anything wrong with each other.
—Rene Yasenek, quoted by "Dear Abby," Universal Press Syndicate

Some couples can't even agree before they get married. I heard one couple talking in the shopping mall. They couldn't agree on two rather picky little details for a wedding. She wanted the bridesmaids to wear long blue gowns, and he didn't want to get married.
—Ron Dentinger

Men who have pierced ears are better prepared for marriage. They've experienced pain and have bought jewelry.   —Rita Rudner

I belong to Bridegrooms Anonymous. Whenever I feel like getting married, they send over a lady in a housecoat and hair curlers to burn my toast for me.
—Dick Martin

A man and a woman met and married through a personal ad in the paper. Now there's a problem: Every time he picks the paper off the porch, she thinks he's cheating on her.
—Paul Dickson

On getting married: You lose the ability to get dressed by yourself.
—Paul Reiser

Yesterday somebody asked me what I did before I was married. I said, "Anything I wanted to."

—Ron Dentinger

Thurgood Marshall, the first black member of the Supreme Court, was mowing the lawn at his posh residence in a Washington suburb when a car stopped in the street. The woman driving the car noted a black man mowing a lawn and called out, "How much do you charge for mowing a lawn, my good man?" Marshall hesitated, and the woman said, "Well, what does the lady of the house pay you?"

Marshall replied, "She doesn't pay me anything, ma'am. She just lets me sleep with her."

Marriage is when a man and woman become as one; the trouble starts when they try to decide which one.

The longest sentence known to man: "I do."

My wife exclaimed to me as our twenty-fifth wedding anniversary approached, "This year let's give each other sensible gifts—like neckties and diamond bracelets."

I've known my wife so long, when we started dating the Dead Sea was only sick.

—Gene and Linda Perret

Following an especially angry argument, Uncle Ted and his wife went to bed not speaking to each other. Needing to arise early the following morning, Uncle Ted left a note on his wife's bedside table that said "Wake me at six."

An exasperated Uncle Ted awoke at ten the following morning and rolled stiffly out of bed to see a note on his bedside table: "It's six! Get out of bed!"

Whoever perpetrated the mathematical inaccuracy "Two can live as cheaply as one" has a lot to answer for.

—Caren Meyer

The other night my wife said, "Do you feel that the excitement has gone out of our marriage?"

I said, "I'll discuss it with you during the next commercial."

—H. Aaron Cohl

One night, the Potato family sat down to dinner—Mother Potato and her three daughters. Midway through the meal, the eldest daughter spoke up.

"Mother Potato?" she said. "I have an announcement to make."

"And what might that be?" said Mother, seeing the obvious excitement in her eldest daughter's eyes.

"Well," replied the daughter, with a proud but sheepish grin, "I'm getting married!"

The other daughters squealed with surprise as Mother Potato exclaimed, "Married! That's wonderful! And whom are you marrying, Eldest Daughter?"

"I'm marrying a Russet!"

"A Russet!" replied Mother Potato with pride. "Oh, a Russet is a fine tater, a fine tater indeed!"

As the family shared in the eldest daughter's joy, the middle daughter spoke up. "Mother? I, too, have an announcement."

"And what might that be?" encouraged Mother Potato.

Not knowing quite how to begin, the middle daughter paused, then said with conviction, "I, too, am getting married!"

"You, too!" Mother Potato said with joy. "That's wonderful! Twice the good news in one evening! And whom are you marrying, Middle Daughter?"

"I'm marrying an Idaho!" beamed the middle daughter.

"An Idaho!" said Mother Potato with joy. "Oh, an Idaho is a fine tater, a fine tater indeed!"

Once again, the room came alive with laughter and excited plans for the future, when the youngest Potato daughter interrupted. "Mother Potato? Um, I, too, have an announcement to make."

"Yes?" said Mother Potato with great anticipation.

"Well," began the youngest Potato daughter with the same sheepish grin as her eldest and middle sisters before her, "I hope this doesn't come as a shock to you, but I am getting married, as well!"

"Really?" said Mother Potato with sincere excitement. "All of my lovely daughters married! What wonderful news! And whom, pray tell, are you marrying, Youngest Daughter?"

"I'm marrying Peter Jennings!"

"Peter Jennings?" Mother Potato scowled suddenly. "But he's just a common tater!"

Oscar Levant to Harpo Marx upon meeting Harpo's fiancée: "She's a lovely person. She deserves a good husband. Marry her before she finds one."

Marrying a man is like buying something you've been admiring for a long time in a shop window. You may love it when you get it home, but it doesn't always go with everything else in the house.

—Jean Kerr

A Miami newspaper relates the touching story of a married couple who had not spoken to each other since 1982, but were reconciled during a recent hurricane. They were blown simultaneously through the roof of their home, and the wife explained later, "It seemed silly for us to go out together and not be speaking."

Further Reading:
Confessions of a Gold Digger, Emile Ticket
Repent at Leisure, Marion Hayste

■ Math

Back in ancient times a brilliant mathematician came up with the concept of "zero." Prior to that there were positive and negative numbers, but zero hadn't been used. Knowing that the zero was an important new concept, a dinner was given in honor of the scholar. A banner behind the head table read: "Thanks for nothing!"

—Ron Dentinger

Equations you might need to know when helping the kids with homework:

1000 microphones	=	1 megaphone
10 cards	=	1 decacards
2000 mockingbirds	=	2 kilamockingbirds
453.6 gram crackers	=	1 pound cake
100 rations	=	1 C ration
1,000,000 piccolos	=	1 gigolo
8 nickels	=	2 paradigms
2 snake eyes	=	1 paradise

When rock singer Ginger Spice announced she was leaving the group Spice Girls, a reporter mentioned to the remaining four that they were now a quartet. To which one of them replied: "Please, no math."

—Chris Pina in the *Los Angeles Times*

Question: If two's company and three's a crowd, what are four and five?
Answer: Nine.

Half of all high school students have trouble with basic math. That means that out of 14 million students . . . uh . . . uh . . . .

—Sue Sebesta in *Quote Magazine*

Further Reading:
I Love Fractions, Lois C. Denominator
I Love Sums, Adam Up

■ Memory

I have a memory like an elephant. In fact, elephants often consult me.
—H. Aaron Cohl

My wife accuses me of being absent-minded just because once when I was taking a shower, she heard me mumble to myself, "Now let me see—which pocket did I put that soap in?"

Nobody ever forgets where he buried the hatchet.   —Kin Hubbard

When I was younger, I could remember anything, whether it happened or not.   —Mark Twain

> **O**f all the things I've lost
> I miss my mind the most

■ Men versus Women

Once upon a time, in a land far away, a beautiful, independent, self-assured princess happened upon a frog as she sat contemplating ecological issues on the shores of an unpolluted pond in a meadow.

The frog hopped into the princess' lap and said, "Elegant Lady, I was once a handsome prince, until an evil witch cast a spell upon me. One kiss from you, however, and I will turn back into the dapper, young prince that I am, and then, my sweet, we can marry and set up housekeeping in yon castle with my mother, where you can prepare my meals, clean my clothes, bear my children, and forever feel grateful and happy doing so."

That night, as the princess dined sumptuously on a repast of lightly sautéed frog legs seasoned in a white wine and onion cream sauce, she chuckled to herself and murmured, "I don't think so."

Don't let a man put anything over on you except an umbrella.
—Mae West

Bumper sticker: Men are from Mars. Women are from Venus. Then some bozo had to go and invent space travel.

If we can put a man on the moon . . . why not all of them?

WHAT MEN REALLY MEAN

- "I'm going fishing" really means, "I'm going to stand by a stream with a stick in my hand, while the fish swim by in complete safety."
- "It's a guy thing" really means, "There is no rational thought pattern connected with it, and you have no chance at all of making it logical."
- "Can I help with dinner?" really means, "Why isn't it already on the table?"
- "Uh huh," "Sure, honey," or "Yes, dear," really means absolutely nothing. It's a conditioned response.
- "It would take too long to explain" really means, "I have no idea how it works."
- "I'm getting more exercise lately" really means, "The batteries in the remote are dead."
- "We're going to be late" really means, "Now I have a legitimate excuse to drive like a maniac."
- "Take a break, honey, you're working too hard" really means, "I can't hear the game over the vacuum cleaner."
- "Honey, we don't need material things to prove our love" really means, "I forgot our anniversary again."
- "That's women's work" really means, "It's difficult, dirty, and thankless."
- "You know how bad my memory is" really means, "I remember the theme song to *F Troop*, the address of the first girl I ever kissed, and the Vehicle Identification Numbers of every car I've ever owned, but I forgot your birthday."
- "Oh, don't fuss. I just cut myself, it's no big deal" really means, "I have severed a limb, but will bleed to death before I admit I'm hurt."
- "I do help around the house" really means, "I once put a dirty towel in the laundry basket."

- "Hey, I've got my reasons for what I'm doing" really means, "I sure hope I think of some reasons pretty soon."
- "I can't find it" really means, "It didn't fall into my outstretched hands, so I'm completely clueless."
- "What did I do this time?" really means, "What did you catch me doing?"
- "I heard you" really means, "I have no idea what you just said, and I'm desperately hoping I can fake it well enough so that you don't spend the next three days yelling at me."
- "You look terrific" really means, "Oh, please don't try on one more outfit. I'm starving."
- "I missed you" really means, "I can't find matching socks, the kids are hungry, and we are out of toilet paper."
- "I'm not lost. I know exactly where we are" really means, "I'm lost. I have no idea where we are, and no one will ever see us alive again."
- "We share the housework" really means, "I make the messes; you clean them up."
- "I don't need to read the instructions" really means, "I am perfectly capable of screwing it up without printed help."

For years journalists have portrayed Elizabeth and me as the only two attorneys in Washington, D.C., who trust each other. Even now, some people seem astonished that I'm comfortable sharing the spotlight with a powerful woman. I'm just glad she lets me share it. In 1985, when Elizabeth was appointed secretary of transportation by President Reagan, her selection inspired a raft of stories. *People* magazine sent a photographer to follow us around for days. He took about three hundred pictures, of which the magazine used three. One of these showed us making the bed in our Watergate apartment.

Shortly after, I got a letter from an irate Californian whose wife had seen the story. "Senator," he told me, "I don't mind your wife getting a job. I'm sure she is qualified and does good work. But you've got to stop doing the work around the house. You're causing problems for men all across the country."

"You don't know the half of it," I wrote back. "The only reason she was helping was because they were taking pictures." —Bob Dole

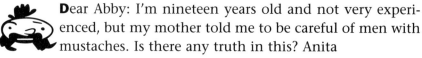

Dear Abby: I'm nineteen years old and not very experienced, but my mother told me to be careful of men with mustaches. Is there any truth in this? Anita

Dear Anita: Yes . . . and also be careful of men without them.

Two guys are talking. The first says, "I asked her to marry me, and she turned me down."

The other guys says, "Don't feel too bad. Often a woman's 'No' really means 'Yes.'"

The first guy says, "But she didn't say 'No.' She said, 'Get lost.'"

If you're in a car with a man and he stops and asks for directions, listen carefully, because he won't and it will be your fault if you get lost.

—Rita Rudner

Nagging: The constant reiteration of the unhappy truth.

Sign on an Indiana highway: Don't just sit there. Nag your husband.

TOP TEN THINGS ONLY WOMEN UNDERSTAND
10. Dog's facial expressions
 9. The need for the same style of shoes in different colors
 8. Why bean sprouts aren't just weeds
 7. Fat clothes
 6. Taking a car trip without trying to beat your best time
 5. The difference between beige, off-white, and eggshell
 4. Cutting your bangs to make them grow
 3. Eyelash curlers
 2. The inaccuracy of every bathroom scale ever made
. . . and, the Number One thing only women understand:
 1. Other women.

When Winston Churchill once was asked if he knew any professional women, he answered promptly, "I've never met any amateur ones."

I hate women because they always know where things are.

—James Thurber

A study in the *Washington Post* says that women have better verbal skills than men. I just want to say to the authors of that study: Duh.

—Conan O'Brien

A woman's mind is cleaner than a man's. She changes it more often.

—Oliver Herford

It is a known fact that men are practical, hardheaded realists, in contrast to women, who are romantic dreamers and actually believe that estrogenic skin cream must do something, or they couldn't charge sixteen dollars for that little tiny jar. —Jane Goodsell

Men do not like to admit to even momentary imperfection. My husband forgot the code to turn off the alarm. When the police came, he wouldn't admit he'd forgotten the code . . . he turned himself in. —Rita Rudner

Men do cry, but only when assembling furniture of Scandinavian design.

Ever since Eve gave Adam the apple, there has been a misunderstanding between the sexes about gifts. —Nan Robertson

At a huge gathering a female psychology student was rebuked when she stated that men were much vainer than women. Naturally, she was immediately challenged by a fellow standing near her. In order to prove her statement, she said in a clear voice that carried through the room, "It's a shame that most intelligent and sensitive men attach so little importance to the way they dress. Why, right this minute, the most cultivated man in this room is wearing the most clumsily knotted tie."

Whereupon, as if on cue, every man in the room immediately put his hand to his tie.

—Myron Cohen

If a woman has to choose between catching a fly ball and saving an infant's life, she will choose to save the infant's life without even considering if there are men on base.

—Dave Barry

I took up a collection for a man in our office. But I didn't get enough to buy one.

—Ruth Buzzi

Think how much happier women would be if, instead of endless fretting about what the males in their lives are thinking, they could relax, secure in the knowledge that the correct answer is—very little.

—Dave Barry, *The Complete Guide to Guys*

■ Ministers

The minister of a church in Wyckoff, New Jersey, told the sexton to put on the bulletin board his sermon topic for the following Sunday—"Are Ministers Cracking Up?" The sexton looked puzzled but did as he was told and put up the letters to announce: "Our Minister's Cracking Up."

Notice in church bulletin: The preacher for next Sunday will be found pinned up in the side porch.

When Franklin D. Roosevelt was president, the pastor of the church he attended in Washington was asked over the phone, "Is the President expected to attend church this Sunday?"

"I do not know," replied the minister. "But I can assure you that God will be there, which should be incentive enough."

—Larry Wilde

At a faculty-student reception, Yale's chaplain, the Rev. William Sloane Coffin Jr., met an intense sophomore with the light of battle in his eye. "Sir," said the boy belligerently, "religion is a crutch!"

"Sure it is," agreed Coffin, "but who isn't limping?"

Carl Winters is one minister who appreciates the value of humor. He declares, "When I preach, I definitely try to make people laugh. And while their mouths are open, I put something in for them to chew on."

An elderly woman is sitting on a plane and getting increasingly nervous about the thunderstorm raging outside. She turns to a minister sitting next to her:

"Reverend, you are a man of God. Why can't you do something about this problem?"

"Lady, I'm in sales, not management."

—Paul Dickson

Rev. Eugene Magee is an enthusiastic preacher, who likes to wave his arms to emphasize important points in his sermons. Unfortunately, he has trouble keeping his shirttails in his trousers and has developed the habit of stuffing them in surreptitiously whenever he has the opportunity. Last Easter Sunday, while admonishing the faithful, he fished around behind his back in the usual way, and found more material than usual to push out of sight. He persisted doggedly, however. At the close of his sermon he discovered that he had about half of the American flag stuffed into his pants.

Even without TV and special effects, some old-time traveling preachers still managed to be quite theatrical. One of them would hire a young boy to climb into the rafters and hide there with a caged dove. At the climax of his appeal, the preacher would raise his hands, look toward heaven, and call, "Holy Ghost, come down!" The boy would release the dove on cue, and it would fly down with great effect.

But one day when the preacher called, "Holy Ghost, come down!" nothing happened. He tried again, a little louder, "Holy Ghost, come down!"

Scuffling sounds were heard from the rafters, followed by a little voice that said, "Preacher, a big yellow cat just ate the Holy Ghost. You want me to throw down the yellow cat?"

Jean Roth, the wife of my dear friend Father Ralph Roth, shook him awake in the middle of one night and whispered, "Wake up! There are burglars in the house."

Ralph rolled over and muttered, "What of it? Let them find out their mistake themselves."

■ Misanthropy

"Be yourself" is about the worst advice you can give some people.

—Tom Masson

The trouble with treating people as equals is that the first thing you know they may be doing the same thing to you.   —Peter De Vries

All the problems we face in the United States today can be traced to an unenlightened immigration policy on the part of the American Indian.

—Pat Paulsen

I know there are people in the world who do not love their fellow human beings, and I hate people like that!   —Tom Lehrer

One thing I like is long walks—especially when they're made by people who annoy me.
—Fred Allen

I am free of all prejudice. I hate everyone equally.
—W. C. Fields

Further Reading:
Go Away!, Ron Onhome
Don't Tread on Me, Amanda B. Reckonwith

■ Misers

We have a guy in our office who is so cheap that he even tries to buy tattoos secondhand.

Two bellhops were discussing the best tippers in the hotel. "Watch out for that preacher's convention," cautioned the older bellhop.

"Are they cheap?" asked the younger man.

"Let me put it this way," answered the voice of experience. "Last year they showed up with the Ten Commandments in one hand and a ten-dollar bill in the other, and when they left, they hadn't broken either."
—George Jessel

This guy has a wallet that won't let dollar bills out of it. It's like a Roach Motel for money.

During one of his presidential campaigns, Ross Perot registered at the St. Francis Hotel in San Francisco and asked for the cheapest room.

The hotel clerk was dumbfounded. "But, Mr. Perot," he protested. "When your son stops here, he always occupies the finest suite we have."

"My son has a rich father," said Perot sternly. "I am not so fortunate."

An indignant Scotchman sent a letter to the editor of a newspaper. "If you don't stop writing about Scotchmen being so stingy," he penned, "I'll stop borrowing your paper."   —Joe Laurie Jr.

My uncle Ted has reached for fewer checks than Venus De Milo.

The funniest joke ever heard on radio consisted of nothing but silence. On one of his Sunday evening radio shows, Jack Benny, known by all as the cheapest man in the world, was stopped by a thief who said, "Your money or your life."

There followed a long silence, and in due course the audience, catching on, began to laugh louder and louder and louder. Finally, just in case there were a few people who didn't get the point, the thief persisted, "Come on, your money or your life!"

To which Benny replied snappishly, "I'm thinking! I'm thinking!"

He read in the paper that it takes ten dollars a year to support a kid in India. So he sent his kid there.   —Red Buttons

I cannot remember my mother ever spending a dime on herself for something she didn't desperately need. I can never remember her buying more than five dollars' worth of gas at a time, either. I think she was afraid if she filled up the tank and died, she would have wasted money on whatever gas remained in her car.

            —Lewis Grizzard

My uncle Ted and his wife dined out almost every night. Ted was not what one would call a generous tipper. In fact, Ted expressed himself as highly sympathetic to the viewpoint and aims of the National Anti-Tipping Society, but his enthusiasm waned perceptibly when he heard the annual dues were twenty dollars a year. "Twenty dollars," he grumbled. "Why that's more than I spend a year in tips!"

You heard about the man who quit playing golf, then took it up again fourteen years later? He found his ball.   —Bob Kaliban

Melvin Westerman, a notorious skinflint in our community, became desperately ill with emphysema. One day he startled the pastor of the First Baptist Church by wheezing, "Pastor, pray for my recovery, and if I get well, I'll give the church building fund one hundred thousand dollars."

He recovered, but did everything he could to avoid encountering the pastor. He even refused to come to the door when the pastor called at his home on numerous occasions. The minister finally cornered him in the post office, and sternly reminded him, "You promised the church building fund one hundred thousand dollars if you recovered your health."

"I did?" responded Melvin in mock bewilderment. "That'll give you a rough idea of how sick I was!"

■ Modern Life
Martin Levin predicts this airwave bulletin one hundred years from today:

- Washington: The president checked into the Walter Reed Army Hospital early this morning. Doctors say it may be twins.
- New York: Traffic Commissioner Bargle has warned motorists that the city will crack down on litterbugs who fail to deposit their disposable automobiles in trash receptacles.
- UN Headquarters: A visiting Dodger spokesman has denied a rumor that the team will move to Tangier. "We'll never leave Kuwait," he declared.
- Detroit: The Ford Foundation has granted $750,000 to an educational experiment which will investigate the use of books as possible visual aids.   —Bennett Cerf

I bought some poison to kill some bugs. When I took off the cap I had to remove a tamper seal. Is this to keep someone from putting something bad in there?   —John Aceti

USEFUL TERMS FOR MODERN LIVING

Argument: A discussion that occurs when you're right, but he hasn't realized it yet.

Cantaloupe: Gotta get married in a church.

Clothes dryer: An appliance designed to eat socks.

Diet soda: A low-calorie drink you consume with a big bag of M & Ms.

Eternity: The last two minutes of a football game.

Exercise: To walk up and down a mall, occasionally resting to make a purchase.

Grocery list: What you spend an hour writing, then forget to take to the store.

Hair stylist: Someone who is able to create a style you will never be able to duplicate again. See "Magician."

Patience: The most important ingredient for dating, marriage, and children. See also "tranquilizers."

Waterproof mascara: Eye makeup that comes off if you cry, shower, or swim, but will not come off if you try to remove it.

Valentine's Day: A day when you have dreams of a candlelight dinner, diamonds, and romance, but consider yourself lucky to get a card. If you are a parent, see also "Birthday."

How do you explain "counterclockwise" to a child with a digital watch?

Progress might have been all right once, but it has gone on too long.

—Ogden Nash

■ Modesty

Sweet praise is like a perfume. It's fine if you don't swallow it.

—Dwight Eisenhower

I often quote myself. It adds spice to the conversation.

—George Bernard Shaw

A young reporter in Wichita rode in an open car down the main street with Jack Kennedy during his 1960 campaign tour. While the onlookers cheered lustily, the reporter begged, "Won't you tell the driver he's going too fast?"

"It's all right," the soon-to-be president assured him. "They all know who I am."

"I know," grinned the reporter. "But I'd like to give them a chance to see who's riding with you."   —Bennett Cerf

Franklin Delano Roosevelt certainly never lacked self-confidence at crucial moments, but I personally witnessed an exhibition of extraordinary modesty on his part. Invited to visit with him in his White House study shortly before the outbreak of World War II, I found him busily writing his name on the flyleaf of every book in his personal library. He was completely surrounded by piles of volumes. When I asked the reason for this methodical labor, the president explained, "Visitors to the White House don't seem to realize these books are my personal property, and not the government's. They pilfer them as souvenirs." It never had occurred to FDR that his personal autograph would make every book a hundred times more tempting to souvenir hunters!   —Bennett Cerf

■ Money

Mark Twain once attended a party where he was bored by a paunchy tycoon who was pontificating on the subject of wealth. "Money is not everything, gentlemen," he said. "It cannot buy happiness, nor can it buy a happy home, nor can it lift the spirits of the saddened, nor alleviate the sufferings of the afflicted, nor buy the love of a good woman."

Commented Twain, "You refer, of course, to Confederate money."

On a Chicago billboard: Now you can borrow enough to get completely out of debt.

Extravagance: Anything you buy that is of no earthly use to your wife.

—Franklin P. Adams

Two guys were chatting at a cocktail party. "Your wife certainly brightens the room," one said to the other. "Her mere presence is electrifying."

"It ought to be," the other man replied. "Everything she's wearing is charged."

—Ron Dentinger

Signs of stock market madness:
- You think MTV is a stock symbol.
- You think middle-age spread is an options hedge.
- You hear "new impotence medicine" and you think "pumped up drug stocks."
- You think "downsizing" has a nice ring to it.
- You have Charles Schwab on speed dial, but not your mother.
- You now think, "Well, maybe not the root of *all* evil."

—*Newsweek*

Workers earn it
Spendthrifts burn it
Bankers lend it
Women spend it
Forgers fake it
Taxes take it
Dying leave it
Heirs receive it
Thrifty save it
Others crave it
Robbers seize it
Rich increase it
Gamblers lose it . . .
I could use it.

—Richard Armour

A penny saved is worthless.

—Dave Barry

My uncle Joe has discovered a sure-fire way to save. He forgets who he's borrowed it from.

Change is inevitable, except from a vending machine.

The rich industrialist from the North was horrified to find the southern fisherman lying lazily beside his boat, smoking a pipe.

"Why aren't you out fishing?" said the industrialist.

"Because I have caught enough fish for the day," said the fisherman.

"Why don't you catch some more?"

"What would I do with them?"

"You could earn more," was the industrialist's reply. "With that you could have a motor fixed to your boat, and go into deeper waters and catch more fish. Then you would make enough to buy nylon nets. These would bring you more fish and more money. Soon you would have enough to own two boats . . . maybe even a fleet of boats. Then you would be a rich man like me."

"What would I do then?" asked the fisherman.

"Then you could really enjoy life."

"What do you think I am doing right now?"

From the pastor's note in a bulletin of Glad Tidings Assembly of God church in Greeley, Colorado: Thanks to all of you for your prayers, love, support, faithful attendance, and financial giving for 1997. It is because of you that we pad all of our bills.

I'm living so far beyond my income that we may almost be said to be living apart.

— e. e. cummings

(It's been said that e. e. cummings' problem was that he was undercapitalized!)

I'm going to start living within my means. Even if I have to get a loan to do it.
— *Ziggy* (Tom Wilson*)*

I once asked my Aunt Harriet, "If you found a million dollars in the street, what would you do with it?"

"That depends," answered my aunt. "If I found it belonged to somebody very poor, I'd give it back."

God shows his contempt for wealth by the kind of person he selects to receive it.
—Austin O'Malley

After having an extremely profitable year, the wealthy dress manufacturer went to his Florida home.

While he was in Florida, he met a lovely widow and immediately fell in love with her. Since he was somewhat older than she, he knew that a little diplomacy and bribery were called for.

"Marry me," he told her, "and I'll buy you a new Cadillac convertible."

"I've got two already," she told him.

"How about a new diamond ring?" he offered.

"I've got a beautiful ring already," she said, lifting her hand and displaying a huge, shiny stone.

"I'll give you an exquisite mink coat."

"I've got a mink and a sable, too."

Confused, the manufacturer asked, "Well, what do you want?"

"Cash," she replied, "just cold, hard cash!"
—Myron Cohen

Two young wives were discussing the pitfalls of love and marriage. They railed against their husbands and men in general. One of the chief complaints was the improvidence of their respective mates. "If only I were the wife of a millionaire," moaned one.

"You mean, of course, if only you were the widow of a millionaire," corrected the other.
—Myron Cohen

Cheer up! After all, you can still use a dime for a screwdriver.

Plenty of people are willing to give God credit, yet few are willing to give him cash.

—Carol Rumsey

I have enough to last me the rest of my life—unless I buy something.

—Jackie Mason

After giving the situation quite a thorough bit of thinking, Mrs. Willie Mae Finn gave a financially nonchalant friend a bit of advice in her home in Montgomery, Alabama. "I think, my dear," said Willie Mae, "that you ought to find out who the Joneses are trying to keep up with before you try to keep up with the Joneses."

—Walter Davenport

Ever notice that price and worth mean the same thing, but priceless and worthless are opposites?

—Jay Trachman in *One to One*

A study of economics usually reveals that the best time to buy anything is last year.

—Marty Allen

Sam always loved to make his friend Max envious, so after refurnishing his home, Sam invited Max over. Sam didn't overlook anything, especially the price of every article, stressing the point that everything was very "expensive."

Poor little Max returned home very depressed. Then someone tipped him off that Sam had bought all the new furniture on the installment plan. Elated, Max couldn't wait until he got him on the phone. "Bluffer, you!" he said with contempt. "I found out you bought your furniture on installments!"

"Sure," admitted Sam. "It's more expensive that way."

—Harry Hershfield

Further Reading:
More for Your Money, Max Amize
Debt Management, Owen Cash
Where to Put Your Paper Money, Bill Fold
I Work with Diamonds, Jules Sparkle
Girl on a Budget, Penny Pincher
Bad Investment, Les Riches
We Take Credit Cards, But . . . , Cassius Better
Neither a Borrower, Nora Lender Bee

■ Mothers

It's not easy being a mother. If it were easy, fathers would do it.
—Dorothy on *The Golden Girls*

My mother got up every morning at 5:00 A.M. no matter what time it was.
—Sam Levenson

Every time I find a girl who can cook like my mother, she looks like my father.
—Tony Randall

A mother on my street walked into her son's room, four o'clock in the afternoon. He was asleep, a grown-up son, forty-two years old. And she went right up to the bed in pointy shoes, and she kicked him and said, "Look-a you. You forty-two years old, you no work, sleep, ya big-a bum. You don't bring-a no money home, I cry-a my eyes out! Shame, shame on-a you, you bum."

And the fella stood up with tears in his eyes and said, "Mother, why do you talk like that? We're not Italian." —Norm Crosby

Hey, the way I figure it is this: if the kids are still alive by the time my husband comes home, I've done my job. —Roseanne Barr

There's not a lot of warmth between me and my mother. I asked her about it. I said, "Mrs. Stoller . . ."

—Fred Stoller

A woebegone lady clad only in a suit jacket and sheer slip pushed ahead of the line at a department store's lost-and-found window and inquired anxiously, "Has anybody turned in a black skirt with four children from two to five hanging on to it?"

—Bennett Cerf

My mom is a clean freak. She vacuumed so much, the guy downstairs went bald.

—Steve Bridges

I will never understand children. I never pretended to. I meet mothers all the time who make resolutions to themselves. "I'm going to go out of my way to show them I am interested in them and what they do. I am going to understand my children." These women end up making rag rugs, using blunt scissors.

—Erma Bombeck

Four matronly women were sitting under their beach umbrellas at Atlantic City. It was a hot afternoon, and none of them felt like talking. Finally, one heaved a deep sigh and uttered, "Oh!"

The second responded with "Oh, dear."

The third said, "Oh, dear me!"

And the fourth stood up angrily and said, "If you're all going to start talking about your children again, I'm leaving."

When my seventy-seven-year-old mother was in a nursing home during the last year of her life, I called her frequently. She was always delighted to hear from me and seized the opportunity of telling me the latest news. She said to me: "Yesterday, I was speaking to an old woman of ninety-four, and in the middle of the conversation, she just dropped dead. Oh, Isaac, everything happens to your mother."

—Isaac Asimov, *Asimov Laughs Again*

My friend Myron tells me, "Last year on Mother's Day the whole family got together for a dinner, and afterward, when Mom started to clean up, I said to her, 'Don't bother with those dishes, Mom. Today is Mother's Day. You can always do them tomorrow.'"

—Joey Adams

My mom was a little weird. When I was little, she would make chocolate frosting. And she'd let me lick the beaters. And then she'd turn them off.

—Marty Cohen

A man is speaking into the telephone, and you hear only his side of the conversation.

"Yes, Mother, I've had a hard day. Gladys has been most difficult—I know I ought to be more firm, but it is hard. Well, you know how she is. Yes, I remember you warned me. I remember you told me she was a vile creature who would make my life miserable, and you begged me not to marry her. You were perfectly right. You want to talk to her? All right."

He looks up from the telephone and calls to his wife from the next room, "Gladys, your mother wants to talk you."

—Isaac Asimov

My mother calls at five-thirty in the morning. I'm not a dairy farm. I don't like phone calls before six in the morning. —Richard Lewis

During one of my visits to my parents' home in Florida, my mother made blintzes—one of her specialties. They were wonderful, as usual. Mother turned to me and beamed, "Lowell, I know how you love blintzes. Why don't you take a couple more?"

I replied, "I would love to take some more, Mom, but I am positively stuffed. I have already had eight."

"You've had eleven," corrected my mother, "but who's counting?"

An angry mother took her son to the doctor and asked, "Is a nine-year-old boy able to perform an appendectomy?"

"Of course not," the doctor said impatiently.

The mother turned to her son and said, "What did I tell you? Now put it back." —H. Aaron Cohl

My fastidious mother awoke one morning with a ringing in her ears—so she got an unlisted ear.

I think I'd be a good mother. Maybe a little overprotective. Like I would never let the kid out—of my body. —Wendy Liebman

Some women are lucky, you know. They gave birth to babies. I gave birth to teenagers. Our daughter was born with a princess phone growing out of her ear. Our son was born with his foot extended in an accelerator position and a set of car keys in his little fist. The third was born hostile. (Even in the nursery he staged a protest to lower the age of birth to a five-month fetus.) —Erma Bombeck

A child of two can be taught not to do certain things, like touch a hot stove, knock over a table, or wake Mommy before noon.

—Joan Rivers

There's a very old saying: "Neurotics build castles in the air and psychotics live in them." My mother cleans them. —Rita Rudner

The phrase "working mother" is redundant. —Jane Sellman

Any mother could perform the jobs of several air traffic controllers with ease. —Lisa Alther

■ Movies

During the Depression, movie theater owners resorted to a wide variety of marketing gimmicks to attract paying customers. Howard Dietz, a publicity director for MGM, felt that exhibitors were giving the public too much for its money. "I will tell you how far things have gone," he said. "I just heard about a man in Oklahoma who went to a theater where for fifteen cents, he got two feature pictures, a Mickey Mouse cartoon, a newsreel, and two sets of dishes, and then demanded his money back because he didn't strike oil under his seat."

Famed motion picture producer Billy Wilder tells of the day he tried to persuade Sam Goldwyn to let him do a picture on the life of the great Russian ballet star Nijinsky. Said star unfortunately had come to a disastrous end, spending the last years of his existence in an insane asylum convinced he was a horse.

"Now listen to me, Billy," argued Goldwyn. "If you think I'm going to invest three million dollars in a picture about a man who thinks he's a horse, you're even crazier then he is."

"We can give the story a happy ending," urged Wilder. "We'll have him win the Kentucky Derby!"
—Bennett Cerf

Karate is a form of martial arts in which people who have had years and years of training can, using only their hands and feet, make some of the worst movies in the history of the world.   —Dave Barry

David Helfgott, the subject of the movie *Shine,* said playing for the Academy Awards audience reminded him of playing at the mental hospital. Half the people were on medication and half have delusions of grandeur.
—Bill Maher

I don't think I could take a mellow evening because I don't respond well to mellow. You know what I mean? I have a tendency to—if I get too mellow—I ripen and then rot.   —Woody Allen, in *Annie Hall*

My uncle Phil is a bit eccentric. He once bought an old double-decker bus to go to the drive-in. He explained, "I like to sit in the balcony."

The badness of a movie is directly proportional to the number of helicopters in it.

—Dave Barry

I saw the sequel to the movie *Clones,* and you know what? It was the same movie!

—Jim Samuels

Sometimes when I'm sitting in my car at a stop light, I imagine myself as Luke Skywalker, and I close my eyes and concentrate on using the Force. Sometimes I have to concentrate longer than others, but I know it works, 'cause the light always turns green.

—Troy Peterson

The candy at the movies is really expensive. I had to get a box of Raisinettes on layaway.

—Scott Wood

STAR TREK: AN EPISODE BY DR. SEUSS

Picard:	Sigma Indri, that's the star,
	So, Data, please, how far? How far?
Data:	Our ship can get there very fast,
	But still the trip will last and last.
	We'll have two days till we arrive,
	But can the Indrans there survive?
Picard:	La Forge, please give us factor nine.
La Forge:	But, sir, the engines are off-line!
Picard:	Off-line! But why? I want to go!
	Please make it so, please make it so!
Riker:	But sir, if Geordi says we can't,
	We can't, we mustn't, and we shan't.
	The danger here is far too great!

Picard:	But surely we must not be late!
Troi:	I'm sensing anger and great ire.
Computer:	Alert! Alert! The ship's on fire!
Picard:	The ship's on fire? How could this be?
	Who lit the fire?
Riker:	Not me!
Worf:	Not me!
Picard:	Computer, how long until we die?
Computer:	Eight minutes left to say good-bye.
Data:	May I suggest a course to take?
	We could, I think, quite safely make
	Extinguishers from tractor beams
	And stop the fire, or so it seems.
La Forge:	Hurray! Hurray! You've saved the day!
	Again I say, Hurray! Hurray!
Picard:	Mr. Data, thank you much.
	You've saved our lives, our ship, and such.
Troi:	We still must save the Indran planet!
Data:	Which by the way is made of granite.
Picard:	Enough, you android. Please desist.
	We understand, we get your gist.
	But can we get our ship to go?
	Please make it so, please make it so!
La Forge:	There's sabotage among the wires,
	And that's what started all the fires!
Riker:	We have a saboteur? Oh, no!
	We need to go! We need to go!
Troi:	We must seek out this traitor spy,
	And lock him up and ask him why.
Worf:	Ask him why? How sentimental.
	I say we give him problems dental.
Troi:	Are any Romulan ships around?
	Have scanners said that they've been found?
	Or is it Borg or some new threat
	We haven't even heard of yet?
	I sense no malice in this crew.
	Now what are we supposed to do?

Crusher:	Captain, please, the Indrans need us.
	They cry, "Help us, clothe us, feed us!"
	I can't just sit and let them die!
	We must attempt, we must try!
Picard:	Doctor, please, we'll get there soon.
Crusher:	But they'll be dead by tomorrow noon!
	[Commercial break, commercial break!
	How long will all these dumb ads take?]
Worf:	The saboteur is in the brig!
	He's very strong and very big!
	I had my phaser set on stun—
	A zip! A zap! Another one!
	He would not budge, he would not fall.
	He would not stun, no, not at all!
	He changed into a stranger form
	All soft and purple, round and warm.
Picard:	Did you see this, Mr. Worf?
	Did you see this creature morph?
Worf:	I did and then I beat him fairly.
	Hit him on the jaw, quite squarely.
Riker:	My commendations, Klingon friend!
	Our troubles now are at an end.
Crusher:	Now let's get our ship to fly,
	And orbit yonder Indran sky!
Picard:	La Forge, please tell me we can go?
La Forge:	Yes, sir, we can.
Picard:	Then make it so!

Further Reading:

Tear-jerker Movie, Maud Lynn Story

Home Alone IV: The Sequel, Annie Buddyhome

■ Music

An ambitious and aggressive mother conned pianist Artur Rubinstein into listening to her ten-year-old son murder a nocturne by Chopin. At the conclusion of the massacre, Rubinstein announced, "Madam, that is undoubtedly the worst piano playing I ever heard."

Whereupon the mother nodded happily and told her son, "You see? Now will you give up those expensive piano lessons and try out for the Little League baseball team?   —Art Buchward

Radio and TV personality Charles Osgood recalls the time he entertained at a St. Patrick's Day affair. As he strummed an Irish tune, he caught a listener weeping. "Irish?" asked Osgood.

"No," came the reply. "Musician."

—Quoted by Irv Kupcinet in the *Chicago Sun-Times*

Mrs. Cornelius Vanderbilt, fabulously wealthy arbiter of New York's social *creme de la creme*, once asked violin virtuoso Fritz Kreisler how much he would charge to play a short recital at a very posh affair she was planning in her palatial home. "My fee is eighteen thousand dollars," said Mr. Kreisler.

"That's agreeable," replied Mrs. Vanderbilt. "But I hope you understand that you should not mingle with my guests."

"Oh! Well, in that case, my fee is only five hundred dollars," said Mr. Kreisler.   —Art Linkletter

Boston Pops: Carbonated beverages with a New England accent.

A young student asked Wolfgang Amadeus Mozart how to write a symphony. Mozart told the ambitious young man to begin with something simple, like ballads.

"But you composed symphonies when you were only ten years old," objected the youth.

"True," replied Mozart, "but I didn't ask how."   —Art Linkletter

Q: What happens if you play country music backward?

A: Your wife returns to you, your dog comes back to life, and you get out of prison.

I worry that the person who thought up Muzak may be thinking up something else. —Lily Tomlin

Jack Benny likes to credit his father with a gem of musical criticism. Back in Waukegan, Jack practiced faithfully on his violin each day. One Saturday a neighboring dog passed by and started howling dolefully under the window of the room where Jack was sawing away. Finally his father shouted downstairs, "For pity's sake, Jack, can't you play some piece the dog doesn't know!" —Art Linkletter

On George Burn's singing: "He sounds like a disposal with a spoon caught in it."

—Quoted by Cheryl Blythe and Susan Sackett in *Say Goodnight, Gracie!*

Jack Benny swears that one evening when he was invited to play for the president, a guard stopped him outside the White House gate and asked, "Whatcha got in that case, Mr. Benny?"

Benny answered solemnly, "A machine gun."

With equal solemnity, the guard nodded. "Enter, friend. I was afraid for a minute it was your violin!" —Bennett Cerf

She was a town-and-country soprano of the kind often used for augmenting the grief at a funeral. —George Ade

Mark Twain after sitting through a performance of Tannhauser in Vienna commented: "Wagner isn't as bad as it sounds."

A trio was making music for the residents of a nursing home. After the third song an old gent asked if they played requests. The leader said, "Yes, we do. What would you like us to play?"

The old guy said, "Pinochle."

Son: When I grow up, I want to be a musician.
Father: I'm sorry—you can't have it both ways.
—Quoted by Garrison Keillor on *A Prairie Home Companion*

Thinking it was about time his four children courted a little culture, a gentleman in Bismarck, North Dakota, bought them a piano. He got home that evening and found his kids gazing admiringly at the instrument. What they wanted to know, however, was how you plugged it in.
—Walter Davenport

Shortly after Charles Gounod died, in 1893, a second-rate German composer called on Johannes Brahms and proudly showed him the score of his latest work. "It is a funeral march in honor of our dear friend Gounod," he explained. "What do you think of it?"

The testy Brahms looked it over through the smoke of his ever-present cigar. Finally, he handed it back and said, "It would have been better if you had died and Gounod had written the march."
—Art Linkletter

An international opera company was touring Mexico when it was set upon by bandits and brought before the notorious Pancho Villa. The soprano demanded that she be released as a world treasure. "I am a prima donna," she sniffed.

"Prima donna?" the infamous bandit sneered. "Prove it! Sing for me!"

"Sing? Now?" she said, looking at him with disdain. "Without accompaniment or payment? In this filthy camp? To a vulgar man like you? I'd rather die!"

"Release her!" Villa told his men. "She *is* a prima donna!"
—The Jokesmith

Samuel Johnson was at a gathering one evening when a young man essayed a bassoon solo. Johnson visibly winced, and his neighbor whispered reassuringly, "You know, Doctor, that the bassoon is very difficult to play."

"You may well say so, sir," said Johnson. "And I only wish to God it were impossible!" —Art Linkletter

Smack in the middle of an Oscar Levant performance of Gershwin's pyrotechnic *Piano Concerto in F,* in a small college auditorium, the audience became aware of a telephone ringing in an office just off-stage. Levant ignored the annoying jangle as his fingers flew over the keyboard, but finally took advantage of a slightly pianissimo passage to turn to the audience and say, without missing a note, "If that's for me, tell them I'm busy." —Art Linkletter

Fullerton High School in southern California has a new provision in contracts with rock bands that play at school dances. A decibel meter will be used during their performance, and if the sound goes over ninety-two decibels, they don't get paid.

—cited by Bud and Lolo Delaney, *The Laugh Journal*

Wallace Swine now has an orchestra in his restaurant, but the music is so bad that last night a waiter dropped a tray of dishes and everybody got up and started to dance. —Charley Weaver (Cliff Arquette)

In search of an apartment some years ago, jazz bandleader and guitarist Eddie Condon ran into a building supervisor who bragged, "In this building we allow no wild parties, musical instruments, or loud radio, hi-fi, or TV playing after eleven at night."

"Fine," said Condon. "But before you accept me as a tenant, there's something I have to tell you: my fountain pen scratches."

—Art Linkletter

An American impresario, preparing a concert program, instructed his new secretary to expand all abbreviations—Op. into Opus, for example—before sending the program to the printer. Later, in the printer's proof, he found: "Bach: Massachusetts in B Minor."

DON'T TRY THIS AT HOME!

August 1998, Montevideo, Uruguay—Paolo Esperanza, bass-trombonist with the Simphonica Mayor de Uruguay, in a misplaced moment of inspiration decided to make his own contribution to the cannon shots fired as part of the orchestra's performance of Tchaikovsky's *1812 Overture* at an outdoor children's concert. In complete seriousness he placed a large, ignited firecracker, which was equivalent in strength to a quarter stick of dynamite, into his aluminum straight mute and then stuck the mute into the bell of his quite new Yamaha in-line double-valve bass trombone.

Later, from his hospital bed he explained to a reporter through bandages on his mouth, "I thought that the bell of my trombone would shield me from the explosion and instead, would focus the energy of the blast outwards and away from me, propelling the mute high above the orchestra, like a rocket."

However, Paolo was not up on his propulsion physics nor qualified to use high-powered artillery and in his haste to get the horn up before the firecracker went off, he failed to raise the bell of the horn high enough so as to give the mute enough arc to clear the orchestra. What actually happened should serve as a lesson to us all during those delirious moments of divine inspiration.

First, because he failed to sufficiently elevate the bell of his horn, the blast propelled the mute between rows of players in the wood-wind and viola sections of the orchestra, missing the players and straight into the stomach of the conductor, driving him off the podium and directly into the front row of the audience.

Fortunately, the audience were sitting in folding chairs and thus they were protected from serious injury, for the chairs collapsed under them, passing the energy of the impact of the flying conductor backwards into row of people sitting behind them, who in turn were driven back into the people in the row behind and so on, like a row of dominos. The sound of collapsing wooden chairs and grunts of people falling on their behinds increased logarithmically, adding to the overall sound of brass cannons and brass playing as constitutes the closing measures of the *Overture*.

Meanwhile, all of this unplanned choreography notwithstanding, back on stage Paolo's Waterloo was still unfolding. According to Paolo, "Just as I heard the sound of the blast, time seemed to stand still. Everything moved in slow motion. Just before I felt searing pain to my mouth, I could swear I heard a voice with a Austrian accent say, 'Fur every akshon zer iz un eekvul un opposeet reakshon!' Well, this should come as no surprise, for Paolo had set himself up for a textbook demonstration of this fundamental law of physics. Since he failed to plug the lead pipe of his trombone, the energy of the blast sent a superheated jet of gas backwards through the pipe of the trombone which exited the mouthpiece, burning his lips and face.

The pyrotechnic ballet wasn't over yet. The force of the blast was so great it split the bell of his shiny Yamaha right down the middle, turning it inside out while at the same time propelling Paolo backwards off the riser.

And for the grand finale, as Paolo fell backwards he lost his grip on the slide of the trombone, allowing the pressure of the hot gases coursing through the horn to propel the trombone's slide like a double golden spear into the head of the third clarinetist, knocking him unconscious.

The moral of the story? Beware the next time you hear someone in the trombone section yell out, "Hey, everyone, watch this!"

Further Reading:
Songs from South Pacific, Sam and Janet Evening
Musical Gunfighters, The Okay Chorale
The Little Richard Story, Judy Frudy
Wind Instruments, Tom Bone
Not a Guitar!, Amanda Lin
Punk Rock Rulez!, Lotta Noyze

■ New York

New York. It's a great city. It's very culturally enriching. I now understand English in seven foreign accents. —Anita Wise

Only real New Yorkers can find their way around in the subway. If just anybody could find his way around in the subway, there wouldn't be any distinction in being real New Yorkers except talking funny.

—Calvin Trillin

Let me give you a tourist tip. If you want to go to New York, bring your camera there, because you'll see things you'll never see again. The first thing you'll never see again is your camera.

—Mike Reynolds

I used to live about an hour's drive outside of New York. Twenty minutes if you walked. —Mike Guido

New York—in the event of a nuclear attack it'll look the same as it did before. —Billy Connolly

New York: Where everyone mutinies, but no one deserts.

—Harry Hershfield

I was walking down 126th Street on my way to work. Met a fella. He said, "Moms, I hate this, I really hate this, but, Moms, gimme some money! I ain't got no home. I ain't got no family, no children, no wife! My mother, my father are dead! Moms, gimme some money! I ain't got nowhere to eat, I ain't got nowhere to sleep. I ain't got nothin', Moms. But this gun."

—Moms Mabley

A car is useless in New York, essential everywhere else. The same with good manners.

—Mignon McLaughlin

New York really messes up your perspective, doesn't it? Even in the little things. Like the other night I was watching *The Diary of Anne Frank*. Now I used to have a normal reaction to that movie—I felt bad for that poor family trapped in their tiny little attic. Now I'm looking at it going, "This is a great apartment. That skylight, that bookcase you go through—it's fabulous."

—Frank Maya

Q: Why are New Yorkers always depressed?
A: The light at the end of their tunnel is New Jersey.

—*Motivational Manager*

Most people who don't live in New York think of it as the home office for obnoxious behavior.

—Lewis Grizzard

St. Peter was manning the Pearly Gates when forty people from New York City showed up. Never having seen anyone from the Big Apple at heaven's door, St. Peter said he would have to check with God.

After hearing the news, God instructed him to admit the ten most virtuous from the group.

A few minutes later, St. Peter returned breathless and said, "They're gone!"

"What?" said God. "All of them are gone?"

"No!" replied St. Peter. "I'm talking about the Pearly Gates!"

—*Trading Post*

Being a New Yorker is never having to say you're sorry. —Lily Tomlin

In New York crime is getting worse. I was there the other day. The Statue of Liberty had both hands up. —Jay Leno

Any time four New Yorkers get into a cab without arguing, a bank robbery has just taken place. —Johnny Carson

I grew up in New York, so I didn't really fish. You fish in New York, you get, like, a snow tire, or a union organizer. Nothing you would actually serve up to your buddies with a slice of lemon. —Paul Reiser

The old panhandler living in New York hears that his brother is very sick in Los Angeles. By working day and night for a week he is able to beg enough to buy his airline ticket. He arrives at Kennedy Airport, goes to he ticket counter, and plunks down all the money. The clerk at the counter counts it and says to the man, "I'm sorry sir, but you're a nickel short."

The panhandler tells the clerk that he'll be right back. He runs out in front of the terminal and stops the first man he sees. "Mister, can you let me have a nickel, so I can get to California?"

The stranger flips him a quarter and says, "Here, take four of your friends."

■ Newspapers

Help-wanted ad in the Camden, Maine, *Herald:* "Man with flair for public relations needed to superintend Camden dump. Ability to visualize total job perspective beyond immediate appearance could be an asset. Chance to meet and work closely with all types of people. First choice on antiques, bric-a-brac, and leftovers. Selection of all leading newspapers and periodicals for coffee breaks. Unequaled opportunity for bird-watching enthusiast specializing in gulls."

To the Editor:
I'm writing this letter,
Quite frankly, to say
I abhorred the column
You wrote yesterday!
It was weak and insipid
And words synonymous—
In short, it lacked courage!
Yours truly, Anonymous.

—Mary Grace Dembeck in *The Wall Street Journal*

Accuracy to a newspaper is what virtue is to a lady, except that a newspaper can always print a retraction.   —Adlai Stevenson

Help-wanted ad in *The Wall Street Journal*: "Mediocre accountant. Disreputable company has recently acquired obscure widget firm as a tax loss and wishes to continue its unprofitable operation by hiring an inept, apathetic accountant. A disinterested attitude while working for this bewildered management is the key to securing this job. Position offers little and gives less with probable reduction in your current earnings."

Two ads from the Scarborough, Ontario, *Mirror:* "Jack, please come home," ran the first one. "I have rented reducing equipment from Stephensons' Rent-All."

"Jack, don't go home," warned the second ad. "She's also rented a floor sander, wallpaper steamer, paint sprayer, power saw, and rug shampooer from Morningside Rent-Alls."

I won't say the papers misquote me, but I sometimes wonder where Christianity would be today if some of those reporters had been Matthew, Mark, Luke, and John.   —Barry Goldwater

Genuine classified ads from newspapers around the country:

- 1 man, 7 woman hot tub—$850 or best offer
- Amana washer $100. Owned by clean bachelor who seldom washed.
- Snow blower for sale. Only used on snowy days.
- Free puppies—part German shepherd, part dog.
- Free puppies: half cocker spaniel, half sneaky neighbor's dog.
- Free Yorkshire terrier. 8 years old. Unpleasant little dog.
- German Shepherd, 85 lbs. Neutered. Speaks German. Free.
- Free 1 can of pork & beans with purchase of 3 br 2 bath home.
- Nice parachute: never opened—used once—slightly stained.
- Notice: to the person or persons who took the large pumpkin on Highway 87 near Southridge storage: please return the pumpkin and be checked. Pumpkin may be radioactive. All other plants in vicinity are dead.
- Exercise equipment: queen size mattress & box springs, $175.
- Our sofa seats the whole mob and it's made of 100 percent Italian leather.

Classified ad in the Elmwood, Illinois, *Home Shopper*: "Apt. for rent: water, heat, garbage provided."

LONDONER FATALLY INJURED BY TURNIP

London—Police are investigating the death of a man who was fatally injured after being hit by a turnip thrown from a passing car. The attack apparently was carried out by a gang who toss vegetables at random at passers-by. "It sounds very amusing but clearly it is not because a man has died," a police official said.

They kill good trees to put out bad newspapers.
—Secretary of the Interior James G. Watt, *Newsweek*, March 8, 1982

These three successive notices from the classified column of a small Connecticut weekly paper tell their own story:

March 22nd: "For sale. Slightly used farm wench in good condition. Very handy. Phone 366-R-2. Cartwright."

March 29th: "Correction. Due to an unfortunate error, Mr. Cartwright's ad last week was not clear. He has an excellent winch for sale. We trust this will put an end to jokesters who have called Mr. Cartwright and greatly bothered his housekeeper, Mrs. Hargreaves, who loves with him."

April 5th: "Notice! My W-I-N-C-H is not for sale. I put a sledge-hammer to it. Don't bother calling 366-R-2. I had the phone taken out. I am *not* carrying on with Mrs. Hargreaves. She merely L-I-V-E-S here. A. Cartwright."

■ Observational Humor

My favorite Steven Wright one-liners:

- Hermits have no peer pressure.
- How can there be self-help groups?
- How come you never hear about gruntled employees?
- If someone with multiple personalities threatens to kill himself, is it considered a hostage situation?
- It doesn't matter what temperature a room is, it's always room temperature.
- There's a fine line between fishing and just standing on the shore like an idiot.
- What's another word for synonym?
- When sign makers go on strike, what is written on their picket signs?
- When your pet bird sees you reading the newspaper, does he wonder why you're just sitting there, staring at carpeting?
- Where do forest rangers go to get away from it all?
- Why are there interstate highways in Hawaii?
- Why in a country of free speech, are there phone bills?
- Why is it that when you transport something by car, it's called a shipment, but when you transport something by ship, it's called cargo?
- Why isn't "phonetic" spelled the way it sounds?
- Why isn't there mouse-flavored cat food?

More questions from various sources:
- Why doesn't glue stick to the inside of the bottle?
- If a parsley farmer is sued, can they garnish his wages?
- When it rains, why don't sheep shrink?
- Should vegetarians eat animal crackers?
- Do cemetery workers prefer the graveyard shift?
- What do you do when you see an endangered animal that eats only endangered plants?
- If the cops arrest a mime, do they tell him he has the right to remain silent?
- Instead of talking to your plants, if you yelled at them would they still grow? Only to be troubled and insecure?

Ever notice that in the movies, when someone buys something, they never wait for their change?   —George Carlin

WHY IS IT . . .

. . . that the same guy who has a $1000 treadmill has a $2000 riding mower?

. . . that when you wash tight clothes they get tighter, but when you wash loose clothes they get looser?   —Ron Dentinger

. . . that what people call congestion in a train becomes atmosphere in a nightclub?   —*Nuggets*

. . . that when people say, "I want to share this with you," it's never money?   —Hugh Glasgow in *National Enquirer*

Sometimes I lie awake at night in my bed and I watch the stars, and I wonder, where the heck is my ceiling?   —Tiffany-Joanne

■ Opera and Orchestra

Tired of huge sopranos portraying the title role in *Carmen,* H. T. Parker, critic of the *Boston Transcript,* upon hearing that the petite Lily Pons was to make her debut in *Carmen,* he said, "Thank God! At last we'll have a Carmen who weighs less than the bull!"

One night the great Viennese tenor Leo Slezak was singing in *Lohengrin,* in which the tenor always makes a triumphal exit on a huge swan, which is hauled offstage by a rope. But this night, the stagehands missed their cue and started pulling too soon. Slezak finished his aria, looked around for the swan and saw it disappearing into the wings. He was stunned—but not speechless. Turning to the audience, he shrugged his shoulders in helplessness and called out, "What time does the next swan leave?"

—Art Linkletter

Outside an Italian opera house: Tonight—*The Barber of Seville.* 2,000 chairs. No waiting.

Koussevitzky was conducting d'Indy's *Mountain Symphony* in Boston. The score calls for an offstage horn passage, to give the effect of an echo from the distance. The horn player took his stance in the wings, dutifully watching Koussevitzky's baton. Just as the player raised the horn to his mouth for his solo, a stagehand rushed up and snatched the instrument from him. "Hey, you can't play that thing here," he whispered. "Don't you know there's a concert going on?"

—Art Linkletter

When Uncle Sid sold his trucking company in 1973, he was a multimillionaire. At age fifty-one, he was still a relatively young man and could do most anything he wanted. One of his great dreams was to conduct an orchestra. He never let the fact that he knew nothing about music interfere with his dream. He assembled an orchestra of classically trained musicians on the lawn of his palatial home, and proceeded to lead them in selections from Wagner.

The musicians of the orchestra understood at once that they must totally disregard what Sid was doing with his baton. But that scarcely solved their problems. Without the guidance of a real conductor, they produced enough cacophony to frighten the animals for miles around. In total disregard of the awful sounds, Uncle Sid continued to wave his baton as he had seen Arthur Fiedler and Leonard Bernstein do on television. Appreciating their well-paid gig, the musicians went along with him, and continued meeting regularly to rehearse for two months.

Finally, the cymbalist could take it no longer. Willing to risk his lucrative tenure, he lifted his cymbals during a soft and delicate passage, and with one mighty swipe, delivered the loudest and most resonant cymbal crash the musicians had ever heard. Shocked by the thunderous crash, Uncle Sid dropped his baton, and the entire orchestra came to a stop. The resounding cymbal clap rang on and on as though it would never stop.

Finally, after long minutes, the last echoes of that thunder clap died away, and Uncle Sid, his face beet red with fury, said, "All right, which one of you wise guys did that?"

Further Reading:
Handel's Messiah, Ollie Luyah
Season Tickets, Oprah Maven
Back Row of the Orchestra, Clara Nett
String Instruments, Viola Player
Imitating Mozart, Sam Phony

■ Oxymorons

Webster defines an oxymoron as "a combination of contradictory or incongruous words." This list thoroughly illustrates the concept:

act naturally	Amtrak schedule
almost exactly	British fashion
alone together	business ethics

cafeteria food
calm wind
clean coal
clearly confused
computer security
conservative liberal
constant variable
cowardly lion
dangerously safe
deafening silence
definite maybe
deliberately thoughtless
diet ice cream
double solitaire
educational television
even odds
exact estimate
extensive briefing
extinct life
federal budget
found missing
free love
freezer burn
fresh-frozen
friendly fire
friendly takeover
genuine imitation leather
good grief
government organization
hell's angels
humanitarian invasion
ill health
instant classic
intense apathy
jumbo shrimp
larger half
least favorite
legally drunk

light rock
liquid gas
mild interest
mild-mannered reporter
minor crisis
minor miracle
modern history
new classic
non-dairy creamer
normal deviation
now, then
old news
only choice
open secret
original copies
paid volunteer
passive aggression
peace offensive
peacekeeper missile
plastic glasses
polite salesman
political science
postal service
qualified success
randomly organized
rap music
real potential
religious tolerance
Republican party
resident alien
rock opera
rolling stop
rush hour
same difference
sanitary landfill
second best
serious musician
seriously funny

small crowd
soft rock
standard deviation
sweet sorrow
synthetic natural gas
taped live
temporary tax increase
terribly enjoyable
tragic comedy
twelve-ounce pound cake
unbiased opinion
United Nations
unsung hero
virtual reality
war games
working vacation

Further Reading:
I Saw It Coming, Sue Prize
Eventual Awareness, Oliver Sudden

■ Paranoia

Telltale signs you are being stalked by Martha Stewart:

- You get a threatening note made up of letters neatly cut out of a magazine with pinking shears.
- You find a slice of lemon floating in your dog's water dish.
- On her TV show she makes a replica of your home out of gingerbread, including your fallen-down licorice downspout and stuck-half-open graham-cracker garage door.
- Every napkin in your house has been folded into the shape of a swan.
- You find your pet bunny simmering on the stove in an exquisite tarragon, rose-petal, and saffron demiglace. —Patti Teague

He's so nervous that he wears a seat belt in a drive-in movie.

—Neil Simon

He was an angry man, Uncle Swanny. He had printed on his grave: "What are you lookin' at?" —Margaret Smith

She's such a hypochondriac she cooks with penicillin.

—Betty Walker

I wanted to go to the Paranoids Anonymous meeting, but they wouldn't tell me where it was. —H. Aaron Cohl

Friday afternoon I'm walking home from school, and I'm watching some men build a new house. And the guy hammering on the roof calls me a paranoid little weirdo. In Morse code.   —Emo Phillips

Further Reading:
Quit Asking My Name, Ima Nonymous
Better Mental Health, Cy Kosis
Unsolved Mysteries, N. Igma
Who Killed Cock Robin?, Howard I. Know

■ Parents

Parenthood is a lot easier to get into than out of.   —Bruce Lansky

When a persistent reporter challenged Bernard Baruch to state the secret of longevity in three words, he responded, "Choose healthy parents."

The quickest way for a parent to get a child's attention is to sit down and look comfortable.   —Lane Olinghouse

I didn't make the same mistakes my parents made when they raised me. I was too busy making new ones.   —Bruce Lansky

For years I thought I was adopted. Until one day I just got bold. I went up to my dad and asked him straight out. I said, "Ling Chow . . ."
—Scott Wood

A prosperous silk manufacturer took an out-of-town client to his home for dinner. When the meal was over, the host took his business associate into the study, and they began talking about various topics. While they were talking, the manufacturer's three young sons came running into the room, making a fearful racket.

"Be good," warned the mother from the kitchen, "or you won't have any ice cream for lunch."

But the boys took no heed of their mother's warning.

"My system is better," the father told his associate. "I give Tom, my oldest son—he's seven—a dollar, and he keeps still." He handed the boy the bill, and sure enough he shut up. "And," continued the father, "I give Bob—he's five—a half-dollar and he quiets down."

"Sounds interesting," said the guest, "but what about your youngest son?"

"Oh him," came the mother's voice from the kitchen, "he's like his father—good for nothing."   —Myron Cohen

One thing they never tell you about child raising is that for the rest of your life, at the drop of a hat, you're expected to know your child's name and how old he or she is.

—Erma Bombeck

The thing that impresses me most about America is the way parents obey their children.   —King Edward VII

Setting a good example for children takes all the fun out of middle age.

—Babs Bell Hajdusiewicz

Parents are not interested in justice. They want quiet.   —Bill Cosby

Parents: A peculiar group who first try to get their children to walk and talk, and then try to get them to sit down and shut up.

—*Wagster's Dictionary of Humor and Wit*

It goes without saying that you should never have more children than you have car windows.   —Erma Bombeck

299

My parents have been visiting me for a few days. I just dropped them off at the airport. They leave tomorrow.   —Margaret Smith

Spotted in the Everett, Washington, *Herald:* "Dick's and Peggy's fiftieth anniversary party has been canceled due to lack of interest. They are now going around the world—courtesy of their children's inheritance."

■ Peace

Dr. Konrad Adenauer once observed, "An infallible method of conciliating a tiger is to allow oneself to be devoured."

They can hold all the peace talks they want, but there will never be peace in the Middle East. Billions of years from now, when Earth is hurtling toward the Sun and there is nothing left alive on the planet except a few microorganisms, the microorganisms living in the Middle East will be bitter enemies.   —Dave Barry

■ Pets

My wife and I are pet lovers. It all started with Cuddles, a rag-mop-impersonator identified as a cockapoo that we rescued from an animal shelter in Delaware. Cuddles was soon joined by Gus, a platinum poodle, who would live to a ripe old age of twenty-two or twenty-three. Currently our menagerie includes Duffy, a West Highland terrier; Katie, a Scottish terrier; Nehi, an Australian cattle dog; our Himalayan house cat, Ana-purr-na; a black and white barn cat named Tassie (short for "Cat-tas-strophe" —she had a hard life before we found her); and, last but certainly not least, a seven-year-old paint mare named Stormy.

Pets are much more intelligent than we humans give them credit for. Duffy is a case in point. Not only does he watch television every evening, interacting with all the animals that appear, growling, barking, and chasing them, he also has memorized all the TV programs and commercials in which animals appear. At the first bar of the theme from such a program or commercial, Duffy goes on full alert, sitting on his haunches before the TV set, waiting for his prey. A few years ago, my wife and I left our house and pets in the care of my mother-in-law, Betty, and her sister, Aggie, while we visited my wife's relatives in Norway. On the first day after our departure, Aggie was alone in our living room, working on her needlepoint. At 4:30 P.M. Duffy took up a position at her feet, staring intently at her. Aggie did not know that Duffy has trained his humans to feed him promptly at 4:30, so she continued with her work.

Duffy cleared his throat. Aggie did not respond. Duffy yelped twice. Still no response. Duffy barked sharply. Aggie wondered if he were hungry but, assuming that his dinner hour was much later, paid no attention. Duffy growled, barked, pushed off with his paws against her thighs. Aggie was annoyed but tried to ignore him. At this point, Duffy picked up her knitting basket in his jaws and carried it to the kitchen, depositing it near his food dish. Aggie got the point. Duffy got his dinner.

Fleas are a part of the ecological cycle, but I doubt if a dog thinks he is doing something to destroy ecology by wearing a flea collar.

—Ronald Reagan, March 7, 1973

My neighbor Ray Jean has found a way at last to dissuade her neighbors —and their children—from coming over to swim in her pool. She's bought a pet shark.

My parakeet died. We were playing badminton. —Danny Curtis

Sign in a pet shop window: For sale cheap, a talking parrot. Owner no longer can stand parrot's political opinions.

Over a cocker spaniel in a pet shop window: Reduced—Obedience School Dropout.

When I was a child, a sign in the window of a spotless new fish store in Chicago proudly proclaimed: "We sell anything that swims!" The sign disappeared after my uncle Sid walked in and demanded Esther Williams.

My brother had a hamster. He took it to the vet—it's like bringing a disposable lighter in for repair.   —Wayne Cotter

Your kids will feed their new puppy the day you buy it and the days you threaten to take it back to the pet store.   —Bruce Lansky

Back in the Middle East, I had a pet goat. It was our main source for milk. It even had pictures of missing children on it.   —*Nazareth*

■ Police

We live in an age when pizza gets to your home before the police.
                                                              —Jeff Marder

Our son, Todd, the sheriff's deputy, looks imposing. He has more things hanging from his belt than I have hanging in my closet.

A sheriff's office in Colorado received a call about a cat that was trapped somewhere in a house. When the deputies arrived at the scene, they were greeted by a concerned woman who described the cries of the distressed cat.

She guided the deputies to the spot where the sound was apparently coming from. The officers found a wall with no apparent openings, so they were stumped on how to get to the cat. The woman said the deputies could tear into the walls and floorboards and even signed a release absolving them from responsibility for any damages. They tore into the walls but didn't find anything. They tore into the floorboards. No cat. They tore into other places.

No cat. Finally, the deputies figured out where the sound of the cat was coming from: the screen saver on the family's computer featured a loud meowing cat as a reminder that the computer was still turned on. "We never even thought to ask her if she owned a cat," said the deputy. "We just assumed she did." —David Naster

Annoyed driver to patrolman who has pulled her over: "Why can't you people get organized? One day you take my license away, and the next day you ask to see it." —Hageman in the *National Enquirer*

Announcement in the Pullman, Washington, *Herald:* "Wanted: State trooper applicants. Applicants must be six feet tall with a high-school education, or 5' 11" with two years of college."

Herb Caen once reported that conditions have become so chaotic in one Midwestern community that the police department now has an unlisted telephone number.

A not-too-bright cop was taking a desperado to jail. While crossing a street the desperado's hat blew off, and he started as if to chase it. "No you don't, wise guy!" warned the cop. "You stay where you are, and I'll get it!" —Harry Hershfield

■ Political Correctness

LITTLE POLITICALLY CORRECT RED RIDING HOOD

There once was a young person named Red Riding Hood who lived with her mother on the edge of a large wood. One day her mother asked her to take a basket of fresh fruit and mineral water to her grandmother's house—not because this was womyn's work, but because the deed was generous and helped engender a feeling of community. Furthermore, her grandmother was not sick, but rather was in full physical and mental health and was fully capable of taking care of herself as a mature adult.

So Red Riding Hood set off with her basket of food through the woods. Many people she knew believed that the forest was a foreboding and dangerous place and never set foot in it. Red Riding Hood, however, was confident in her own budding sexuality that such obvious Freudian imagery did not hinder her.

On her way to Grandma's house, Red Riding Hood was accosted by a Wolf, who asked her what was in her basket. She replied, "Some healthful snacks for my grandmother, who is certainly capable of taking care of herself as a mature adult."

The Wolf said, "You know, my dear, it isn't safe for a little girl to walk through these woods alone."

Red Riding Hood said, "I find your sexist remark offensive in the extreme, but I will ignore it because of your traditional status as an outcast from society, the stress of which has caused you to develop your own, entirely valid worldview. Now, if you'll excuse, me I must be on my way."

Red Riding Hood walked on along the main path. But, because his status outside society had freed him from slavish adherence to linear, Western thought, the Wolf knew of a quicker route to Grandma's house. He burst into the house and ate Grandma, an entirely valid course of action for a carnivore such as himself. Then, unhampered by rigid, traditionalist notions of what was masculine or feminine, he put on grandma's nightclothes and crawled into bed.

Red Riding Hood entered the cottage and said, "Grandma, I have brought you some fat-free, sodium-free snacks to salute you in your role of a wise and nurturing matriarch."

From the bed, the Wolf said softly, "Come closer, child, so that I might see you."

Red Riding Hood said, "Oh, I forgot you are as optically challenged as a bat. Grandma, what big eyes you have!"

"They have seen much, and forgiven much, my dear."

"Grandma, what a big nose you have—only relatively, of course, and certainly attractive in its own way."

"It has smelled much, and forgiven much, my dear."

"Grandma, what big teeth you have!"

The Wolf said, "I am happy with who I am and what I am," and leaped out of bed. He grabbed Red Riding Hood in his claws, intent on devouring her. Red Riding Hood screamed, not out of alarm at the Wolf's apparent tendency toward cross-dressing, but because of his willful invasion of her personal space.

Her screams were heard by a passing woodchopper-person (or log-fuel technician, as he preferred to be called). When he burst into the cottage, he saw the melee and tried to intervene. But as he raised his ax, Red Riding Hood and the Wolf both stopped.

"And what do you think you're doing?" asked Red Riding Hood.

The woodchopper-person blinked and tried to answer, but no words came to him.

"Bursting in here like a Neanderthal, trusting your weapon to do your thinking for you!" she said. "Sexist! Speciesist! How dare you assume that women and wolves can't solve their own problems without a man's help!"

When she heard Red Riding Hood's speech, Grandma jumped out of the Wolf's mouth, took the woodchopper-person's ax, and cut his head off. After this ordeal, Red Riding Hood, Grandma, and the Wolf felt a certain commonality of purpose. They decided to set up an alternative household based on mutual respect and cooperation, and they lived together in the woods happily ever after.

INDIGENOUS PEOPLES/COLUMBUS DAY

In 1990, the Berkeley City Council passed a law changing the name of Columbus Day to Native American Day because Columbus wasn't nice to the Indians. Of course, no Indians were asked if they wanted the holiday's name changed or if they wanted to be called Native Americans.

In 1991, the Berkeley City Council changed the name again, to Indigenous People Day. A group of "P.C.ers" argued that Indians are not native to America but to Asia, so calling them Native Americans might be insulting to Asians. Of course, neither the Indian or Asian communities were consulted about this.

In 1992, the Italian American Anti-Defamation League gave the City of Berkeley their Insensitivity Award. The Italian-American group said that they agreed that Indians haven't been treated well, but that the Italians weren't the ones who did it, so why take away their holiday? Nobody asked Italian-Americans how they felt about renaming Columbus day.

In 1994, the Berkeley City Council changed the holiday back to Columbus Day.

In 1995, representatives of the Winnamucca Indians protested at City Council meetings. They argued that Indians had never asked that Columbus Day be renamed to honor Indians, but since it had, the City Council couldn't take it back, lest they become "indigenous peoples givers."

In 1996, the City Council changed the name to Indigenous Peoples/Columbus Day.

Currently there are people lobbying to rename the holiday Animal Rights Day.

■ Politics and Politicians

The first mistake in politics is the going into it. —Benjamin Franklin

I'll say this much about George Washington. He never once blamed his problems on the previous administration.

—Ron Dentinger, *Down Time*

Asked what it takes to be a politician, Winston Churchill responded, "It's the ability to foretell what will happen tomorrow, next month, and next year—and to explain afterward why it did not happen."

During the 1952 presidential campaign, Democratic candidate Adlai Stevenson said, "I will make a bargain with the Republicans. If they stop telling lies about Democrats, we will stop telling the truth about them."

As they watched a TV newscast, a woman said to her husband, "It seems to me that the majority of people in this country belong to some minority group."

Bad officials are elected by good citizens who do not vote.

—Walt Whitman

There are only two political parties in America—the one you're aligned with, and the Know-Nothing Party.

Conservative: A statesman who is enamored of existing evils, as distinguished from the liberal, who wishes to replace them with others.

—Ambrose Bierce, *The Devil's Dictionary*

A liberal is someone who wants to spend what he doesn't have. A conservative is someone who wants to keep him from getting it.

Q: What do you call a wise liberal?
A: A conservative.

A liberal: Someone who won't take his own side in a quarrel.

—Robert Frost

In the U.S. today, you are considered innocent until appointed to a public position by the president.   —Ambassador William Crowe

I voted for the Democrats because I didn't like the way the Republicans were running the country. Which is turning out to be like shooting yourself in the head to stop your headache.

—Jack Mayberry

As vice president, George Bush quipped, "It's important for a vice president not to upstage his boss, and you don't know how hard it has been to keep my charisma in check these last few years."

To make my "retirement" a little more exciting, in the early months of 1998 when Monica Lewinsky became a media preoccupation, I was in the rather embarrassing position of being Lewinsky's next-door neighbor at the Watergate. The *New York Times* asked me if I had seen my famous neighbor. I acknowledged that I had. "I walk by fast," I reassured the *Times*. "I don't want to be subpoenaed!"

—Bob Dole

When Winston Churchill was defeated in his bid for reelection as prime minister, his wife consoled him with the thought that the defeat was a blessing in disguise. "If so," responded Churchill, "then it is very effectively disguised."

—H. Aaron Cohl

One old-time politician always advised his young political protégés, "Remember that every time you do a favor for a constituent, you make nine enemies and one ingrate."

Ronald Reagan, commenting on the Democratic presidential primary debate in New Hampshire: "There were so many candidates on the platform that there were not enough promises to go around."

They're getting pretty vicious in politics nowadays. The oath of office ends with a denial of all the charges.

One candidate was so happy about winning that he accidentally kept one of his campaign promises.

Papers today say, "What would Lincoln do today?" Well, in the first place, he wouldn't chop any wood, he would trade his ax in on a Ford. Being a Republican he would vote the Democratic ticket. Being in sympathy for the underdog he would be classed as a radical progressive. Having a sense of humor he would be called eccentric.

—Will Rogers

One of the dullest political meetings I ever attended was finally rescued when, following a long and boring introduction of another party hack, the public-address system miraculously picked up the wavelength of a nearby radio station, and this announcement came crackling out of the loudspeaker: "Now's the time to put in your spring supply of fertilizer!"
—Art Linkletter

When Will Rogers went to the White House to meet President Harding, Rogers said, "Mr. President, I would like to tell you all the latest political jokes."

"You don't have to, Will," Harding replied. "I appointed them."

The president returned from a trip abroad, and the press asked him how he felt about foreign aid. "Well, the good news is that I'm all for it. The bad news is I can't find any country that'll give it to us."

Liberals believe in giving everyone a second chance. Conservatives believe in giving everyone a second mortgage.

Cordell Hull, the U.S. secretary of state from 1933 to 1944, was a notoriously cautious man, loathe to jump to conclusions, not given to advancing an inch past the evidence.

Once, while on a train trip, Hull and his administrative assistant watched as the train crept slowly past a large flock of sheep. Making idle chit-chat, Hull's companion said, "Those sheep have been recently sheared."

Hull stared thoughtfully at the animals for a full minute before answering: "Appears so. At least on the side facing us."

The short memories of American voters is what keeps our politicians in office.
—Will Rogers

Politicians can do more funny things naturally than I can think of
to do purposely.

—Will Rogers

In his best-selling biography *Huey Long*, the eminent historian T.
Harry William's tells about the first time the ebullient Huey cam-
paigned in rural, predominantly Catholic Southern Louisiana. A
veteran local boss advised him at the outset of the tour, "Remember
one thing, Huey. South Louisiana's a lot different from your northern part of the state. We've got a lot of Catholic voters down here."

"I know," nodded Long. And so at every whistle stop on the tour
Huey would declaim for openers, "When I was boy, I'd get up at
6:00 A.M. every Sunday, hitch our old horse up to the buggy, and
take my Catholic grandparents to Mass. I'd bring them home, and
take my Baptist grandparents to church."

The audiences responded heartily, and the boss finally told Huey
admiringly, "You've been holding out on us. We didn't know you
had any Catholic grandparents."

"Don't be a fool," replied Huey. "We didn't even have a horse!"

—Bennett Cerf

Three lobbyists in Washington, D.C. were debating how to determine their degree of power with the White House. "I would know I
was influential," began one, "if the president would ask me over for
a private dinner."

"That would be impressive," replied the second. "However, I
would know I had influence if the president would invite me to dinner, and while we were dining, his hotline rang and he didn't get it.
That would be the ultimate."

"Let me tell you the real measure of power," said the third lobbyist. "I would know I was powerful if the president invited me to
dinner. Then, while talking over coffee, his hotline rang. The president answered and listened momentarily. I'd know I had real
power if he then looked at me, and said, 'Here, it's for you.'"

Politics is supposed to be the second oldest profession. I have come to realize that it bears a very close resemblance to the first.

—Ronald Reagan, speech at a business conference in Los Angeles, March 2, 1994

Talk-show host to political expert: "Campaigns have become so simplistic and superficial. In the twenty seconds we have left, could you explain why?"
—Bennett in *The Christian Science Monitor*

Political elections . . . are a good deal like marriages; there's no accounting for anyone's taste.

Nothing is so permanent as a temporary government program
—Milton Friedman (attributed)

Common sense is not an issue in politics; it's an affliction. Neither is honesty an issue in politics. It's a miracle. Politicians are interested in people. Not that this is always a virtue. Fleas are interested in dogs.
—P. J. O'Rourke

The difference between horse races and political races is that in a horse race the whole horse wins.
—George Phair

The phone rang as we sat at the dinner table. My wife answered and was asked by a pollster what her opinion was about the forthcoming election. Her reply: "My opinion is that whoever is elected, my husband will be furious."

Politician: Someone who divides his time between running for office and running for cover.

In politics if you want anything said, ask a man. If you want anything done, ask a woman.

—Margaret Thatcher, British Conservative Party Leader, *People,* September 15, 1975

State legislators are merely politicians whose darkest secret prohibits them from running for higher office. —Dennis Miller

At a summit meeting, President Reagan told this story: An American told a Russian, "I can walk into the White House. I can slam my hand on the desk. And I can say that I don't like the way Ronald Reagan is running the country."

The Russian replied, "I can do that same thing in my country. I can walk into the Kremlin. I can slam my hand on the desk. And I can say that I don't like the way Ronald Reagan is running the country."

Being in politics is like being a football coach. You have to be smart enough to understand the game and stupid enough to think it's important. —Eugene McCarthy

A statesman is a politician who's been dead for ten or fifteen years. —Harry S Truman

A statesman is any politician that it's considered safe to name a school after. —Bill Vaughan

The more you read and observe about this politics thing, you've got to admit that each party is worse than the other. —Will Rogers

Diplomacy: Lying in state. —Oliver Herford

The major difference between the two parties in America is when one does absolutely nothing, the other one always says they're doing it wrong.
—Gene and Linda Perret

Politics is the art of looking for trouble, finding it everywhere, diagnosing it incorrectly, and applying the wrong remedies.
—Groucho Marx

I never vote for the best candidate; I vote for the one who will do the least harm.
—Franklin K. Dane

I am a man of fixed and unbending principles, the first of which is to be flexible at all times.
—Everett Dirksen

I would like to nominate a man who is honest and courageous. I'd like to, but this party doesn't have one of them kind of people. My candidate does not know the meaning of the word "compromise," does not know the meaning of the word "appeasement," does not know the meaning of the word "cowardice"—and has done quite well despite this lousy vocabulary.
—Vaughn Meader

You show me a politician who says he doesn't believe in polls, and I'll show you a politician who's so far behind he's about to dump his campaign manager.
—Gene and Linda Perret

I had an uncle who was a Democrat in Chicago. He received a silver cup from the party for voting fifteen straight elections—he'd been dead for fourteen of them.
—Ronald Reagan

I think the next four years we should try it with no president.
—Dana Fradon

We have a presidential election coming up. And I think the big problem, of course, is someone will win.
                                                    —Barry Crimmins

As far as the men who are running for president are concerned, they aren't even people I would date.
                                                    —Nora Ephron

Congress, our leaders, voted against a proposal to have a national seven-day waiting period to buy a gun. I don't want to sound like a Quaker, but when you think about it, is a week a long time to wait to see if a former mental patient is qualified to own an Uzi? Come on, will ya, Congress? It takes three weeks to get a phone!
                                                    —Jimmy Tingle

Further Reading:
The Criminals of Watergate, Barton Mee

■ Post Office and the Mail

Hallmark is so furious over postal-rate increases that they're sending the post office a nasty poem.

If the post office raises the rates much more, the mail carriers will be safe from dogs. It'll be the customers that bite them.
                                                    —Gene and Linda Perret

The postal service will be issuing new stamps that show life in the 1950s, including 3-D glasses and cars with fins, reports Jerry Perisho. "But if they want something to show what life was really like," he says, "they should print 'four cents.'"

Postage is getting too expensive. For short notes now, it's cheaper to just hire a skywriter.
                                                    —Gene and Linda Perret

A worried-looking citizen came to the FBI to ask if they couldn't do anything about a series of threatening letters he had been receiving. "Any idea who might be sending them?" asked the FBI agent.

"I have one little clue," said the helpful citizen. "The envelopes are marked Department of Internal Revenue."

Letter received by the editor of a rural weekly: "Sir: My wife and I, unbeknownst to each other, bought subscriptions to your paper, so now two issues are delivered to us every week. One is carefully slipped under our welcome mat, the other is thrown by a boy riding a bicycle and lands somewhere on our front porch, where the pages usually blow apart. Kindly cancel our subscription to the one that blows apart."

—Bennett Cerf

The high cost of postage is presenting hardships to some people. Kids in college can no longer afford to write home for money.

—Gene and Linda Perret

Neosho Rapids, Kansas (AP)—As Dwight Hodson rushed out the front door to go to work for the Santa Fe Railroad in nearby Emporia, Kansas, his wife handed him a small package to be mailed and a sack containing his lunch. He mistakenly dropped his lunch in a mailbox en route to work. When he reached his office, he found he still had the package. Fellow employees called the post office, but learned that a letter carrier had opened the mailbox, found the food, and thinking it was dropped in as a joke, had given the sandwiches to a dog. —cited by Bud and Lolo Delaney, *The Laugh Journal*

According to Juliet Lowell, a western senator received this letter from a constituent last month: "Dear Senator: I have voted for you three times, and I think you're terrific. Please send me $900 at once, so I can buy an ice box and repaint my car. PS: The three times I voted for you were in the election of 1996."

—Bennett Cerf

The way postage rates keep rising, pen pals will be a thing of the past. It'll be cheaper to just have them move into your house and live with you.

After my cousin Mark completed a tour of Yellowstone Park, he sent his mother the following message on a postcard: "The bears here come right up to your car and beg for candy. At night they eat the garbage. For anybody who eats nothing but candy and garbage, they seem awful healthy."

Why is it that the perforated area between postage stamps is stronger than the stamps themselves?

I get every catalog in the world. I don't know what mailing list I got on. Once you buy something stupid, they sell your name to other people who make stupid things.

—Paul Reiser

Further Reading:
The Philippine Post Office, Imelda Letter

■ Poverty

Thousands upon thousands are yearly brought into a state of real poverty by their great anxiety not to be thought poor.

—William Cobbett

I used to think I was poor. Then they told me I wasn't poor, I was needy. Then they told me it was self-defeating to think of myself as needy. I was underprivileged. Then they told me that "underprivileged was overused." I was disadvantaged. I still don't have a dime. But I have a great vocabulary.

—Jules Feiffer

We were so poor that we used to use a substitute for margarine. . . . In school I took algebra, history, and overcoats. . . . We didn't have a TV set; we used to sit around and watch the mirror. —Jackie Vernon

Remember the poor—it costs nothing.

—Josh Billings

Further Reading:
The Housing Problem, Rufus Quick
My Life on Skid Row, Titus A. Drum
Hunger in America, Heywood Jafeedme
A Great Plenty, E. Nuff

■ Prayer

When I was a kid, I used to pray every night for a new bicycle. Then I realized that the Lord, in his wisdom, didn't work that way. So I just stole one and asked him to forgive me.

—Emo Phillips

A missionary is chased through the jungle by a ferocious lion, who corners him. With no other option left, the missionary falls to his knees in prayer. To his great surprise, the lion also begins to pray.

"This is miraculous," says the missionary, "joining me in prayer when I had given myself up for lost."

"Don't interrupt," says the lion, "I'm saying grace."

—Paul Dickson

Asked by Lyndon Johnson to say grace before a White House dinner in 1965, Press Secretary Bill Moyers spoke very quietly.

"Speak up, Bill!" President Johnson bellowed. "Speak up!"

"I wasn't addressing you, Mr. President," Moyers replied.

■ Pregnancy

QUESTIONS AND ANSWERS
ABOUT PREGNANCY AND ITS AFTERMATH

Q: What is the easiest way to figure out exactly when I got pregnant?

A: Have sex once a year.

Q: What is the most common pregnancy craving?

A: For men to be the ones who get pregnant.

Q: My husband and I are very attractive. I'm sure our baby will be beautiful enough for commercials. Whom should I contact about this?

A: Your therapist.

Q: I'm two months pregnant now. When will my baby move?

A: With any luck, right after he finishes college.

Q: How will I know if my vomiting is morning sickness or the flu?

A: If it's the flu, you'll get better.

Q: My brother tells me that since my husband has a big nose, and genes for big noses are dominant, my baby will have a big nose as well. Is this true?

A: The odds are greater that your brother will have a fat lip.

Q: Since I became pregnant, my breasts, rear end, and even my feet have grown. Is there anything that gets smaller during pregnancy?

A: Yes, your bladder.

Q: My wife is five months pregnant and so moody that sometimes she's borderline irrational.

A: So what's your question, you insensitive idiot?

Q: Will I love my dog less when the baby is born?

A: No, but your husband might get on your nerves.

Q: My childbirth instructor says it's not pain I'll feel during labor, but pressure. Is she right?

A: Yes, in the same way that a tornado might be called an air current.

Q: When is the best time to get an epidural?

A: Right after you find out you're pregnant.

Q: Is there any reason I have to be in the delivery room while my wife is in labor?

A: Not unless the word alimony means anything to you.

Q: I'm modest. Once I'm in the hospital to deliver, who will see me in that delicate position?

A: Authorized personnel only—doctors, nurses, orderlies, photographers, florists, cleaning crews, journalists, etc.

Q: Does labor cause hemorrhoids?

A: Labor causes anything you want to blame it for.

Q: Where is the best place to store breast milk?

A: In your breasts.

Q: Is there a safe alternative to breast pumps?

A: Yes, baby lips.

Q: What does it mean when a baby is born with teeth?

A: It means that the baby's mother may want to rethink her plans to nurse.

Q: What is the best time to wean the baby from nursing?

A: When you see teeth marks.

Q: What happens to disposable diapers after they're thrown away?

A: They are stored in a silo in the Midwest, in the event of global chemical warfare.

Q: Do I have to have a baby shower?

A: Not if you change the baby's diaper very quickly.

Q: What causes baby blues?

A: Tanned, hard-bodied bimbos.

Q: What is colic?

A: A reminder for new parents to use birth control.

Q: What are night terrors?

A: Frightening episodes in which the new mother dreams she's pregnant again.

■ Presidents

George Washington never told a lie. Of course, ever since then, presidents held press conferences.

George Washington was being practical when he stood up in that boat crossing the Delaware. Every time he sat down, somebody handed him an oar.

At a White House dinner for Nobel Prize winners, John F. Kennedy commented, "I think this is the most extraordinary collection of talent and human knowledge that has ever been gathered together at the White House—with the possible exception of when Thomas Jefferson dined alone."

STORIES OF LINCOLN

General George B. McClellan was always telling Abraham Lincoln how to run the country. A friend asked Lincoln, "What are you going to do about it?"

"Nothing, for now," said Lincoln. But it did remind him of a story: "A cowboy was riding a horse. All of a sudden, the horse kicked up and stuck his leg through the stirrup. The cowboy looked down and said, 'If you're getting on, I'm getting off.' "

—Melvin Berger

President Lincoln told the story of a governor who visited the state prison. The governor talked to the prisoners and asked what crimes they had committed. Each prisoner said he had never done anything wrong. To hear them talk, you would have thought they were all innocent, good men. At last the governor came to one prisoner who said, "I am a thief and I deserve to be in jail."

"Then I must pardon you," said the governor, "and get you out of this place. You seem to be the only criminal in this prison, and I don't want you here setting a bad example to all these good men I have been talking to."
—Beatrice Schenk de Regniers

Abraham Lincoln told the story of the hired man in Illinois who was driving a team of oxen: The hired man came running to the farmer with bad news— one ox had dropped dead. The farmer was sorry to hear it. The hired man stood around and waited a while. At last he told the farmer, "The other ox died, too."

"Why didn't you tell me in the first place that both oxen were dead?" asked the farmer.

"I didn't want to hurt you by telling you too much at one time," replied the hired man.
—Beatrice Schenk de Regniers

Lincoln was riding horseback on a country road and found his way blocked by a big load of hay that had fallen off a wagon. The boy driving the wagon was upset. "Now don't worry," Lincoln told the boy. "Come with me to the farmhouse, and we'll find someone to help us get the hay back on the wagon."

At the farmhouse, the kindly farmer invited Lincoln and the boy to have dinner. Lincoln enjoyed his dinner, but he saw that the boy was still worried.

"Pa won't like this," the boy muttered. "Pa won't like this at all."

"Now don't you worry," Lincoln told the boy. "Your pa knows that an accident can happen to anybody. No need to hurry." And Lincoln took a second helping of potatoes.

"Pa won't like my being away so long."

"Oh come now," said Lincoln. "Your pa will understand. I'll go with you and explain what happened. By the way, where is your pa?"

Wailed the boy, "Under the load of hay!"

—Beatrice Schenk de Regniers

Abraham Lincoln always said you can't fool all the people all of the time. But Abraham Lincoln was fooling when he said that.

—Mark Russell

WAS TAFT DAFT?

The fattest president by far that we've ever had in the U.S. was the good-natured William Howard Taft. Visiting friends one summer day in Long Branch, New Jersey, he was disporting himself languidly in the surf when his host's two young sons asked if they could have a swim before lunch. "You'll have to wait till later," their father told them gravely. "The president is using the ocean."

—Bennett Cerf

Not only was William Howard Taft the largest president in pounds, but also one of the sharpest in dealing with hecklers. A heckler once tossed a cabbage at Taft during a political speech. He paused, peered at the vegetable, and then placidly said, "Ladies and gentlemen, I see that one of my opponents has lost his head."

President William Howard Taft was holding a reception one day when his tailor arrived to try on his new Prince Albert. The tailor was hustled into the reception line by zealous guards. When he reached the president, Taft remarked, "You look very familiar to me."

"Naturally, Mr. President," chuckled the tailor, "I made your pants."

"Ah, yes," nodded the president. "How do you do, Major Pants."

—Bennett Cerf

Like all presidents, William Howard Taft had to endure his share of abuse. One evening at the dinner table his youngest kid made a disrespectful remark to him. There was a sudden hush. Taft became thoughtful.

"Well," asked Mrs. Taft, "aren't you going to punish him?"

"If the remark was addressed to me as his father, he certainly will be punished," replied Taft. "However, if he addressed it to the president of the United States, that is his constitutional privilege."

Ohio claims they are due a president as they haven't had one since Taft. Look at the United States, they haven't had one since Lincoln.

—Will Rogers

CALVIN COOLIDGE: GREAT COMMUNICATOR?

On one occasion Ronald Reagan shared, "I take a lot of ribbing for praising silent Cal Coolidge, but he was a real communicator. He was having his hair cut once in a one-chair barbershop up in Vermont, and the town doctor came in, sat down, and said, 'Cal, did you take the pills I gave you?'

"Coolidge said nothing for a minute or two, then in his usual articulate style he said, 'Nope.'

"A little later the doctor asked, 'Well, are you feeling any better?'

"Another long silence and then he said, 'Yup.'

"Well, his haircut was finished, and he started to leave. The barber hesitantly said, 'Aren't you forgetting something?'

"An embarrassed Coolidge replied, 'Oh, yeah, I'm sorry. I forgot to pay you. I was so busy gossiping with the doctor, it slipped my mind.'"

Calvin Coolidge possessed humor and sense enough to escape that exaggeration of the ego which afflicts a good many of our presidents. Awakening from a nap in the middle of a presidential executive day, he opened his eyes, grinned, and asked a pal, "Is the country still here?"

Sometimes we overestimate the people at the top of the ladder. President Coolidge once asked several guests over to sail with him along the Potomac in the presidential yacht. Some of the guests noticed that the president stood by himself at the rail gazing over the waters. They wondered what historic thoughts were racing through his mind, what weighty decisions he might be meditating on. They left him alone to his private contemplation. Later Coolidge turned and asked the others to join him. When they did, he pointed out over the sea and said, "That gull over there hasn't moved in twenty minutes. I think it's dead."

Once a friend bet Will Rogers that he couldn't make President Coolidge laugh. But Will won. When he was introduced to Coolidge, he said, "Beg your pardon, I didn't catch the name."

Near the end of Calvin Coolidge's term in office, reporters asked him if he planned to run again.

"I do not choose to run," he said.

One reporter persisted. "Don't you want to be president again, Mr. Coolidge?" he asked.

"No," replied Coolidge. "There's no chance for advancement."

Besides Washington and Lincoln, what other American presidents happened to have been born on American holidays?

When Teddy Roosevelt was campaigning in the West, a delegation of prim ladies urged him to come out openly against a candidate for the Senate from Utah who was a power in the Mormon Church.

"Ladies," said Roosevelt, "I prefer a polygamist who does not polyg to a monogamist who does not monog." —Bennett Cerf

To hunt, fish, drive, or own a dog, you need a license. But anybody who wants to can run for president.

When I was a boy I was told that anybody could become president; I'm beginning to believe it.

—Clarence Darrow

President Warren G. Harding was not known for his speaking ability. Senator William McAdoo once said of him: "His speeches leave the impression of an army of pompous phrases moving over the landscape in search of an idea. Sometimes these meandering words actually capture a straggling thought and bear it triumphantly a prisoner in their midst until it dies of servitude and overwork."

Woodrow Wilson was a man of acerbic wit. The former history professor observed of his less than brilliant successor that Warren G. Harding had a "bungalow mind." Asked to explain the phrase, Wilson pointed to his forehead and said, "No upper story."

—Bob Dole

A reporter once asked Woodrow Wilson how long it took him to prepare a ten-minute speech. "About two weeks," he replied.

"And a one-hour speech?"

"That would take me a week," he estimated.

"And a two-hour speech?"

"Oh," laughed the President, "if you'll let me ramble on for two hours, I'm ready now."

"We've got good news about the economy," President Hoover's chief consultant told him. "There's one group of people that are making a ton of money!"

"Glad to hear it," said the commander in chief.

"Uh . . . the bad news," said the consultant, "is it's all the people who are making 'Going Out of Business' signs."

A young boy was on a tour of the White House with his family. President Herbert Hoover greeted the guests in person and offered to sign autographs. The boy asked Hoover for his autograph. The president agreed. When he had finished signing his autograph, the boy held out four more pieces of paper. "Could you sign four more times?" he asked.

"Why?" Hoover asked.

"I can get one Babe Ruth autograph for five of yours," the honest youngster answered.

—Melvin Berger

If there had been any formidable body of cannibals in the country, [Franklin Delano Roosevelt] would have promised to provide them with free missionaries fattened at the taxpayer's expense.

—H. L. Mencken

Writing to his sister in 1947, Harry Truman described his job as follows: "All the president is, is a glorified public relations man who spends his time flattering, kissing, and kicking people to get them to do what they are supposed to do anyway."

A country club attendant stepped up to former President Eisenhower in the locker room and asked, "Do you notice anything different since you left the White House?"

"Yes," was the rueful answer. "A lot more golfers are beating me."

THAT KENNEDY CLAN

I used to wonder when I was a member of the House how President Truman got into so much trouble. Now I am beginning to get the idea. It is not difficult.

—John F. Kennedy

Asked by a small boy at Cape Cod, "Mr. President, how did you become a war hero?"

Kennedy replied, "It was absolutely involuntary. They sank my boat."

Shortly after President Kennedy's famous inauguration in 1961, Nixon and presidential aide Ted Sorensen met. Their conversation turned to Kennedy's inaugural address.

"I wish I had said some of those things," Nixon said.

"What part?" Sorensen asked, justifiably proud of his speech-writing prowess. "That part about 'Ask not what your country can do for you'?"

"No," replied Nixon. "The part that starts, 'I do solemnly swear.'"

—Bob Dole

John Kennedy's father, Joseph, was a very wealthy man. Rumors spread that he was going to bribe people to vote for his son. Turning these rumors into a joke, John Kennedy said, "I just got a letter from my father. He says, 'Don't buy one more vote than you need. I'm not going to pay for a landslide.'"

Jack Kennedy . . . played the game of politics by his own rules. . . . During his early years in politics, he hated shaking hands, which was highly unusual in a city where some politicians had been known to shake hands with fire hydrants and wave to telephone poles.

—Bob Dole

Robert Kennedy was the campaign manager for his brother John, so sometimes Robert addressed the crowd before John did. Robert usually broke the ice with the story of two brothers who went fishing. One brother caught all the fish. The other caught none. The unlucky one finally borrowed his brother's fishing pole, but still didn't get any bites. Finally a fish jumped out of the water and said, "We're waiting for your brother."

—Melvin Berger

Campaigning for the U.S. Senate in 1964, Robert Kennedy told an audience, "People say I am ruthless. I am not ruthless. And if I find the man who is calling me ruthless, I shall destroy him."

Senator Edward Kennedy recalls, "I ran for the Senate at a very young age, and one of the issues used by the opponents was that I had never worked a day in my life. One day I was going through one of the factories in my state to meet the workers. And I will never forget the fellow who came up to me, shook my hand, and said, 'Mr. Kennedy, I understand that you have never worked a day in your life. Let me tell you, you haven't missed a thing.'"

President Lyndon Johnson's devotion to his wife Ladybird was apparent to all. He frequently declared: "Only two things are necessary to keep one's wife happy. First is to let her think she's having her own way. Second is to let her have it."

STORIES OF REAGAN: THE WITTIEST PRESIDENT

Reagan responded to an introduction given by Clare Boothe Luce, in which she read some gloomy passage from the memoirs of former presidents. After Ms. Luce dramatized the personal sacrifices it takes to be president, Reagan responded: "Well, Clare, I must be doing something wrong. I'm kind of enjoying myself."

—The Uncommon Wisdom of Ronald Reagan

Shortly before he took office, Ronald Reagan was briefed by his advisors on the many problems that the country faced. He joked, "I think I'll demand a recount."

At the annual awards dinner of the White House News Photographers Association on May 27, 1987, Reagan got off a great remark about correspondent Sam Donaldson, who was notorious for bellowing questions at the president during press conferences: "Somebody asked me one day why we didn't put a stop to Sam's shouting out questions at us when we're out on the South Lawn. We can't. If we did, the starlings would come back."

After reports that the president always first pointed at female reporters dressed in red during questions at his press conferences, Reagan said at the annual dinner of the White House Correspondents Association on April 17, 1986: "At my last press conference, I thought that gimmick of wearing a red dress to get my attention went a little too far. But it was a nice try, Sam."

—The Uncommon Wisdom of Ronald Reagan

As President Reagan ran across the South Lawn, Sam Donaldson yelled over the noise of the presidential helicopter, "What about Walter Mondale's charges?"

Reagan shot back, "He ought to pay them."

An excellent example of the self-deprecating Reagan wit: "I've been getting some flack about ordering the production of the B-1. How did I know it was an airplane? I thought it was a vitamin for the troops."

I recall the unforgettable day in the Reagan administration when an American plane shot down two Libyan jets, and the White House was engulfed in controversy because aides failed to wake the President in the middle of the night. The next day, Reagan got off a trademark quip: "I've laid down the law to everyone from now on about anything that happens that no matter what time it is, I'm to be awakened . . . even if it's in the middle of a cabinet meeting."

—Bob Dole

Bob Mills, on President Clinton signing a bill for a Ronald Reagan Building: "The new building, second in size only to the Pentagon, will be made entirely of glass, stucco, and Teflon."

The White House birth of puppies to Millie, George and Barbara Bush's beloved springer spaniel (and best-selling author), led President Bush to gloat, "The puppies are sleeping on the *Washington Post* and *Times*. It's the first time in history these papers have been used to prevent leaks."

—Bob Dole

President George Bush met an emigrant from Russia. "I guess you left Russia because you wanted more freedom," the president said.

"No, I had plenty of freedom," replied the Russian. "I could not complain."

"Then it must be that there were no opportunities in Russia," the president tried next.

"I had opportunities!" the Russian insisted. "I could not complain."

"Was it that you could not find a nice place to live?"

"Not at all. I had a beautiful apartment. I could not complain."

President Bush looked confused. "If everything was fine in Russia, why did you come to America?"

"Aha!" the Russian chortled. "Here I can complain!"

At a party celebrating the fiftieth anniversary of his arrival in America, famed restaurateur George Lang received this letter of tribute: "My great dream was to eat at one of your restaurants. I began to make inquiries and was told, 'You have to learn to appreciate good food.' And I thought, I can do that. Then I was told, 'You have to travel around the world.' And I thought, I can do that. Then I was told, 'It might help if you were the president of the United States,' and I thought . . . well, you know what I thought." It was signed "Bill Clinton." —*Nobody Knows the Truffles I've Seen*

President Ford was a good athlete. Yet he was known for being very clumsy. Ford, though, was able to laugh at himself. For example, he said, "I can ski for hours on end." —Melvin Berger

Suggested names for Ben and Jerry's new presidential ice cream:
- Impeach-Mint
- Subpoena Colada
- Rocky Road Ahead

Paul Steinberg, on President Clinton teaching daughter Chelsea to drive: "Is this such a good idea? He prides himself on steering down the middle of the road."

Further Reading:

Laughing in the White House, Polly Tickle

Retreats of Former U.S. Presidents, Kenny Bunkport and Sam Clemente

■ Prices

Somebody broke into our car the other day and stole eighty dollars worth of groceries—from the glove compartment!

A lion walks into a bar and orders a dry martini. "What does a lion know?" thinks the bartender, and charges the lion ten dollars. After a while, the bartender's curiosity gets the best of him. He walks over to him, starts wiping the bar casually, looks up, and says, "Say, you know, we don't get too many lions in here."

Says the lion, "I'm not surprised, at these prices."   —Paul Dickson

■ Pride

In the 1930s, a British novelist arrived in America for his first visit and Bennett Cerf, his publisher, bursting with local pride, took him uptown in an open car. "There is the Municipal Building," he pointed out. "It's sort of our city hall. American workmen put up the whole building in 132 days."

"That's not very remarkable," said the Londoner. "Our city hall was built in ninety-four days."

A little later Cerf pointed out the Williamsburg Bridge. "They built that in four months flat," he boasted.

"Our new Waterloo Bridge," answered the novelist, "was put up in two months and a half."

Cerf pointed out several other architectural triumphs, but the novelist topped him every time. Cerf became nettled.

Suddenly the novelist gasped in surprise as their car passed by the Empire State Building. "What's the name of that building?" he inquired.

Cerf shrugged his shoulders. "I couldn't tell you," he said. "It wasn't there when I came downtown this morning."

This is the tale of the haughty family of Willoughby-ffinch of Somersetshire, who one and all were prostrated with grief and shame when the beautiful Millicent Willoughby-ffinch had the bad taste to fall in love with and to marry a handsome and athletic young man of appalling laboring background, by the name of Alfie Suggs. Naturally, as any decent family of breeding would, they cut her off, and Mr. and Mrs. Suggs were forced to live a life of penury. Through it all, Millicent clung loyally to her husband. Then came strokes of fate. A lucky business venture sent Mr. Suggs on the road to prosperity, and with unparalleled industry and pluck, he piled profit upon profit and grew rich. The Willoughby-ffinches, on the other hand, suffered reverses and grew poor. Faithful Millicent, on her deathbed, begged her husband to be forgiving and repay the hardheartedness of her family with kindness, and sorrowing, Alfie agreed. Consequently, when it was Alfie's turn to pass on, he left a sizable portion of his fortune to the Willoughby-ffinches on the sole condition—and this he could not resist—that they change their name legally to Suggs. The fallen aristocrats had no choice but to accept this utter humiliation. They had their name changed and accepted the inheritance. From then on they carefully spelled their name "S-U-G-G-S"—but they pronounced it "Willoughby-ffinch."

—Isaac Asimov

■ Procrastination

Procrastination is like a credit card: it's a lot of fun until you get the bill.

—Christopher Parker

I have not yet begun to procrastinate.

Procrastinate now!

Never overnight today what you can fax tomorrow.

—Jay Trachman, *One to One*

Punctuality: The art of arriving for an appointment just in time to be indignant at the tardiness of the other party.

My uncle Sid owned a trucking firm that was once offered a chance at a pension plan with remarkable advantages. There was one important condition: every employee without exception had to sign on, and it had to be done within thirty days.

There was great enthusiasm for the plan among Sid's employees, and within a week, everyone had signed up. Everyone, that is, except Phil Roth in the shipping department. Everyone in the plant argued with him—his fellow workers, the union representative, his immediate superiors. But he kept putting it off. "It's too complicated," he said, "and I don't understand it."

The deadline was approaching, and Phil Roth was ushered into Uncle Sid's plush office. A copy of the pension plan was on the desk as was an uncapped pen.

Uncle Sid said, "Mr. Roth, I have the approval of your union in what I am about to say." Uncle Sid pointed to two burly shop stewards and continued, "We are now on the seventh floor. If you do not sign this paper by the time I have counted ten, I will have you thrown out the window."

Without waiting for Uncle Sid to start counting, without a word, without the slightest sign of displeasure—Roth immediately wrote his name on the paper.

Uncle Sid glanced at it, folded it neatly, and said, "Now, why on earth couldn't you have signed on for the pension plan before?"

And Roth said, "Because you're the first person who explained it clearly."

Further Reading:
Let's Do It Now!, Igor Beaver

■ Psychiatry

A psychiatrist is a fellow who asks you a lot of expensive questions that your wife asks you for nothing.   —Joey Adams

Neurotic: A person who, when you ask how she is, tells you.

332

OREO PSYCHO-PERSONALITY TEST

Psychiatrists have discovered that the manner in which people eat Oreo cookies provides great insight into their personalities. Which method best describes your favorite approach?

1. the whole thing in one bite
2. one bite at a time
3. slow and methodical nibbles, examining the results of each bite
4. in little feverish nibbles
5. dunked in some liquid (milk, coffee . . .)
6. the inside first
7. the inside only
8. the outside only
9. just lick them, not eat them
10. don't have a favorite way because I don't like Oreos.

YOUR PERSONALITY:

1. the whole thing in one bite
This means you consume life with abandon, you are fun to be with, exciting, carefree with some hint of recklessness. You are totally irresponsible. No one should trust you with their children.

2. one bite at a time
You are lucky to be one of the 5.4 billion other people who eat their Oreos this very same way. Just like them, you lack imagination, but that's okay, not to worry, you're normal.

3. slow and methodical
You follow the rules. You're very tidy and orderly. You're very meticulous in every detail with everything you do to the point of being anal retentive and irritating to others. Stay out of the fast lane if you're only going to go the speed limit.

4. little feverish nibbles
Your boss likes you because you get your work done quickly. You always have a million things to do and never enough time to do them. Mental break downs and suicides run in your family. Valium and Ritalin would do you good.

5. dunked

Every one likes you because you are always upbeat. You like to sugar coat unpleasant experiences and rationalize bad situations into good ones. You are in total denial about the shambles you call your life. You have a propensity towards narcotic addiction.

6. the inside first

You have a highly curious nature. You take pleasure in breaking things apart to find out how they work, though you're not always able to put them back together, so you destroy the evidence of your activities. You deny your involvement when things go wrong. You are a compulsive liar and exhibit deviant, if not criminal, behavior.

7. the inside only

You are good at business and take risks that pay off. You take what you want and throw the rest away. You are greedy, selfish, mean, and lack feelings for others. You should be ashamed of yourself. But that's okay, you don't care, you got yours.

8. the outside only

You enjoy pain.

9. just like to lick them, not eat them.

Stay away from small furry animals and seek professional medical help—immediately.

10. don't have a favorite way because I don't like Oreo cookies.

You probably come from a rich family and like to wear nice things and go to upscale restaurants. You are particular and fussy about the things you buy, own, and wear. Things have to be just right. You like to be pampered. You are a prima donna. There's just no pleasing you.

Psychiatrist to Uncle Sid: "You're quite right. A man *is* following you constantly. He's trying to collect the two thousand dollars you owe me."

Two colleagues were discussing a patient: "I was having great success with Mr. Green," said the first doctor. "When he first came to me, he was suffering from a massive inferiority complex related to his size."

"How did you treat this patient?" asked the second doctor.

"I started out with intensive analysis and then group therapy. I convinced him that many of the world's greatest leaders were men of small physical stature. I really hated to lose Mr. Green."

"What do you mean? How did you lose him?"

Replied the physician, "A kitten ate him."

—George Jessel

He told me that at night when he is trying to sleep he sees shadows all over his bedroom. I asked him if he has ever seen a psychiatrist. He said, "No. Just shadows."

—Ron Dentinger

Psychiatrist: Congratulations, Mr. Young. You're finally cured of your delusion. But why are you so sad?

Patient: Wouldn't you be sad if one day you were president of the United States and the next day you were nobody?

Further Reading:

Nuts About You!, Cy Cosis

Split Personalities, Jacqueline Hyde

It's All In Your Head, Madge Ination

The Empath, Ophelia Sadness

Self-Denial Made Easy, Abner Gation

Positive Reinforcement, Wade Ago

■ Puns and Punnier

In Great Neck, a doctor, summoned to treat a weekender who had swallowed an oyster containing an indigestible hard and gritty substance, removed the offending substance with the observation, "A gritty pearl is like a malady."

—Bennett Cerf

My uncle Ted retired and became a church sexton. "This job is a push-over," he explained. "All I have to do is mind my keys and pews."

Two ropes walk into a bar to get some drinks. The bartender leans over to address the first rope and asks, "Are you one of them ropes?"

"Why yes," quavers the rope.

"We don't serve ropes here," growls the bartender, grabbing the rope, twirling him around his head, and throwing him out the door.

The second rope decides that he had best disguise himself, so he ruffles his threads and twists his two ends together.

Glaring, the bartender looks at the second rope and asks, "You one of them ropes?"

"No!" was the indignant reply. "I'm a frayed knot!" —Paul Dickson

A group of people are touring the White House in Washington, D.C. As the tour ends, they are waiting in line to sign the visitors register. A group of nuns are in line to sign the book, followed by a Jewish family with their young son Sheldon.

As they near the visitors registry, young Sheldon loses patience and runs ahead to sign the book.

However, his mother stops him and admonishes him saying, "Wait till the nun signs, Shelly!"

My dad believes that cheerful people resist disease better than chronic moaners and complainers. In other words, according to his theory, "The surly bird catches the germ."

John Lennon's mom, trying to get him to eat his vegetables when he was a child: "All I am saying, John, is give peas a chance!"

There was a man who entered a local paper's pun contest. He sent in ten different puns, hoping that at least one of the puns would win. Unfortunately, no pun in ten did.

A doctor made it his regular habit to stop off at a bar for a hazelnut daiquiri on his way home. The bartender knew of his habit and would always have the drink waiting at precisely 5:03 P.M. One afternoon, as the end of the work day approached, the bartender was dismayed to find that he was out of hazelnut extract. Thinking quickly, he threw together a daiquiri made with hickory nuts and set it on the bar. The doctor came in at his regular time, took one sip of the drink, and exclaimed, "This isn't a hazelnut daiquiri!"

"No, sorry," replied the bartender. "It's a hickory daiquiri, Doc."

A dwarf psychic was arrested for being a phony. She escaped from jail, and the next day the newspaper headline said: Small Medium at Large.

—John Hakel

A group of chess enthusiasts had checked into a hotel and were standing in the lobby discussing their recent tournament victories. After about an hour, the manager came out of the office and asked them to disperse.

"But why?" they asked, as they moved off.

"Because," he said, "I can't stand chess nuts boasting in an open foyer."

Did you hear about the Buddhist who refused his dentist's novocaine during root canal work? He wanted to transcend dental medication!

Two atoms are walking down the street, and they bump into each other. One says to the other, "Are you all right?"

"No, I lost an electron!"

"Are you sure?"

"Yeah, I'm positive!"

A neutron goes into a bar and asks the bartender, "How much for a beer?" The bartender replies, "For you, no charge."

Fascinate: There were nine buttons on her nightgown, but she could only fascinate.
—Homer Haynes

James Stewart and Josh Logan, when they returned to Princeton for their twenty-fifth reunion, found themselves bedded down in Old Nassau, the hall in which they had roomed together so many years before. It was the first night of festivities and no formal activity had been planned.

"How about a game of gin just to pass the time?" suggested Logan.

"Okay," nodded Stewart. "Any old sport in a dorm."
—Bennett Cerf

A three-legged dog walks into a saloon in the Old West. He sidles up to the bar and announces, "I'm looking for the man who shot my paw."

A renowned lady gardener in the New Haven area, her living room festooned with blue ribbons she had garnered, decided to plant some special fronds and anemones this spring. The fronds turned out in spectacular fashion, but the anemones, to put it mildly, were a distinct flop. The lady, unaccustomed to failure, was lamenting this minor setback, but a good friend hastened to bolster her sagging spirits. "Remember, Debbie," she counseled, "that with fronds like this, you don't need anemones."
—Bennett Cerf

Two boll weevils grew up in South Carolina. One went to Hollywood and became a famous actor. The other stayed behind in the cotton fields and never amounted to much. The second one, naturally, became known as the lesser of two weevils.

Two Eskimos sitting in a kayak were chilly, but when they lit a fire in the craft it sank, proving once and for all that you can't have your kayak and heat it, too.

During World War II, why did Winston Churchill put ugly female sheep in the woodlands of England to keep the Luftwaffe from bombing? Because . . . homely ewes can prevent forest flyers.

A frog goes into a bank and hops up on a chair in front of the loan officer's desk. "Hi!" says the frog. "What's your name?"

The loan officer replies, "My name is John Paddywack. How can I help you?"

The frog says, "I'd like to borrow some money."

The loan officer finds this a little odd, but gets out a form anyway. He asks, "Okay, what's your name?"

"Kermit Jagger," says the frog.

"Really?" says the loan officer, "Any relation to Mick Jagger?"

"Yeah," says the frog, "he's my dad."

"Okay," the loan officer continues, "do you have any collateral?"

The frog hands the loan officer a pink ceramic elephant and asks, "Will this do?"

"Hmm," ponders the loan officer. "I'm not so sure. Please let me go check with the bank manager."

The frog says, "Oh, by the way, tell him I said hello. He knows me."

The loan officer goes back to the manager's office and says, "Excuse me, sir, but there's this frog out front named Kermit Jagger who wants to borrow some money. All he has for collateral is this pink elephant thing—I'm not even sure what it is."

Obviously irritated, the manager roars back at the loan officer, "Well, what's the problem here? It's a knick-knack, Paddywack, give the frog a loan! His old man is a Rolling Stone!"

Long, long ago an old Indian chief was about to die, so he called for Geronimo and Falling Rocks, the two bravest warriors in his tribe. The chief instructed each to go out and collect buffalo skins. Whoever returned with the most skins would be the new chief.

About a month later, Geronimo came back with one hundred pelts, but Falling Rocks never returned. Even today as you drive through the West you can see signs saying: Watch Out for Falling Rocks.

—Toni Sortor

A maker of eyeglasses has just moved his shop to an island off Alaska, which is now known as an optical Aleutian.   —Bennett Cerf

From my Norwegian friend Bjarne comes an encouraging word to all active punsters: "Don't let those who hate your puns get you down. In this country, at least, the pun is still mightier than the fjord."

TOM SWIFTIES

- "That's the last time I'll ever pet a lion," Tom said, offhandedly.
- "I'll never sleep on the railroad tracks again!" Tom said, beside himself.
- "That's the third electric shock I've gotten this week!" Tom said, revolted.
- "I'm never anywhere on time," Tom related.
- "I won't let a flat tire get me down," Tom said, without despair.
- "That car you sold me has defective steering!" Tom said, straight-forwardly.
- "I've been on a diet," Tom expounded.
- "I'll have to send that telegram again," Tom said, remorsefully.
- "I keep banging my head on things," Tom said, bashfully.
- "Look at that jailbird climb down that wall," Tom observed with condescension.
- "I remember the Midwest being flatter than this," Tom explained.
- "That's the third time my teacher changed my grade," Tom remarked.
- "I'll have to dig another ditch around the castle," Tom sighed remotely.
- "I've lived through a lot of windstorms," Tom regaled.
- "I haven't caught a fish all day!" Tom said, without debate.
- "That mink coat is on wrong side out," Tom inferred.
- "I'm never going to be president of the U.S.," Tom said dolefully.

Further Reading:

Fred Can Philosophize!, Immanuel Kant

The World's Deadliest Joke, Theophilus Punoval

■ Rednecks and Country

November 1998 marked a dramatic transition in my life. After nearly sixty years of urban and suburban existence, my wife and I moved to rural Cottonwood near Redding, California. My wife is a native of the area, so the change was easier for her. But my relatives are in a state of shock. A cousin wrote to me as follows:

Memphis, Tennessee
Dear Cousin Lowell:
I hear y'all have moved to the country up in Shasta County and that you're now wearing overalls and plaid flannel shirts, driving a red pickup truck, and raising a cattle dog. I reckon we'll make a redneck out of you yet!

Just so's you can get in the right frame of mind, I'd best educate you. So here is a list for you to study up on.

As always,
Your rebel cousin,
Bobby Lee

THINGS YOU WOULDN'T HEAR A REDNECK SAY

- We don't keep firearms in this house.
- Has anybody seen the sideburn trimmer?
- You can't feed that to the dog.
- I thought Graceland was tacky.
- No kids in the back of the pickup, it's not safe.
- Wrastlin's fake.

- Honey, did you mail that donation to Greenpeace?
- We're vegetarians.
- Do you think my hair is too big?
- I'll have grapefruit instead of biscuits and gravy.
- Honey, these bonsai trees need watering.
- Who's Richard Petty?
- Give me the small bag of pork rinds.
- Deer heads detract from the decor.
- Spitting is such a nasty habit.
- I just couldn't find a thing at Wal-Mart today.
- Trim the fat off that steak.
- Cappuccino tastes better than espresso.
- The tires on that truck are too big.
- I'll have the arugula and radicchio salad.
- Unsweetened tea tastes better.
- Would you like your fish poached or broiled?
- My fiancée, Paula Jo, is registered at Tiffany's.
- Little Debbie snack cakes have too many fat grams.
- Checkmate.
- Does the salad bar have bean sprouts?
- Hey, here's an episode of *Hee Haw* that we haven't seen.
- I believe you cooked those green beans too long.
- Elvis who?
- Be sure to bring my salad dressing on the side.

Sign at the box office of an Ozark movie house: Children under fifteen not admitted unless accompanied by their husbands.

Bumper sticker on Arkansas car: If you can read this, you're not from here!

I was in Tennessee, and they hated me. They knew I came in from California. A guy stood up and said, "At least here in Tennessee we don't drive all over our freeways and shoot and kill people!"

I said, "No, but you should." —Pam Stone

Nice people down South—they take their guns seriously. We passed a pickup truck. It had a bumper sticker: Guns Don't Kill People, I do!

—Jon Haymen

 A young ventriloquist is touring the South and stops to entertain in a bar in Arkansas. He's going through his usual stupid redneck jokes, when a big burly guy in the audience stands up and says, "I've heard just about enough of your durn hillbilly jokes! We ain't all stupid here in Arkansas!"

Flustered, the ventriloquist begins to apologize, when the big guy pipes up, "You stay out of this mister, I'm talking to the smart-mouth little fella on your knee!"

YOU MIGHT BE A REDNECK JEDI IF . . .

- You ever heard the phrase, "May the force be with y'all."
- Your Jedi robe is camouflage color.
- At least one wing of your X-wing fighter is primer colored.
- You have bantha horns on the front of your land speeder.
- You can easily describe the taste of an Ewok.
- You have ever had an X-wing fighter up on blocks in your yard.
- You ever lost a hand during a light saber fight because you had to spit.
- The worst part of killin' time on Dagobah is the dadgum skeeters.
- Wookies are offended by your BO.
- You have ever used the Force in conjunction with fishing or bowling.
- Your father has ever said to you, "Shoot, son, come on over to the dark side . . . it'll be a hoot!"
- You have ever had your R2 unit use its self-defense electro-shock thingy to get the barbecue grill to light.
- You think Han Solo would look better in a flannel shirt, 'cuz he looks like a little sissy in that vest.
- You have the doors of your X-wing fighter welded shut and you have to get in through the window.
- In your opinion, that Darth Vader fellow just ain't right.

Q: What's the difference between a southern zoo and a northern zoo?

A: A southern zoo has a description of the animal on the front of the cage, plus it has a recipe, too.

Q: What do they call *Hee Haw* in Oklahoma?

A: A documentary.

Q: What do they call it in Kentucky?

A: *Lifestyles of the Rich and Famous.*

If an infinite number of rednecks driving an infinite number of pickup trucks fire an infinite number of shotgun rounds at an infinite number of highway signs, they will eventually produce all the world's great literary works. In Braille.

Since my cousin Bobby Lee is always accusing me of becoming a redneck, it is only fair that I point out that she is in equal danger of becoming a Yankee. Here, dear cuz, are the warning signs:

YOU MIGHT BE A YANKEE IF YOU . . .

- Would rather vacation on Martha's Vineyard than at Six Flags.
- Don't see anything wrong with putting a sweater on a poodle.
- Eat fried chicken with a knife and fork.
- Don't know anyone with two first names (e.g., Joe Bob, Billy Ray, Nancy Jo, Bubba Dean).
- Have never eaten okra.
- Think more money should go to scientific research at your university than to pay the salary of the head football coach.
- Would rather have your son become a lawyer than grow up to get his own TV fishing show.

CUMPLEET REDNECK CUMPUTER MEENINS

32-bit resolution: Motion to spend four dollars.

Apple: Needed for pan dowdy and fritters.

Backup: Takin the truck outta the driveway.

Byte: Wut them dang flys and muskitos do.

C++: Superior grade in skool.

Cache: Needed when yur credit cards max out and ya have no food stamps.

CD-ROM: Place in the bank ware they sell those big notes.

Chip: Munchies fer the TV.

Code: Wen yu gotta snooty nose and coff.

Debugger: A roach motel.

Digital control: Wut yur fingers do on the TV remote.

Disc Operating System: Wut the doc uses to fix your floppy disc (see floppy disc).

DOS: Opposite of don'ts.

Dot matrix: Tom Matrix's wife.

Down: Feelin blue.

Download: Gettin the farwood off the truk.

Drive compatibility: A long car ride with your wife without fightin.

Edit: Wucha did with the food.

Encryption: What the undertaker duz to ya.

Enter: Notherner talk fer "cum in, ya all."

Ethernet: Wut the doc puts on your face in surgery to make ya sleep.

Expansion Slot: extra hole in yur belt ya use wen ya overeat.

File: Wut yur wife uses on her nails.

Firewall: Ware ya practises yur target shutin.

Floppy disk: Soggy pizza; and, wucha git in yer spine from liftin too much farwood.

Font: Discover, as in "I font it at a garage sale."

Format: Small rug to wipe your feet on wen ya go inta the house on a muddy day.

Java applets: Fritters for dunkin.

Hard drive: Gettin home in the muddy season with a flat tire.

Homepage: Place in the newspaper with houses for sale.

Icon: Braggin, as in "icon lift yur truck with one arm."

Interface: Wat happens when two teens with braces kiss.

Internet Explorer: A curious fish.

Keyboard: Ware ya hang yur truk keys.

Laptop: Ware the little kids jump on to sit.

Log on: Making a wood stove hotter.

Log off: Takin the wood off the pile fur usin.

Mac: Yur kids' favorite food.

Main frame: Wut holds up the barn roof.

Manual: Truck without automatic geers.

Megabyte: Wucha git from Meg durin luvmakin.

Megahertz: Watcha git when yer not keerful gettin the farwood.

Microchip: Wuts left in the munchie bag when the chips are gone.

Microfiche: Tiny fish used fur bait.

Microprocessor: Fine meat chopper fur making sausages.

Modem: Whacha do to the grass twisa yeer.

Monitor: Teachur's helper at lunch.

Mouse: Fuzzy white thing wut eats the horses grain in the barn and
   ya can stuff in your beer bottle to get a free case.

Multisync: Two washing areas in the same bathroom.

Overwrite: What makes yur checks bounce.

Plug-in: Push the end of the TV cord into the wall.

Program: Wuts on the TV when there's receptshun.

Programmer: Fella with the TV remote.

Prompt: Wucha wish the mail was, in mud season.

RAM: Lamb's daddy.

RAM chip: Male sheep droppins.

Random access: Wen ya can't member wen yer wife asks ware ya were.

ROM: The Pope's home.

Screen: Thing to keep the flies out.

Server: Gal in resterant that brings yur food.

Superconductors: Glenn Miller, Doc Severnsen, Lawrence Welk.

Terminal: Time to call the undertaker.

Token ring: Wat ya usta grab on the merry-go-round to git a free ride.

Update: Wen ya rite a check so it cant be used until next month.

Vector: Winner of the fite or race.

Version: Wucha dislike, as in "he has a version to broccoli."

Virus: same as a code but wurse.

Website: ware spiders catch flies.

Zip drive: goin fast at NASCAR.

ADVICE FOR YANKEES MOVING SOUTH

When cousin Roberta married a southerner and decided to move to the South, her husband's relatives sent this helpful advice.

- Save all manner of bacon grease. You will be instructed later how to use it.
- If you forget a southerner's name, refer to him (or her) as Bubba. You have a 75 percent chance of being right.
- Just because you can drive on snow and ice doesn't mean we can. Stay home the two days of the year it snows.
- If you do run your car into a ditch, don't panic. Four men in the cab of a four wheel drive with a twelve-pack of beer and a tow chain will be along shortly. Don't try to help them. Just stay out of their way. This is what they live for.
- Don't be surprised to find movie rentals and bait in the same store.
- Do not buy food at the movie store.
- If it can't be fried in bacon grease, it ain't worth cooking, let alone eating.
- Remember: "Y'all" is singular. "All y'all" is plural. "All y'all's" is plural possessive.
- Get used to hearing, "You ain't from around here, are you?"
- Don't be worried that you don't understand anyone. They don't understand you either.
- The proper pronunciation you learned in school is no longer proper.
- Be advised: The "he needed killin'" defense is valid here.
- If attending a funeral in the South, remember, we stay until the last shovel of dirt is thrown on, and the tent is torn down.
- If you hear a southerner exclaim, "Hey, y'all, watch this!" stay out of his way. These are likely the last words he will ever say.
- Most southerners do not use turn signals, and they ignore those who do. In fact, if you see a signal blinking on a car with a southern license plate, you may rest assured that it was on when the car was purchased.
- Northerners can be identified by the spit on the inside of their car's windshield that comes from yelling at other drivers.
- Satellite dishes are very popular in the South. When you purchase one, it is to be positioned directly in front of your trailer.

This is logical bearing in mind that the dish cost considerably more than the trailer and should, therefore, be displayed.

- Tornadoes and southerners going through a divorce have a lot in common. In either case you know someone is going to lose a trailer.
- Florida is not considered a southern state. There are far more Yankees than southerners living there.

Further Reading:
Fifty Yards to the Outhouse, Willy Makit and Betty Woant

■ Relatives

Gracie: My sister had a baby.

George: Boy or girl?

Gracie: I don't know, and I can't wait to find out if I'm an uncle or an aunt.
　　　　　　　　　　　　　　　　　　　—George Burns and Gracie Allen

I just got a "Wish You Were Here" card from my brother. . . . He's in prison.
　　　　　　　　　　　　　　　　　　　　　　　　　—Scott Wood

My cousin Mel is the kind of fellow who throws a drowning man both ends of a rope.
　　　　　　　　　　　　　　　　　　　　　　　　　—Myron Cohen

"I'm sorry you don't like my gift," the aunt said to her nephew. "But I asked if you preferred a large check or a small check."
　　"I know," he replied, "but I didn't think you meant neckties."
　　　　　　　　　　　—Todd Murphy in *Louisville Courier-Journal Magazine*

Happiness is seeing your mother-in-law on a milk carton.

■ Religion

Different people look for different things in the Ten Command-ments. Some are looking for divine guidance, some for a code of liv-ing, but most people are looking for loopholes.   —Sam Levenson

One medieval monk, transcribing scripture, to another: "Some-body's going to get a break. I skipped a couple of commandments."

Getting inoculated with small doses of religion prevents people from catching the real thing.   —Sam Levenson

Converts tend to take their religion much more seriously than do those reared in a given tradition. Clare Boothe Luce, well-known playwright and wife of the publisher of *Time* magazine, provided an example. Mrs. Luce became a Catholic in middle life and had all the enthusiasm of the convert. President Eisenhower appointed her as ambassador to Italy, and while she was there, the story goes, a reporter once spied her in earnest conversa-tion with Pope Pius XII.

The reporter thought that a conversation between the Pope and an ambassador might have enormous news value, so he drifted clos-er in an attempt to overhear. He finally maneuvered himself into earshot, and the first words he heard were those of His Holiness, saying in accented English, "But you don't understand, Mrs. Luce. I already am a Catholic."

One Sunday I missed church because I was tied up with con-stituents, and some people said being down in Washington had made an atheist out of me. Several weeks later, when I was back home again and did get to church, they said, "Why, that pious fraud, he's just trying to dig up votes!"   —Tip O'Neill

E. H. Taylor tells this tale at the expense of Bishop Bompas, the first Anglican missionary to venture into the Yukon. The good bishop discovered a tribe of Indians who had never recorded a baptism, a confirmation, or a marriage service. The bishop soon rectified this situation, baptizing and confirming everybody in sight, and winding up by uniting every beaming couple in holy wedlock. Later the tribal chief told Bishop Bompas that his tribe hadn't had so much fun in a month of Sundays.

"And what part of the ceremonies," asked the bishop, "did you enjoy most?"

"The marriage service!" replied the chief happily. "We all got new wives!"
—Bennett Cerf

When Bishop Stephen Bayne Jr. was appointed executive officer of the Anglican Communion, he was asked how he regarded his new duties. "I am rather like a mosquito in a nudist camp," confessed the bishop with a wry smile. "I know what I ought to do, but I don't know where to begin."

■ Restaurants

After eating a meal in a first-class restaurant nowadays, you need an after-dinner mint—preferably the one in Denver.
—Irving Laza

Ever notice that the harder it is to read a menu, the higher the prices on it are?
—*Executive Speechwriter Newsletter*

Fancy Restaurant: One that serves cold soup on purpose.
—Doug Larson, United Feature Syndicate

Your request for no MSG has been denied.
—fortune cookie

The murals in restaurants are on par with the food in museums.
—Peter De Vries

During another visit to the Cape Coral Grill, my dad beckoned the waiter. "Please close the window," he said nervously. "I'm afraid this steak is going to blow away."

Never eat any place where they mark the rest room doors in any fashion but "Men" and "Women" or "Ladies" and "Gentlemen." Especially do not eat in a restaurant that specializes in seafood and marks its rest room doors "Buoys" and "Gulls," because they have been too busy thinking up cutesy names for the rest room doors to really pay attention to the food.

—Lewis Grizzard

Never eat in a restaurant where you see a cockroach bench-pressing a burrito.

—Pat McCormick

My cousin Sid was a notoriously crude fellow when he dined out at a fancy restaurant. His worst habit was tucking his napkin under his chin. Naturally, this caused the entire staff to stare at him. The maitre de quickly ran over to the waiter who was serving him and said, "Inform that man that he shouldn't wear a bib in here. But remember, do it very tactfully."

With this, the waiter walked over to Sid and asked, "Would you like a shave and a haircut also?"

—Myron Cohen

Waiters can sometimes be like children. It seems as though they can take nine months to arrive.

A customer was so infatuated with his waitress that he decided to ask her for a date, but couldn't get her attention. When he finally caught her eye, she quickly looked away. Then he followed her into the kitchen and confronted her, blurting out his invitation. To his amazement, she consented. He said, "Why have you been avoiding me since you served me? You wouldn't even make eye contact."

"Oh," replied the waitress, "I thought you wanted more coffee."

—Ron Dentinger

When I lived in Philadelphia, I took my teenage son and daughter to a delicatessen for lunch. When the waiter came to our table, my daughter said, "I think I'll have a chicken sandwich with white meat."

"White meat isn't good for a young girl," said the waiter. "Take roast beef."

"Okay," said my daughter. "Roast beef will be fine."

"Better make it whole wheat," said the waiter. "It has more vitamins."

My son ordered corned beef hash. "Don't take that," said the waiter. "It's made up of all the things that other people leave on their plate. The London broil is what you should take."

"All right," said my son. "Make it London broil and a cup of coffee."

"Coffee!" exclaimed the waiter. "You won't sleep a wink tonight. You take a nice glass of fresh buttermilk."

"Very well," said my son. "London broil and buttermilk it is."

I was a bit overwhelmed by the waiter, to say the least, so I said, timidly, "What do you think I should order?"

"How do I know?" said the waiter indignantly. "Who's got time around here to make recommendations?"

Customer: There's a fly in my soup!
Waiter:
    1. Ssh! Everybody will want one!
    2. What do you expect for a dollar? Elephants?
    3. Wait'll you see the coffee!
    4. That's all right. How much can a fly drink?
    5. Force of habit, sir. Our chef used to be a tailor.　—Bennett Cerf

All things come to those who wait . . . except hot soup.

In most restaurants today, you find that the food is frozen, and the waiters are fresh.

When we finished a meal at Denny's, my dad commented, "I hate always to eat and run, but the way I tip it's the only safe procedure!"

On the door of Schlotzsky's Deli in Phoenix: No Shoezsky, No Shirtzsky, No Schlotzsky.

Further Reading:
Judging Fast Food, Warren Berger
The Greasy Spoon, Chris Coe
Smash His Lobster!, Buster Crabbe
The Smorgasbord, Buffy Dinner

■ Riddles

RIDDLES TOLD BY CHILDREN IN THE LOS ANGELES AREA

Where do you raise pot?
At the pottery barn!

> —Wilton Kuffel, 7, Los Angeles, Community Magnet School

What do you call a cow with no legs?
Ground beef! —Janelle Burdette, 9, Woodland Hills, Pinecrest School

Where do carpenters go when they run out of nails?
To a manicurist. —Amber Nicolai, 4, Trabuco Canyon, Kindercare Preschool

What did summer say to winter?
Help, I'm going to fall.

> —Ryan Basch, 8, Woodland Hills, Kadima Hebrew Academy

What did one ghost say to the other ghost?
Get a life! —Albert Alvarado, 7, Pasadena, Mayfield School

How do you keep cool in a beauty shop?
Turn on the hair conditioner.

> —Brittany Burne, 12, Rancho Santa Margarita Middle School

What did Cruella's chicken drive?
A Coop De Vil. —Lauren Armanino, 12, Tarzana, Pinecrest Middle School

Why did the sheep cross the road?
He wanted to get to the baa bar shop.
—Justine Coleman, 8, Venice, Westminster Magnet School

Knock, knock.
Who's there?
Clark a Doodle.
Clark a Doodle who?
Oh, I didn't know you were a rooster.
—Rosario Ladera Molina, 8, Venice, Westminster Magnet School

What is white on the outside and green on the inside?
A frog sandwich. —Alex Morales, 8, Venice, Westminster Magnet School

Why did the zombie stay home from the party?
He was dead tired.
—David J. Shophet, 10, Los Angeles, Warner Avenue Elementary

What's a vampire's favorite fruit?
A necktarine. —James Guttridge, 8, Los Angeles, Roscomare Road School

When does a rocket get hungry?
When it's almost launch time.
—Charlotte Jones, 8, Los Angeles, Roscomare Road School

Where do they sell a lot of pencils?
Pennsylvania. —Alexander David, 8, Los Angeles, Roscomare Road School

How does a farmer discipline his corn?
He pulls their ears. —Hanna Lieberman, 8, Encino, Roscomare Road School

Name a Christmas appetizer.
A nutcracker.
—Alice Hall-Partyka, 6, La Canada Flintridge, Paradise Canyon School

What's another name for Santa's helpers?
Subordinate clauses.   —Keith Hershey, 13, North Hills, L.A. Baptist

What does a witch eat at the beach?
A sandwich.   —Annie Garafalo, 5, Calabasas, Lupin Hill Elementary

If Cinderella got married under water, what would she wear?
Glass flippers.   —Laura Ruchinskas, 8, Santa Monica, Franklin Elementary

Where do you take a sick horse?
To the horsepital.   —Ginny Gardner, 4, Trabuco Canyon, Angel Preschool

How can a dog stop a VCR?
He presses the paws button.
                    —Laura Portillo, 10, Sherman Oaks, Chandler Elementary

Where do vampires live?
In the Vampire State Building
                    —Alex Fullman, 8, Encino, Heschel Day School

What do you get when you cross a pair of pants with a telephone?
Bell bottoms.   —Jared Kosareff, 10, Buena Park, Buena Terra Elementary

Further Reading:
Quips for the Young at Heart, Marty Pance

■ Romance

Dear Keith: I have been unable to sleep ever since I broke our engagement. Won't you forget and forgive? Your absence leaves a void nobody else can ever fill. I love you, I love you, I love you.
                    Your adoring Tiffany

PS: Congratulations on winning the Power Ball $38 million lottery

A girl's biggest asset is a man's imagination.   —John Crosby

Sign posted at a perfume exhibit: Don't risk using this scent if you're only bluffing.

Frank ("Harvey") Fay is thought by many to have been the greatest of nightclub ad-libbers. A friend of mine claims to have been present at Broadway's old French Casino when Fay pulled one of his classics.

At a moment's lull in Fay's routine, a drunk hollered, "Ah, you stink!"

Fay drew himself up and said stiffly, "Have a care, sir; you are speaking of the man I love!"   —Art Linkletter

Sales and Salespeople

A salesman was stranded in a small backwoods town due to a critical power shortage. He e-mailed to his boss, "I don't know when I'll be able to get out of here. It might take weeks."

Upon receiving the e-mail, the head man immediately typed back, "As of today you start your two week vacation."

—Myron Cohen

Spartanburg, South Carolina (AP)—A sign on a local home reads, Salesmen Welcome! Dog Food Is Expensive.

—cited by Bud and Lolo Delaney, *The Laugh Journal*

A persistent salesman was ushered into a powerful tycoon's private sanctum at the tag end of a hectic day. "It speaks well for your power of persuasion that you wangled your way in here," said the tycoon. "I've refused to see fourteen other important agents today."

"I know," said the salesman. "I'm all of them."   —Bennett Cerf

A girl was telling her friend that she'd just become engaged to a traveling salesman.

"What's he like?" asked her friend eagerly. "Is he good looking?"

"I wouldn't say he's handsome, just passable."

"Does he have a good personality?"

"He'd never stand out in a crowd."

"Does he have money?"

"If he does, he won't spend it."

"Does he have any bad habits?"

"Well, he drinks an awful lot."

"Lord, girl, if you can't say anything for him, why ever are you marrying the guy?"

"He's on the road all the time. I'll never see him!" —Myron Cohen

A guy applies for a job with a clothing store. He tells the manager, "I really need this job. Please give me a chance. I can sell anything."

The manager says, "Let's see how good you are." He shows the guy a suit so ugly that it has been in stock for years. Nobody could sell it. He tells the salesman, "If you sell this suit, you've got the job." The guy goes to work, and the manager goes out for lunch.

When the manager returns, the new salesman, with his clothes all torn and bloody, tells him, "I sold the suit."

The manager is absolutely elated, but noticing the condition the guy's clothes are in, the manager asks, "Did you have a lot of resistance from the customer?"

The guy says, "No, I didn't have any trouble from the customer, but I got some major resistance from his seeing eye dog."

My son knows a salesman who has a hundred suits . . . and they're all pending.

—Myron Cohen

Further Reading:
Not Bogged Down in Reality, Jason Rainbows

■ School

My school was so tough when the kids had their school picture taken, there was one taken from the front and one from the side.

—Norm Crosby

My school was so tough that we had elections for school coroner.

My school was so tough the school newspaper had an obituary column.

—Norm Crosby

My grandson Jake's alibi for missing school for a week was not convincing, but at least it was original. He explained to his teacher, "I had intentional flu."

The reason you want your kids to pay attention in school is you haven't the faintest idea how to do their homework.

—Babs Bell Hajdusiewicz

Labor Day is a glorious holiday because your child will be going back to school the next day. It would have been called Independence Day, but that name was already taken.   —Bill Dodds

How about the kid whose teacher told him to write a hundred-word essay on what he did during summer vacation? He wrote, "Not much" fifty times.   —H. Aaron Cohl

Extract from a schoolgirl's letter to home: "We all have to have a dictionary here, so I have asked for one to be ordered for me. I hope you don't mind. Apparently Miss Foster thinks they are essensual."

Teacher: Which great event took place in 1809?
Leslie: Lincoln was born.
Teacher: Correct. Now someone tell me what happened in 1812.
Leslie: Lincoln had his third birthday.

Collected from grade school exam papers many years ago:

- There's a big difference between *M* and *N*. Take the word *acme*. With three loops you're at the top, but with two loops you only have pimples.
- Some wine is made by stomping on grapes. This kind of wine is called squash.
- A prune is a plum that didn't take care of itself.
- Obstetrics is a disease my ma catches every year.
- The Indians never smiled at white men, but they had plenty of fun in their teehees.
- Bison roamed the great plains for years under the name of buffalo. Despite this trick they were practically extincted.
- The War of 1812 was fought between American and England in 1776.
- French policemen often disguise themselves as gendarmes.
- Trousers is an uncommon noun because it is singular on top and plural on the bottom.
- Napoleon wanted children, but since Josephine was baroness, she couldn't bare any.

I had a terrible education. I attended a school for emotionally disturbed teachers.
—Woody Allen

The kids at a prep school in West Palm Beach have a sense of humor. A new teacher, determined to impress the boys with the fact that he meant business, wound up his first session by reminding them, "It's going to take more than just the proverbial apple a day to get by in *this* class." So the next morning they brought him a watermelon.
—Bennett Cerf

We've been having some trouble with the school bus. It keeps bringing the kids back.
—Bruce Lansky

I went to correspondence school. But they threw me out because I played hooky. . . . I sent them an empty envelope.
—Baron Munchausen (Jack Pearl)

The Olympia, Washington, *Daily World* offers five signs that your child's preschool doesn't meet quality standards:
1. The kids learn their numbers by counting the teacher's tattoos.
2. It becomes a vocabulary lesson when the kids hear the janitor after he hits his thumb with a hammer.
3. Kids learn eye-hand coordination by playing pin the tail on the Pamela Lee poster.
4. For show and tell, the school brought in the guy who stocks the cigarette machine.
5. A science project involves things kids find in their afternoon milk.

—Quoted in *Los Angeles Times*

I had the worst study habits, the lowest grades . . . then I found out what I was doing wrong. I was highlighting with a black Magic Marker.

—Jeff Altman

Child to father looking over straight-A report card: "You said you wanted to see a good report card—so I brought home Billie Wilson's."

—H. Bosch in the *National Enquirer*

George Orwell, author of the memorable *1984*, once told an interviewer that the principal reason he wrote books was that his old fifth-grade teacher might see his work and be remorseful that she'd misjudged him.

—Bennett Cerf

In elementary school, in case of fire you have to line up quietly in a single file line from smallest to tallest. What is the logic? Do tall people burn slower?

—Warren Hutcherson

Our bombs are smarter than the average high school student. At least they can find Kuwait.

—A. Whitney Brown

When I finished school I took one of those career aptitude tests, and based on my verbal ability score, they suggested I become a mime.

—Tim Cavanagh

Further Reading:
The Truancy Problem, Marcus Absent
How to Succeed in School, Rita Book
Kindergarten Kop II, Bea Hayve

■ Science

Every great scientific truth goes through three stages. First, people say it conflicts with the Bible. Next, they say it has been discovered before. Lastly, they say they have always believed it.   —Louis Agassiz

Drilling fifty yards deep, German scientists discovered small pieces of copper in core samples taken at several sites in their country. After studying the bits of metal, they announced that 25,000 years ago, ancient Germans had a nationwide telephone network.

Naturally, the British didn't want to be outdone. British scientists dug even deeper and found small pieces of glass. After some study, they announced that 35,000 years ago, ancient Brits had a nationwide fiber-optic network.

French scientists were outraged. They dug 100, 200, then 300 yards deep, but found nothing except dirt and rock. Finally they announced proudly that 55,000 years ago, the ancient French used cellular phones.   —Pat Patel

A freshman at Eagle Rock Junior High won first prize at the Greater Idaho Falls Science Fair. He was attempting to show how conditioned we have become to alarmists practicing junk science and spreading fear of everything in our environment. In his project he urged people to sign a petition demanding strict control or total elimination of the chemical dihydrogen monoxide. And for plenty of good reasons, since:

- It can cause excessive sweating and vomiting.
- It is a major component in acid rain.
- It can cause severe burns in its gaseous state.
- Accidental inhalation can kill you.
- It contributes to erosion.
- It decreases effectiveness of automobile brakes.
- It has been found in tumors of terminal cancer patients.

He asked fifty people if they supported a ban of the chemical. Forty-three said yes, six were undecided, and only one knew that the chemical was water. The title of his prize winning project was "How Gullible Are We?"

Further Reading:

Mineralogy for Giants, Chris Tall

The Bird Collection, Arnie Thologie

Robots, Anne Droid

Nuclear Power Bafflement, Ken Fusion

Artificial Weightlessness, Andy Gravity

Cloning, Ima Dubble II

■ Sermons

When I was pastor of the Little Brown Church, I was greatly annoyed by Karl Neufeld, an elderly member, who fell asleep during my sermon every Sunday. So, after service one day, I said to his grandson who always accompanied the senior citizen, "If you can keep the old man awake, I'll pay you a dollar."

This worked for two weeks; the aged man was very alert and listened to the sermons attentively. On the third Sunday, however, there he was, up to his old tricks, sound asleep in his pew.

After the service I called the boy over and said, "I am disappointed in you. Didn't I promise you a dollar a week to keep your grandfather awake?"

"Yes," replied the boy, "but Grandpa gives me five not to disturb him."

A cautious minister ended his sermon with the words, "The sinners referred to in my sermon are fictitious. Any similarity to members of this congregation is strictly coincidental."

A very wise minister surprised his congregation one sweltering mid-summer Sunday morning with this announcement: "Friends, I have here in my hands a hundred-dollar sermon that lasts ten minutes, a fifty-dollar sermon that lasts twenty minutes, and a twenty-dollar sermon that lasts a full hour. We will now take up the collection and see which one I will deliver."   —Bennett Cerf

Young Rabbi Klein finally summoned courage to complain to the richest member of his congregation, "I hesitate to bring this up, but do you always fall asleep while I'm preaching?"

"Look," was the reassuring reply, "would I sleep if I didn't trust you?"

The archbishop had preached a rousing sermon on the beauties of married life. Two Irish ladies left the church feeling uplifted and contented. "'Tis a fine sermon His Reverence gave us this morning," observed one.

"That it was," agreed the other, "and I wish I knew as little about the matter as he does."   —Bennett Cerf

Dr. Tom Walters, a highly successful minister renowned for his preaching, was admonishing a class of seminary students on the importance of making the facial expressions harmonize with the speech in delivering sermons.

"When you speak of heaven," he said, "let your face light up and be irradiated with a heavenly gleam. Let your eyes shine with reflected glory. And when you speak of hell," he continued, staring intently at his audience, turning his head from side to side in order to make eye contact with each one, "well, then your everyday face will do."

One Sunday, the first day of daylight saving time, a sleepy-eyed congregation watched the young priest ascend the pulpit in a Washington church. Not looking too wide-awake himself, he began, "As you all know, we lost an hour last night because of daylight-saving time. I don't know which hour you lost, but I lost the hour in which I usually write my sermon."

He returned to the altar and continued the service.

A new preacher was assigned to a piddling backwoods church. His first sermon, condemning horse racing, fell flat. A deacon admonished him, "You reckless young fool, this area is noted for its fine horses, and many members of this very congregation earn their livelihood in the sport of kings."

The next week, the new preacher enlarged upon the evils of smoking only to incur the wrath of tobacco growers thereabouts.

And the third Sunday, when he ranted about the evils of whiskey drinking, he discovered there was a big distillery less than five miles from his church.

Frustrated, he wailed, "What *can* I preach about here?"

"Preach against them heathen witch doctors," advised the deacon. "There ain't one of them within a thousand miles of us!"

—Bennett Cerf

As Sunday neared, old Reverend Gelder grew desperate, for he couldn't think of a subject for his sermon. His wife suggested that he be modern and preach about water-skiing, so he agreed.

Sunday came and Mrs. Gelder—ill with a virus—remained at home. As the minister drove to church, his doubts about parables in water-skiing increased. Finally, he decided to drop the subject completely, and instead delivered a brilliant, off-the-cuff sermon on sex.

Later that week, a member of the church met Mrs. Gelder in the supermarket and complimented her on her husband's magnificent sermon. "Where on earth did he get all that information?" she asked. "He seemed so sure of himself."

"I'm sure I don't know," replied the minister's wife. "He only tried it twice and fell off both times."

—Larry Wilde

■ Sex

Four-year-old Scott to his sister, eight-year-old Marci: "Are you the opposite sex, or am I?"

Dear Abby: I'm a girl eleven years old. My mother and big sister keep telling me when I get older there is something they have to tell me. I think I know all about what they're going to tell me. I have heard it from friends. Should I tell my mother and sister now or should I wait awhile? Debby

    Dear Debby: Tell them now. It's time they knew.

My father taught me about the birds and the bees. He didn't know anything about girls.

—Joey Adams

Each week a New York youngster would bring home from Sunday school an illustrated card that dramatized one of the Ten Commandments. The first week showed people worshipping at church. Another week, to illustrate "Thou shalt not kill," the picture showed Cain in the act of slaying Abel.

    "I waited with considerable alarm for the seventh week," reports the child's father. "But fortunately, tact and delicacy prevailed. Under the caption 'Thou shalt not commit adultery' was a picture of a dairyman, leering villainously as he poured a huge pail of water into a can of milk!"

■ Shopping

If you want a man to come dress-shopping with you, pick a store that has a chair. Sometimes my husband and I go into a store that has a chair, but there is already a comatose man sitting there. I always bring a folding chair for these situations.

—Rita Rudner

Bargain: Something you can't use at a price you can't resist.

—Franklin P. Adams

TRANSLATIONS FROM SALESLADY INTO ENGLISH

If she says . . .	*It really means . . .*
"I'm afraid we really don't have anything quite like that."	You're a $19.95 girl prepared to spend $29.95 in an $89.95 store.
"Just look at the detailing."	The seams are sewed with thread.
"Just feel the body of that cloth."	It's thick material.
"Just see how that material drapes."	It's thin material.
"That material will wear like iron."	The store owner's mother is helping out for the day.
"I wouldn't lie. That's not for you."	The orange-and-green dress with the lavender bugle beads is too tight to get into.
"The new style? Styles aren't important, dear, it's what suits you."	They have some of last year's stock on hand.
"Madam, that dress (hat, coat, suit) is you!"	It fits and is not chartreuse or purple.

—Robert Paul Smith

I went up to the salesgirl. I said, "I'd like to see something cheap in a man's suit."

She said, "The mirror's on the left."

—Professor Backwards (Jimmy Edmondson)

Sign at a roadside antique shop: If you don't know what you want, we've got it!

I love to shop after a bad relationship. I buy a new outfit, and it makes me feel better. It just does. Sometimes if I see a really great outfit, I'll break up with someone on purpose. —Rita Rudner

I was in a supermarket, and I saw Paul Newman's face on salad dressing and spaghetti sauce. . . . I thought he was missing. —Bob Saget

Further Reading:
Off to Market, Tobias A. Pigg

■ Show Business

Ronald Reagan, speaking to a group of crusty old newspaper reporters, tried to illustrate how hard they are to impress: "You know, in the old days of vaudeville, it used to be that ambitious young vaudevillians would go into an old empty theater and try out in front of a blasé booking agent who'd be sitting there in one of the front seats with a cigar, all alone in the theater, watching them do their act—and he was very hard to please. One young fellow walked out to center stage. The agent asked him what he did, and the kid just took off and flew around the whole theater—made a couple of circles clear up to the ceiling, came back down, and landed back at the center of the stage. The agent says, 'What else do you do besides bird imitations?'"

—The Uncommon Wisdom of Ronald Reagan

A young salesman took a pretty model to see *A Streetcar Named Desire* at one of those off-Broadway theaters. As soon as they found their seats, the girl excused herself and looked for the powder room. Since the theater was in an old building, the poor girl wandered through winding corridors for several minutes until she finally found the place. It was empty except for a girl seated on a sofa. The model quickly fixed her make-up, adjusted the seams of her stocking, took a final glance in the mirror and with the remark, "I look a mess tonight," departed.

She went back into the corridor and found her way back to her seat. As soon as she arrived, she asked her date, "Did I miss much?"

"Not much," he told her. "One girl was sitting on a sofa, then another girl walked in, fixed her stockings, said 'I look a mess tonight,' and walked off."

—Myron Cohen

Comic actor Billy Crystal marked his fifth stint as master of ceremonies for the Academy Awards telecast in 1997. "I'm very excited to be back," he announced. "And I'd like to invite the Hollywood community to help me write the opening monologue. Send any Oscar jokes to my Web site at www.whyistheshowsolong.com."

SHOW-BIZ DICTIONARY

All rights reserved: Engagement ring.
Backstage: On opening night, a branch office of Western Union.
Film with a message: TV commercial.
Monday-morning quarterback: Returning the two bits borrowed Friday.
Rack and ruin: Hanging your coat in a night club.
Smoked ham: Actor fleeing a burning building.
Whodunit: Grammatically incorrect word for "whomdunit."

My uncle Joe was sitting at my dining room table, his head in his hands, looking haggard and dejected. "Uncle Joe," I said, "you look terrible. What's the matter?"

Uncle Joe barely lifted his head as he answered, "Isaac, I'm tired of being a social outcast. I'm with the circus, you see, and clean up the animal cages. The result is that I can't help smelling a little. Naturally, people avoid me, and I don't like it."

"Well," I said, "I know what you mean, and I have to tell you that it's not the best fragrance in the world. But look here, there are openings down at the plywood mill in town. You could get a job there, and it would even pay more than your circus position."

"What!" said Uncle Joe, outraged. "And leave show business?"

—Isaac Asimov

If a farmer fills his barn with grain, he gets mice; if he leaves it empty, he gets actors.
—Bill Vaughan

Eddie Cantor pays tribute to raconteur George Golden: "I wouldn't say he's a ham, but he's the only man I know who uses cloves for shirt studs.

"Take the time he was in the middle of a speech, and a cat wandered onto the platform. Quickly Georgie said, 'Scat. This is a monologue, not a catalogue.'"

Teasing his friend Bob Hope, Ronald Reagan told an audience gathered for a Hope celebration, "He's entertained six presidents. He's performed for twelve."

Further Reading:
A Stuntman to the End, Kenny Doitt
Life as a Comic, Stan Dupp
My Career as a Clown, Abe Ozo

■ Signs of the Times
Sign on city employment-office door: Good girl wanted bad.

Sign in a Chicago gas station: Cubs bumper stickers removed here.

Posted outside an auto dealership in Waco, Texas: Too Hot to Haggle —Come in for a Shady Deal.

Printed on the back of a motorcyclist's leather jacket: If you can read this, my girlfriend fell off.
—Paul Harvey, ABC Radio Network

There's a big sign outside a laundry which says: Don't kill your wife—let us do your dirty work!   —Harry Hershfield

On the back of a private refuse disposer's truck: Satisfaction guaranteed or double your garbage refunded.

On the window of a loan company branch: We're here for the man who already has everything—and hasn't paid for it.

On a roadside near Atlantic City: Our hotel is so near the beach, we have to station a lifeguard in every room!

Hand-painted sign on snow-covered mountain road: Deluxe ski lodge one mile ahead. Eight doctors. No waiting.

On a horrible Ozark back road: Drive with extreme care. This road should be under construction.

In the window of a garage: Mechanic wanted. Must look honest.

Sign in Oregon repair shop: For sale—foreign sports car. Ask for Clyde, the guy with the cramped legs.

Some of the signs hung up by proprietors of musty country stores up New England way are a caution. A counter card in one emporium warned: Please do not play with the cranberries!

Another proclaimed: The cat is put out every night, and it is a lie that she sleeps on the prunes.   —Bennett Cerf

A sign on the locked door of a store in Vermont: I will be closed till 9:30 A.M., as I am being married at 9:00, and don't want to stop beforehand to count eggs or weigh out birdseed.

Foreign entrepreneurs evidently are getting into the act, too:
- A lady in Paris with a Left Bank studio to rent advertised: No bath. Suitable for author, artist, or actor.
- A sign on a Hong Kong restaurant proclaims: Best chop suey! American chef!
- In the window of a Moscow grocery store: Eat Soviet Brand Breakfast Goodies—or Else!

We dust our pies daily.

In big type: Sirloin Steak, 25¢.
In very small type below: With meat, $4.00.

Sign in Bismarck, North Dakota: Watch out for small children— especially when they're driving.

In a business office: This year's Christmas party has been canceled because of last year's Christmas party.

A used-book dealer in Brooklyn has a sign in his seldom washed window proclaiming, "My assets are over ten million dollars."

He isn't kidding, either. His office is directly above a branch of the Chase Manhattan Bank.   —Bennett Cerf

Customers wanted. No experience necessary.

Motto seen on the sweat shirt of a young woman exiting the physical-sciences building at California State University, Los Angeles: St. Andreas, Protect Us from Our Faults.

Near Woodlawn Cemetery: Second-hand tombstone for sale. Extraordinary bargain for family named Schwarzendorfer.

Sign on a restaurant tip jar: If you fear change, leave it here

In an optometrist's window: If you don't see what you want, you've come to the right place.

At a shop specializing in fireplace accessories: Anything your little hearth desires.

On the window of T. Ginsberg's Delicatessen: Mr. Ginsberg himself eats here.

In a Niagara Falls motel: Honeymooners treated with studied neglect.

On a British Columbia automobile association vehicle: Call us at any hour. We're always on our tows.

Near the busy terminal of a trucking firm in Paterson, New Jersey, a large billboard proclaimed: This Is a Trucking Company that Never Sleeps.

    Crayoned neatly beneath: And neither do its neighbors!

On electric-company truck: Let us remove your shorts.

Graffiti on the wall of a New York office building: Legalize Mental Telepathy.

Under it, someone has added: I knew you were going to say that.

At the entrance of the women's clothing section of a Detroit department store: Ladies Ready to Wear Clothes.

Underneath in bold masculine handwriting someone has added: It's about time!

Large sign at the entrance to the Million Dollar Museum in White's City, New Mexico: We do not have the gun that killed Billy the Kid. Two other museums have it.

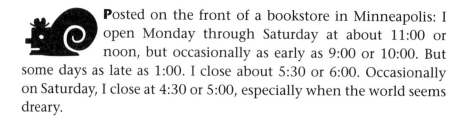

Posted on the front of a bookstore in Minneapolis: I open Monday through Saturday at about 11:00 or noon, but occasionally as early as 9:00 or 10:00. But some days as late as 1:00. I close about 5:30 or 6:00. Occasionally on Saturday, I close at 4:30 or 5:00, especially when the world seems dreary.

Sign above the washbasin in an office: Think!

Directly below, a small hand-lettered sign: Thoap!

■ Sin

A young boy went into the confessional and told the priest that he had thrown peanuts into the pond. The priest thought this was a strange little sin to confess to, but said nothing. The next small boy also confessed to throwing peanuts in the pond, and the next. Finally a very small boy came in, so the priest went ahead and said, "And did you throw peanuts in the river?"

"No, Father," said the kid. "I am Peanuts."

It says something about our times that we rarely use the word sinful, except to describe a really good dessert.

A minister, preaching on the danger of compromise, was condemning the attitude of so many Christians who believe certain things concerning their faith, but in actual practice will say, "Yes, but . . ." At the climax of the sermon, he said, "Yes, there are millions of Christians who are sliding straight to hell on their buts."

The congregation went into gales of laughter, and the minister promptly closed the service with a benediction.

Everything that used to be a sin is now a disease.   —Bill Maher

■ Sleep

Man is the only animal that goes to sleep when he's not sleepy and gets up when he is.

—Dave Gneiser, quoted by Bill Nelson in the *Milwaukee Journal-Sentinel*

> **E**arly to rise,
> Early to bed,
> Makes a man healthy,
> But socially dead!
>
> —Wade the Duck

Alfred Hitchcock, who loved to scare his movie audiences, often embarrassed his wife by going to sleep at parties. At one posh Hollywood gathering, he napped for two hours. Mrs. Hitchcock finally shook him surreptitiously. "I think we'd better go home!" she whispered crossly.

Alfred started, stared at his watch, and muttered, "Go? But it's only twelve-thirty—they'd think we weren't enjoying ourselves."

Sometimes I wake up grumpy. Other times, I let him sleep.

To achieve the impossible dream, try going to sleep.   —Joan Klemper

Two men met. "Gee, I can't sleep at all," complained one.
    "Why don't you count sheep?" suggested the other.
    "I can't count sheep," confessed the complaining one. "I'm near-sighted—I have to count elephants."   —Joe Laurie Jr.

Naps are wonderful, aren't they? Sometimes I have to take a nap to get ready for bed.   —Marsha Warfield

The amount of sleep required by the average person is about ten minutes more.   —Los Angeles Times Syndicate

One good turn usually gets the whole blanket.   —Tom Griffin

Further Reading:
I Hate Monday Mornings, Gaetan Oop
Noise Is Forbidden!, Nada Loud

■ Small Towns

My hometown was so small the local Baskin Robbins had only one flavor.   —Vaughn Meader

Life is a little slower when you live in a small town. For example, the rush hour traffic reports are reported in the weekly newspaper.   —Ron Dentinger

It was such a small town, we didn't even have a village idiot. We had to take turns.
—Billie Holiday

It's such a little town our radio station can't identify itself. It's off the air now. Somebody tripped over the tower.
—Donna Jean Young

It was a small town: Ferguson, Ohio. When you entered there was a big sign which said, "Welcome to Ferguson. Beware of the Dog." The all-night drugstore closed at noon.
—Jackie Vernon

Comedian Herb Shriner spent his boyhood in an Indiana hamlet so tiny that it was located between the first and second line on a Burma Shave ad. "I had to travel to the next town," Herb asserted, "to discover how the poem came out."

It was a little town—when I was a kid we used to play Monopoly on it.
—Donna Jean Young

I pulled into this town called Weedpatch. I check into the Weedpatch Hotel; they give me a *Key* magazine with all the events going on in town. I open it up—there's a picture of me checking into the Weedpatch Hotel.
—Monica Piper

Is it likely that all the people who are described as missing are living together in a small town somewhere?
—George Carlin

The town was so small that it had only one yellow page.
—Orson Bean

Former Arizona congressman Mo Udall grew up in St. Johns, Arizona (which then had a population of 1,400), a town so small that the entering and leaving signs were hung from the same post. He was fond of joking, "A friend was nine years old before he found out that our town was not named 'Resume Speed.'" —Bob Dole

■ Smoking

Buying cigarettes becomes an interview now. I said to the salesgirl in back of the counter. "I'd like a carton of cigarettes."

She said, "There are so many brands, what would you like?"

I said, "Give me a carton of Brand X, they're not doing too good."

She said, "Soft pack or the crush-proof box?"

"Soft pack."

"King size or regular?"

"King size."

"Filter tip or plain?"

"Filter tip."

"Menthol or mint?"

"Menthol."

"Is this cash or credit?"

I said, "Forget it, I broke the habit!" —Bob Melvin

Sign posted in a bed and breakfast: Don't smoke in bed. The next ashes that hit the floor may be your own.

Further Reading:

Smoker's Cough, Nick O'Teen

■ Software Engineers

TOP ENGINEERS' TERMS AND EXPRESSIONS

When they say . . .	*They really mean . . .*
"A number of different approaches are being tried."	We are still guessing at this point.
"We're applying close project coordination."	We sat down and had coffee together.
"An extensive report is being prepared on a fresh approach."	We just hired three punk kids out of school.
"Major technological break-through!"	It works so-so; but *looks* very hi-tech!
"Customer satisfaction is believed assured."	We are so far behind schedule, the customer will take anything.
"Preliminary operational tests were inconclusive."	The darn thing blew up when we threw the switch.
"Test results were extremely gratifying!"	Unbelievable, it actually worked!
"The entire concept will have to be abandoned."	The only guy who understood the thing quit.
"It is in process."	It is so wrapped in red tape that the situation is completely hopeless.
"Please note and initial."	Let's spread the responsibility for this.

A software engineer and a kindergarten teacher are sitting next to each other on a long flight from L.A. to New York. The software engineer leans over to her, introduces himself, asks her name and what she does for a living, and asks if she would like to play a fun game. The kindergarten teacher just wants to take a nap, so she politely declines and rolls over to the window to catch a few winks.

The software engineer persists and explains that the game is really easy and very entertaining. He explains, "I ask you a question, and if you don't know the answer, you pay me five dollars, and visa-versa." Again, she politely declines and tries to get some sleep. The software engineer, now somewhat agitated, says, "Okay, if you don't know the answer you pay me five dollars, and if I don't know the answer, I will pay you fifty dollars!"

This offer catches the kindergarten teacher's attention, and figuring that there will be no end to this torment unless she plays, she agrees to the game.

The software engineer asks the first question. "What's the distance from the earth to the moon?"

The kindergarten teacher doesn't say a word, reaches in to her purse, pulls out a five-dollar bill and hands it to the software engineer. Now, it's her turn. She asks the software engineer, "What goes up a hill with three legs, and comes down with four?"

The software engineer looks at her, puzzled. He takes out his laptop computer and searches all his references. He taps into the Airphone with his modem and searches the Net and the Library of Congress. Frustrated, he sends e-mails to all his coworkers and friends he knows. All to no avail. After over an hour, he wakes the kindergarten teacher and hands her fifty dollars.

The kindergarten teacher politely takes the fifty dollars and turns away to get back to sleep.

The software engineer, who is more than a little miffed, wakes the kindergarten teacher and asks, "Well, so what *is* the answer!?"

Without a word, the kindergarten teacher reaches into her purse, hands the software engineer five dollars, and goes back to sleep.

An applicant for a job in a computer laboratory listed among his qualifications: "I graduated first in my class at MIT. I turned down a vice presidency at IBM. Money means nothing to me, so I don't care what salary I get. And I'm prepared to work sixty-five hours a week."

"Lordy," gasped the superintendent. "Haven't you *any* weaknesses?"

"Just one," admitted the applicant after some reflection. "I'm a terrible liar!"

—Bennett Cerf

Q: How many computer programmers does it take to change a light bulb?

1: Three. One to change it, one to write a manual, and one to work on the upgrade.

2: None. It's a hardware problem.

3: None. It's not a bug, it's a feature.

4: One, but if he changes it, the whole building will probably fall down.

5: Two. One always leaves in the middle of the project.

■ Speeches

Rising to speak after a flowery introduction, President Lyndon Johnson quipped, "I wish my parents were here to hear that introduction. My father would have enjoyed it. And my mother would have believed it."

To a Los Angeles crowd, while campaigning in 1960, John F. Kennedy began his remarks, "I appreciate your welcome. As the cow said to the Maine farmer, 'Thank you for a warm hand on a cold morning.'"

Accepting an award for his humanitarian work, after an embarrassing flowery introduction, Jack Benny said, "I don't deserve this, but I have arthritis, and I don't deserve that either."

Elizabeth and I had hoped to have an opportunity to add our Kansas and North Carolina touches to the White House beginning on January 20, 1997, but that was not to be. I did, however, have the chance to visit the White House three days earlier, when President Clinton honored me by presenting me with the Presidential Medal of Freedom. After President Clinton placed the medal around my neck, I began my remarks by saying, "I, Robert J. Dole, do solemnly swear—oh, sorry, wrong speech."

I added that I had hoped that instead of a medal President Clinton would be giving me the key to the front door.   —Bob Dole

Calvin Coolidge was a master at finding excuses for not speaking. At one whistle stop during his campaign for election he appeared on the observation platform, sized up the crowd, and ducked back into his private car. "This crowd," he said, "is too big for an anecdote and too small for an oration."   —Art Linkletter

A distinguished commentator is one whose predictions are forgotten by the time circumstances prove them wrong.

When Calvin Coolidge occupied the White House, he ducked reporters so consistently that one day they formed a conspiracy against him. Before a conference to which he reluctantly agreed, each one wrote out precisely the same question: "Are you going to run again in 1928?"

Coolidge read each slip carefully, without comment or change of expression, then threw them all in the trash basket. "Gentlemen," he said, "the only question in this lot I care to answer today concerns public schools in Puerto Rico." He then delivered a fifteen-minute talk on the subject, full of statistics. The reporters never tried that trick on him again.   —Bennett Cerf

Will Rogers was once toastmaster at a charity luncheon. There were so many important speakers that a time limit of five minutes had to be imposed. However, one speaker droned on for nearly half an hour and finally said, "I am sorry, Mr. Toastmaster, that I went beyond the limit, but I left my watch at home."

Responded Will, "Don't you even have a pocket calendar?"

Radio/TV personality Art Linkletter had just asked an audience of forty-five hundred people in McCormick Place in Chicago to rise and salute the flag. A hush fell over the crowded dining room. At just that moment, a prolonged, reverberating crash occurred backstage, as some waiter fell with a large tray full of dishes. When the noise subsided, Linkletter turned to the waiting audience and ad-libbed: "The termites holding up the building must have unlocked their arms to salute along with us."

Asked to limit a commencement speech to twelve minutes, Hubert Humphrey, "The last time I spoke for only twelve minutes was when I said hello to my mother."

Muriel Humphrey cautioned her husband, "Hubert, a speech, to be immortal, doesn't have to be eternal."

In the time of Nero, when Romans often crowded the Coliseum to see Christians tossed to the lions, there was one victim who had given authorities untold trouble before he was rounded up. Nero starved eleven of his most ferocious lions for a full week to assure a juicy performance when they were turned on this Christian.

Eighty thousand spectators turned out. The Christian stood alone in the center of the arena, calm and unafraid. The first lion was released and rushed at the Christian. The crowd wetted its lips. But then an amazing thing happened. The Christian bent down and whispered in the lion's ear. The lion put his tail between his legs, lowered his head, and slinked out of the arena.

When six more half-starved kings of the forest did the same, the crowd began to holler for its money back. An angry Nero summoned the Christian and curtly said, "If you will tell me what you say to those lions to make them act that way, I will grant you a full pardon."

"It's simple, Nero," explained the Christian. "I just whisper in their ears: 'Remember, you'll be expected to say a few words after dinner!'"

—Bennett Cerf

■ Sports

One day, I'm gonna finally get up enough courage to actually go skydiving, rather than just being thrown out of the plane like last time.   —LeMel Hebert-Williams

A fellow went to see a Gypsy fortuneteller. "Let me see your crystal ball," he said. She showed it to him. "You've got two holes in it," he remarked in surprise.

"Yes," she replied. "I go bowling nights."   —Joe Laurie Jr.

"Wayne Gretzky is the first person to appear on a can of Campbell's Soup," says Jay Leno. "That makes sense, to put a hockey player on a can of soup. It's probably the only thing you can eat without teeth."   —*The Tonight Show*, NBC

Let me get this straight: the networks won't give gavel-to-gavel coverage of political conventions because they're too dull, but fight for the privilege of broadcasting all laps of the Indianapolis 500?   —Roger Simon

I've got a friend who is a boxer. Once he hung up his coat in a restaurant, but he was afraid someone would run off with it. He hung a note on it reading, "This coat belongs to the champion boxer of the world, and I'll be back."

When he came back, he found another note hanging where the coat had been. This note said, "This coat was taken by the champion runner of the world, and I won't be back!"   —Ed Wynn

Late September is the time of year when the owner of a swimming pool discovers he's not as popular as he thought he was.

—Gilbert Vail

Violent, televised hockey is the chief cause of prison riots in this country. Think about it: You're a convict sitting in your cell at the federal penitentiary watching a hockey player on TV get a two-minute penalty. You're serving seventeen years for the same offense.

—Jeff Cesario

Bowling has one advantage over golf. You very rarely lose a ball.

Ditsy Baummortal went duck shooting with old Uncle George Terwilliger. A flock of ducks flew overhead, and Uncle George took a potshot at them and one fell down on the beach—dead. Ditsy walked over and looked at it. "Hey, Uncle George," he said. "That was a waste of ammunition to shoot that duck. The fall alone would have killed it."

—"Senator" Ed Ford

I used to go fishing until it struck me. You can buy fish. What the heck am I doing in a boat at four-thirty in the morning? If I want a hamburger, I don't track cattle down.

—Kenny Potchenson

Great Reading on Sports:
I Love Bullfighting, Matt Adore
En Garde!, Drew Blood
What You Need for Archery, Beau N. Arrow
Shaky Knees, Cliff Diver
Flips and Tumbles, Jim Nastics
Fish Story, Rod Enreel
A Boxing Cornerman's Story, Dawson DeTowel
Care for a Chop?, Marsha Larts
Joe Wins at a Track Meet, C. Howie Runns
How I Won the Marathon, Randy Hoelway
The L.A. Lakers' Breakfast, Kareem O'Wheat
Russian Tennis Shoes, Ivan Odor
Personal Best, Marco DeStinction
Pull with All You've Got!, Eve Ho
I Win!, U. Lose

■ Stress

I read this article that said the typical symptoms of stress are eating too much, smoking too much, impulse buying, and driving too fast. Are they kidding? This is my idea of a great day!   —Monica Piper

Talk about stress. I'll tell you how much stress there is in my life. You know those coin changers that hang on your belt? I got one that dispenses Rolaids.   —Ron Dentinger

FOR WOMEN ONLY:
SIGNS THAT YOU'RE UNDER TOO MUCH STRESS

- Everyone around you has an attitude problem.
- You're adding chocolate chips to your cheese omelet
- The dryer has shrunk every last pair of your jeans.
- Your husband is suddenly agreeing to everything you say.
- You're using your cellular phone to dial up every bumper sticker that says: How's my driving? Call 1-800-***-****.
- Everyone's head looks like an invitation to batting practice.
- You're counting down the days until menopause.
- You're sure that everyone is scheming to drive you crazy.
- The ibuprofen bottle is empty, and you bought it yesterday.

Further Reading:

How to Overcome Stress, R. E. Lachs
I Hit the Wall, Isadore There

■ Success

If at first you don't succeed, try, try, a couple of times more. Then quit. There's no sense making a fool of yourself.   —W. C. Fields

If at first you don't succeed, destroy all evidence that you tried.
                                                                    —Newt Heilscher

Whenever I go to those motivational success seminars, I am amazed at all the people who drive up in new Mercedes and BMWs. How much more success does a person need?   —Adam Christling

My success has allowed me to strike out with a higher class of women.   —Woody Allen

He's never been very successful. When opportunity knocks, he complains about the noise.   —H. Aaron Cohl

THE TWO RULES FOR SUCCESS:
1. Never tell all you know.

■ Sunday School
The biggest problem I face while teaching Sunday school is convincing the preschoolers that Barney is not God.   —Robert G. Lee

My grandsons, Jonathan and Jake, attend Sunday school regularly. So I asked them which story in the Bible they liked best. Without hesitating, Jake replied, "That one about the multitude—you know, the multitude that loafs and fishes."

A Naval officer asked his small daughter what she had learned at Sunday school. "We studied about the Ten Commanders," she reported. "We learned they are always broke."

The Sunday school teacher asked her class, "Does anyone know who lived in the Garden of Eden?"

"I do, teacher," said little Mary. "It was the Addams Family."

The Sunday school teacher was describing how Lot's wife looked back and turned into a pillar of salt, when little Jimmy interrupted. "My mother looked back once while she was driving," he announced triumphantly, "and she turned into a telephone pole!"

Two youngsters were walking home from Sunday school after hearing a lesson on the devil. One little boy was overheard saying to the other, "What do you think about all this devil business?"

The other youngster replied thoughtfully, "Well, you know how Santa Claus turned out. It's probably just your dad."

■ Swearing

Swearing was invented as a compromise between running away and fighting.

—Finley Peter Dunne

Mark Twain's vocabulary contained a good number of swear words that he used regularly, despite the protests of his wife. One day after Twain had used them all while cutting himself shaving, Mrs. Twain accurately repeated every swear word, just to show Twain how terrible he sounded. Twain calmly told her, "You have the words, dear, but you don't know the tune."

President Harry S Truman was a Missourian with a straightforward, plain manner of speaking. When he made a speech at the Washington Garden Club, he kept referring to the "good manure" that needed to be used on the flowers.

Some of the women members complained to his wife, Bess. "Couldn't you get the president to say 'fertilizer'?" they asked.

Mrs. Truman's reply: "Heavens no. It took me twenty-five years to get him to say 'manure.'"

The minister was whaling away with his niblick, trying to get out of the sand trap. Finally he lofted the ball, only to have it go over the green into a trap on the far side. Red-faced and exasperated, he turned to the other members of the foursome and said, "Won't one of you laymen please say a few appropriate words?"

As Benjamin Franklin exclaimed upon discovering electricity, "Ouch!"

■ Talk, Talk, Talk

We need a twelve-step group for compulsive talkers. They could call it On Anon Anon.

—Paula Poundstone

A good answer is what you think of later.

—Sam Ewing

Sid was a non-stop talker. When his wife Lulu became ill, the doctor said, "I prescribe absolute quiet for your wife. Here's a bottle of sleeping pills."

"When do I give them to her?" asked Sid.

"You don't give them to her," said the doctor. "You take them yourself."

Secret: Something you tell one person at a time.

Loquacious Vice President Hubert Humphrey won the hearts of all the ladies at a Women's National Press dinner when, on the eve of Inauguration Day, he told them, tongue-in-cheek, "President Johnson has given me only two instructions for the next four years. Number one is that I must keep my eyes open. As for number two—well, I don't think I have to mention that!"

—Bennett Cerf

If nobody ever said anything unless he knew what he was talking about, a ghastly hush would descend upon the earth.   —Alan Herbert

Young lawyer Abraham Lincoln once said of another lawyer who talked excessively but never had anything worth saying: "That man can pack the most words into the least ideas of any man I know."

Heiress/poetess Martha Fritz tells this incident from her youth in Boston: In announcing the church's new public address system, the pastor told the congregation that the microphone and wiring had been paid for out of church funds. Then he added, "The loud-speaker has been donated by a member of the congregation in memory of his wife."   —Larry Wilde

No one in the twentieth century marshaled the English language better than Winston Churchill. Presented with an official document of stupefying verbosity, he protested, "This paper, by its very length, defends itself against the risk of being read."   —Bob Dole

Further Reading:
. . . *And Shut Up!,* Sid Downe

■ Taxes
The politician's promises of yesterday are the taxes of today.
                                      —Mackenzie King

There is no truth to the rumor that our local IRS manager is writing a potential best seller called *How We Collected $1,800,000 from the Fellow Who Wrote a Book about Making $2,000,000 in the Stock Market.*

Will Rogers stated that the American tax code produced more liars than anything but golf.

What gets me is that estimated tax return. You have to guess how much you're gonna make. You have to fill it out, fix it up, sign it, send it in. I sent mine in last week. I didn't sign it. If I have to guess how much I'm gonna make, let them guess who sent it.

—Professor Backwards (Jimmy Edmondson)

Income tax returns are the most imaginative fiction being written today.
—Herman Wouk

Last year about three thousand taxpayers erroneously received word from the IRS that they each owed some $300 million in taxes. Corrections and apologies followed. Then, in April, Lorie Marling of Columbus, Ohio, got a tax bill for $270 billion. The IRS did graciously offer to let her pay it in three $90 billion installments.

An IRS agent to an agitated taxpayer: "Yes, Mr. Handelmeier, I'm afraid we *do* want to make a federal case out of it."

Pastor at the offering: "And now, brethren, let us all give in accordance with what we reported on Form 1040."

I'm not sure what I should do about my taxes this year. The way I've got it figured . . . if I use the short form, the government gets my money. And if I use the long form, my accountant gets it.
—Ron Dentinger

HOW TO MESS WITH THE IRS

 My friend Irv hates to pay his taxes. (Who doesn't?) He also loves to get revenge on the Internal Revenue Service. Here are his instructions on how to mess with the IRS:

- Always put staples in the right hand corner. Go ahead and put a row down the whole right side. The extractors who remove the mail from the envelopes have to take out any staples in the right side.
- Never arrange paperwork in the right order, or even facing the right way. Put a few upside down and backwards. That way they have to remove all your staples, rearrange your paperwork, and re-staple it (on the left side).
- Line the bottom of your envelope with Elmer's glue and let it dry before you put in your forms, so that the automated opener doesn't open it and the extractor has to open it by hand.
- If you're very unfortunate and have to pay taxes, use a two or three party check. On top of paying with a three party check pay one of the dollars you owe in cash. When an extractor receives cash, no matter how small an amount, he has to take it to a special desk and fill out a few nasty forms.
- Write a little letter of appreciation. Any letter received has to be read and stamped regardless of what it's about. Write your letter on something misshapen and unconventional, like on the back of a grocery bag.
- When you mail it, mail it in a big envelope (even if it's just a single little form). Big envelopes have to be torn and sorted differently than regular business size ones. An added bonus to the big envelope is that they take priority over other mail, so the workers can hurry up and deal with your mess.
- If you send two checks, they'll have to staple your unsightly envelope to your half-destroyed form.
- Always put extra paper clips on your forms. Any foreign fasteners or the like have to be removed and put away.
- Sign your name in ink on every page. Any signature has to verified and then date stamped.

These are just a few of the fun and exciting things you can do. These methods are recommended only when you owe money.

■ Teachers

A schoolteacher was conducting her class. "What's the opposite of misery?" she asked a pupil.

"Joy!" was the quick reply.

"Correct," she said. "Now what's the opposite of sorrow?"

"Happiness," answered the pupil.

"Correct," she said. "Now what's the opposite of woe?"

Snapped the pupil, "Giddyap!"

—"Senator" Ed Ford

Teacher to colleagues in faculty lounge: "It worked! I told them that the multiplication table was none of their business, and they learned it in a week."

—Hoest, *Parade*

I think a secure profession for young people is to become a history teacher, because in the future, there will be so much more of it to teach.

—Bill Muse

Teacher: Use "conscience stricken" in a sentence.

Jonathan: Don't conscience strickens before they're hatched.

A teacher, offering three reasons for entering her profession: "June, July and August."

■ Technology

Habitual dependence on automation can lead to atrophy of the brain. Incredible as it seems, this news item appeared in the papers after the last blackout: "During the power failure many people complained of having gotten stuck for hours on escalators."

—Sam Levenson

Sometimes technology isn't good. I tried to pray the other day and got God's voice mail.

Fax machine: A device that allows someone in another state to pile work on your desk.
                                                        —*Mrs. Webster's Guide to Business*

The Japanese are threatening to retaliate in the ongoing trade war by making VCRs even more difficult to program.   —Dennis Miller

That new machine is so complex that our office has a problem producing a document that is important enough to feed into it.

We have office machines that perform things today that yesterday weren't even worth doing.

Cordless phones are great. If you can find them.   —Glenn Foster

There's a brand-new invention for people who want to relax in an atmosphere of peace and tranquillity. It's a phoneless cord.

Putt's Law: Technology is dominated by two types of people; those who understand what they do not manage, and those who manage what they do not understand.
Putt's-Brook's Law: Adding manpower to a late technology project only makes it later.

A refrigerator runs by converting the dust behind it into a peculiar mutant, reptilian substance.   —Colin McEnroe

Technological progress has merely provided us with more efficient means of going backward.   —Robert Maynard Hutchins

We spend one-third of our lives sleeping, one-third working, and one-third waiting for the beep.

When microwave ovens didn't exist . . . did people sit around in an emotional vacuum saying, "Heat is so boring. I wish I could bombard a potato with mutant intergalactic energy"? —Colin McEnroe

Voice mail is the technological upchuck of the age. —Herb Caen

Did you hear about the high-tech ventriloquist? He can throw his voice mail.

Quality control has determined that most errors are not serious, unless you're the one who bought that product.

Further Reading:
What's Your Invention?, Pat Tent
The Ham Radio Primer, Loudon Clear

■ Teenagers

Remember that as a teenager, you are in the last stage of your life where you will be happy to hear that the phone is for you.
—Fran Lebowitz

My neighbor Everett finally hit upon a way to get his sixteen-year-old son to mow the lawn. Ev explained, "I told him I lost the car keys in the tall grass."

Father: It says here in the newspaper that teenagers today are smug and condescending.
Son: Well, duh!
—Stivers in *Funny Times*

When my son was a teenager, he used to talk on the telephone for over an hour at a time. One day, when the phone rang, he picked it up and surprised me by hanging up after only half an hour. I asked him how come. He said, "It was a wrong number."

If Abraham's son had been a teenager, it wouldn't have been a sacrifice.

—Scott Spendlove

Puberty is the stage children reach that gets parents to start worrying about pregnancy all over again.　　　—Joyce Armor

After two weeks of unceasing rain it became obvious that the Red River was about to overflow its banks. My friend Herb, a computer programmer and a longtime resident whose homestead bordered the river, packed up his teenage son Herb Jr., and sent him to his uncle in Chicago, asking that he be taken care of until the situation righted itself.

A few days later Herb received an urgent e-mail message that read, "Am returning your son immediately. Send along the flood."

In high school I had my hair spiked up so high somebody put a sign on my back: "Do Not Back Up—Severe Tire Damage!"

—University of Southern California speech major

No need to worry about your teenagers when they're not at home. A national survey revealed that they all go to the same place: "out." And they all do the same thing: "nothing."　　　—Bruce Lansky

A babysitter is a teenager who gets five dollars an hour to eat ten dollars' worth of your food.　　　—Henny Youngman

Between the ages of twelve and seventeen a parent can age thirty years.

—Sam Levenson

A babysitter is a teenage girl you hire to let your children do whatever they want.
—Henny Youngman

My niece Wendy came to visit us a few years ago. Wendy was one of those prematurely world-weary, almost impossible-to-impress teenagers. I knew she was a big Mel Gibson fan, so I took her to see him in the title role of Shakespeare's *Hamlet*. As we left the theater, I asked her what she thought of the film.

"Really," she said, "I don't know why people rave about it. It's nothing but a bunch of quotations strung together."

Mother Nature is providential. She gives us twelve years to develop a love for our children before turning them into teenagers.
—William Galvin

About to be escorted to her first formal dance, a darling teenager, in a dither of excitement, whirled in to show her mother and father how she looked in her brand-new dress. "It must be all right," she reported later to her best friend. "Neither of them can stand it."
—Bennett Cerf

I never met anyone who didn't have a very smart child. What happens to these children, you wonder, when they reach adulthood?
—Fran Lebowitz

There isn't a child who has gone out into the brave new world who doesn't eventually return to the old homestead carrying a bundle of dirty clothes.
—Art Buchwald

There is nothing wrong with teenagers that reasoning with them won't aggravate.

■ Television

A cynical college lecturer was heard to exclaim, "The subject of my talk this afternoon is air pollution—sometimes known as television."

Had it not been for Thomas A. Edison, people today would be watching television by candlelight.   —Dave Gardner

People used to live lives of quiet desperation. Now they go on talk shows.   —Bob Thaves, Newspaper Enterprise Association

Bumper sticker: Friends don't let friends watch *Friends*.

On a TV show, Merv Griffin was asked by a guest, "Where's a good place to go if you find yourself in New York in February?"
   Merv's prompt reply: "Barbados."   —Bennett Cerf

Early to bed and early to rise, you'll miss Leno, Letterman, and all of those guys.   —*Nuggets*

Television—a medium, so called because it is neither rare nor well done.
                                                        —Ernie Kovacs

I wish there was a knob on the TV to turn up the intelligence. There's a knob called brightness, but it doesn't work.
                                                     —Eugene Gallagher

Television is an invention that permits you to be entertained in your living room by people you wouldn't have in your home.
                                                          —David Frost

Ninety-eight percent of American homes have TV sets—which means the people in the other 2 percent of the households have to generate their own sex and violence.

—Franklin P. Jones

"**L**ast year was the fortieth anniversary of the most effective birth-control device in history," says comedian Jay Leno. "The TV remote control."

—*The Tonight Show*, NBC

YOU WON'T HEAR THIS ON TV . . .

- "Since absolutely nothing interesting happened today, we're just going to give you the weather and call it a night."
- "Now that I've had a few minutes to consider it, Mr. Springer, I think my wife has a valid point."
- "Due to the extremely graphic nature of this program, we've changed our minds and decided not to show it at all."
- "I don't really care if our team wins this game. I'm so exhausted I just want to get it over with."
- "Since our ministry has all it needs at present, we won't be asking for any funds for the next six months."
- "We're going to be running at least eight commercials now, so this would be a good time for you to get a snack." —Rudy Minger

Television has proved that people will look at anything rather than each other.

—Ann Landers

In my hometown the TV station owner is a real cheapskate. Recently he has cut down so sharply on expenses that now even the weather reports are reruns.

Some guy broke into our house last week. He didn't even take the TV. He just took the remote control. Now he drives by and changes channels on us.

—Brian Kiley

401

Late-night TV is very educational. It teaches you that you should have gone to bed earlier.

Further Reading:
The TV News Anchorman, Maury Ports

■ Testimonials

Authors and publishers love to use promotional blurbs on the back covers of their books. One author, Stephen Douglas Williford, decided to make up a few of his own for his book *When You Really Embarrass Yourself Nobody Ever Forgets.* As he explains, tongue firmly planted in cheek:

"Like other successful books, I wanted mine to have glowing testimonials from several well-known celebrities. I share with you now some of the responses I have received to the invitation to review my manuscript":

Don't send the manuscript.

—Tom Brokaw

I'm sorry, but I've been swamped with blurb requests, and I'm all blurbed out.

—Dave Barry, Owner, Two Dogs

Mr. Redford is honored that you would think of him to review your book. Unfortunately, he does not have time to read your letter.

—Assistant to Robert Redford

Don't send your manuscript to Mr. Cosby, but does he still get the Elvis pen you offered?

—Assistant to Bill Cosby

■ Texas

My brother Scott boasts that one of his friends in Dallas is so rich he flies his own plane. "So what?" I scoffed. "Lots of people here fly their own planes."

"Inside the house?" my brother rejoined.

A Wall Street financier asked a Texas oil tycoon, "How's business holding up in your part of the world?"

"Son," drawled the oil man, "in Texas we do more business by accident than you do on Wall Street on purpose." —Myron Cohen

There was a Texan visiting a farm up in Maine. The Texan asked this old farmer about his farm and what might be the extent of his spread. The old fellow said, "Well, it runs to that clump of trees and then over to that hill and then down to the creek and over to there. How big is your spread in Texas?"

The Texan bragged, "Well, old-timer, sometimes I get in my car and drive for an hour and a half before I get to the boundary of my farm."

The old fellow from Maine looked at him for a minute and then said, "I know what you mean. I had a car like that myself once."

—Ronald Reagan

Did you hear about the Texan who received a statement from his bank pertaining to a check he had recently deposited? The note read: "INSUFFICIENT FUNDS. NOT YOURS . . . OURS!"

—Myron Cohen

YOU KNOW YOU'RE IN TEXAS WHEN . . .

- You no longer associate bridges (or rivers) with water.
- You can say 110 degrees without fainting.
- You eat hot chilies to cool your mouth off.
- You can make instant sun tea.
- You learn that a seat belt makes a pretty good branding iron.
- The temperature drops below ninety-five, and you feel a bit chilly.
- You discover in July that it takes only two fingers to drive your car.
- You discover you can get a sunburn through your car window.
- You notice the best parking place is determined by shade instead of distance.
- Hot water now comes out of both taps.
- It's noon in July, kids are on summer vacation, and not one person is out on the streets.
- You break into a sweat the instant you step outside. At 7:30 P.M.
- You realize that asphalt has a liquid state.

■ Thanksgiving

A POEM

'Twas the night of Thanksgiving, but I just couldn't sleep.
I tried counting backwards, I tried counting sheep.
The leftovers beckoned—the dark meat and white,
But I fought the temptation with all of my might.
Tossing and turning with anticipation,
The thought of a snack became infatuation.
So I raced to the kitchen, flung open the door
And gazed at the fridge, full of goodies galore.
I gobbled up turkey and buttered potatoes,
pickles and carrots, beans and tomatoes.
I felt myself swelling so plump and so round,
'Til all of a sudden, I rose off the ground.
I crashed through the ceiling, floating into the sky
With a mouthful of pudding and a handful of pie!
But, I managed to yell as I soared past the trees,
"Happy eating to all—pass the cranberries, please!"

YOU ARE PROBABLY OVERDOING THANKSGIVING IF . . .

- You spill more food on you than the local soup kitchen dispenses.
- Paramedics bring in the Jaws of Life to pry you out of the La-Z-Boy.
- Your after dinner moans are loud enough to signal Dr. Kevorkian.
- The gravy boat your wife set out was a real twelve foot boat!
- The potatoes you used set off another famine in Ireland.
- You got grass stains on your bottom after a walk, but never sat down.
- Your Big Elvis Super-Belt won't go around your waist.
- You receive a Sumo Wrestler application in your e-mail.
- You set off three earthquake seismographs on your morning jog Friday.
- Pricking your finger for cholesterol screening only yielded gravy.
- You have five TV sets side-by-side to catch all the football games.
- A guest quotes a biblical passage from "The Feeding of the Five Thousand."
- That rash on your stomach turns out to be steering wheel burn.

- Your wife wears a life jacket at night in your water bed.
- Representatives from the Butterball Hall of Fame called twice.
- You consider gluttony as your patriotic duty.
- It looks like the leftovers are gonna last until Christmas.
- Your arms are too short to reach this book and turn the page.

Tupperware has introduced a new line of merchandise for Thanksgiving. The containers not only burp themselves, they also loosen their belts and fall asleep in front of the television.

BUTTERBALL TURKEY TALK-LINE "GREATEST HITS"

Over the years, the Butterball Turkey Talk-Line staff have had their share of memorable calls—inquiries that stand out from the crowd because they're heartwarming or amusing. We asked some of the veteran staff members to tell us their favorites; plus, we rounded up a bunch of our own personal favorites from the Talk-Line archives.

It's hard to beat the call from a trucker who planned to cook his Thanksgiving turkey on the engine of his truck ("Will it cook faster if I drive faster?"), but some of these come pretty close. These are real incidents, true stories from the front lines.

- *Home alone.* A Kentucky woman was in the doghouse when she called the Butterball Turkey Talk-Line. While preparing the turkey, her Chihuahua jumped into the bird's body cavity and couldn't get out. She tried pulling the dog and shaking the bird, but nothing worked. She and the dog became more and more distraught. After calming the woman down, the Talk-Line home economist suggested carefully cutting the opening in the cavity of the turkey wider. It worked and Fido was freed.
- *Birdie, eagle, or turkey?* Roasting a turkey doesn't have to interfere with daily routine, said a retired Floridian. He called Turkey Central for grilling tips while waiting to tee off from the fourteenth hole.
- *And how do you store already-eaten leftovers?* Taking turkey preparation an extra step, a Virginian wondered, "How do you thaw a fresh turkey?" The Talk-Line staffer explained that fresh turkeys aren't frozen and don't need to be thawed.

- *Don't wait until the last minute!* On Thanksgiving Day, a Georgian woman took the "Be prepared" motto to heart. She had just agreed to host Thanksgiving Dinner and called the Talk-Line a year ahead of time for turkey tips.

- *Happy Thanksgiving, Mr. President!* A Southern woman called to comment, "On Thanksgiving Day, the Butterball Turkey Talk-Line is more important than the President. He can take the day off, but the Talk-Line staff can't." (The Butterball Turkey Talk-Line is open Thanksgiving Day, 6:00 a.m. to 6:00 p.m., Central Standard Time.)

- *Thanksgiving dinner on the run.* A woman called to find out how long it would take to roast her turkey. To answer the question, the Talk-Line home economist asked how much the bird weighed. The woman responded, "I don't know—it's still running around outside."

- Tofu turkey? No matter how you slice it, Thanksgiving just isn't Thanksgiving without turkey. A restaurant owner in California wanted to know how to roast a turkey for a vegetarian menu.

- White meat, anyone? A West Coast woman took turkey preparation to extremes by scrubbing her bird with bleach. Afterward, she called the Talk-Line to find out how to clean off the bleach. To her dismay, she was advised to dispose of the turkey.

- *Then cook it medium well.* A young girl called on behalf of her mother who needed roasting advice. To provide approximate roasting times, the home economist asked what size the turkey was. Without asking her mother the little girl paused, then replied, "Medium."

THERE GOES THE WALLPAPER

Tulsa, OK (DPI)—In what is becoming more and more common on holidays here in America, an entire family exploded shortly after finishing their Thanksgiving dinner. Investigators from the Tulsa Sheriff Department said that while the sheer size of the meal certainly played a part in the Turkey Day Massacre, the straw that broke the gobbler's back was in fact the whipped cream on top of the pumpkin pie. Sheriff Bill Gutt commented, "Yep, it was the Cool-Whip what done it. People just ain't got no common sense."

—*The Daily Probe*, December 1, 1997

DEFINITIONS FOR MY HUSBAND ON THANKSGIVING DAY

Playbook: Also known as my cookbook, to be kept in plain sight at all times. If the book gets moved, the game could get ugly.

Offsides: Silverware is to be set next to the plates . . . off to the side dear, not tossed in the middle of the table in a heap, for all to scramble for.

Game: This is when the food must all be on the table, at the same time, at the same temperature (preferably hot) so that the teams may meet at the arena (table) for the coach to say the prayer.

Team spirit: That which shall be upheld until the end of the game.

End of the game: When the coach (me) has heard the fat lady sing (Aunt Martha saying that she's had enough to eat).

Commercial breaks: There will be *none* for us, until I deem them totally necessary for my sanity, when you have made me crazy!

Penalties: Will be given if there is no team spirit showing and the game time is DELAYED or offsides have occurred due to a certain televised football game engaging your attention.

Holding: May be necessary of several large bowls, so that I may pour gravy without staining my new silk blouse. (And keep in mind, dear, I am "holding" the TV remote control for ransom.)

Touchdowns: Please make them gentle when bowls are being touched down on the table; do not spike them, and do not dance when the mission is complete.

Flag on the play: When something is spilled, *please* by all means throw a towel down on it and mop it up!

Rushing: What we will be doing a lot of! And last but not least . . .

Grooming the field: Dear husband, if you help me through this meal, as I know you will, I promise to recruit new players for the clean up—and yes, in plenty of time for you to enjoy the real game!

—Shan Kish

■ Time

The sooner you fall behind, the more time you'll have to catch up.

We prefer the old-fashioned alarm clock to the kind that awakens you with soft or a gentle whisper. If there's one thing we can't stand early in the morning, it's hypocrisy.

—Bill Vaughan

Time is nature's way of keeping everything from happening at once.

Warning: Dates in calendar are closer than they appear.

How to tell time by children: When they're very sleepy, it's time to go to school. When they never felt more wide awake in their lives, it's time for the late, late, late, late, late movie. When they have a slight fever and an unidentifiable rash, it's three o'clock Sunday morning. When they break a collarbone, it's four o'clock Sunday morning during the doctor's vacation. When they put on underwear and a flannel shirt, it's the middle of the first hot spell in July, and when they put on cotton socks, sneakers, and a mesh T-shirt, it's the day of the worst blizzard since '47. —Robert Paul Smith

Mr. Jones badly needed to know the time, but his wristwatch, alas, turned out to have stopped hours before. The streets were deserted, and the only living soul in sight was a man sunning himself in a deck chair on the large, fenced-off lawn of the local mental hospital. A little dubious, but observing that the man really looked quite harmless, and reflecting that in any case he had no choice, Mr. Jones called out, "Sir, do you by any chance have the time?"

"The time? One moment." The man on the lawn was galvanized into action. Leaping out of his deck chair, he withdrew a small stick from one pocket and a small hammer from another. He tapped the stick into the ground, adjusted it carefully until he was satisfied it was vertical, then whipped out a measuring tape. He measured the length of the stick above the ground and the length of its shadow. Throwing himself prone on the ground, he sighted the top of the stick against some point on the building, made a mark on the ground, and then made a few new measurements. Out from his back pocket came a calculator. Back and forth he manipulated it and finally, perspiring slightly, he said, "It is exactly 3:22 P.M., provided this is June 30, as I think it is."

Mr. Jones, who had watched all this with astonishment, could not help but be convinced, and adjusted his watch carefully. He then said, "This has been a most impressive use of the solar position to tell time, but what do you do at night, or on a cloudy day, when there are no shadows to measure?'

"Oh," said the inmate, holding up his left arm, "then I just look at my wristwatch." —Isaac Asimov

Further Reading:
Almost Missed the Bus, Justin Time

■ Toddlers

There are hundreds of different toilet-training methods—probably because none of them work. —Bruce Lansky

Nothing brings out a toddler's devotion to a toy she has abandoned more quickly than another child playing with it. —Robert Scotellaro

Reasoning with a two-year-old is about as productive as changing seats on the *Titanic.* —Robert Scotellaro

There are two classes of travel: first class, and with children. —Robert Benchley

If your toddlers are giving you a headache, follow the directions on the aspirin bottle. Especially the part that says, "Keep away from children." —Susan Savannah

I was doing the family grocery shopping accompanied by two children, an event I hope to see included in the Olympics in the near future. —Anna Quindlen

Further Reading:
Shhh!, Danielle Soloud
The Hidden Surprise, Pam Perz
Do It Yourself, Tyrone Shoelaces

■ Travel

A woman tourist visiting the Holy Land went to a tourist office for information on roads. Told that it was now possible to go by car all the way from Dan to Beersheba, she confessed, "Do you know, I never knew that Dan and Beersheba were places. I always thought they were husband and wife, like Sodom and Gomorrah."

A journey of a thousand miles begins with a cash advance.

For years, my parents took annual cruises to various parts of the world. Often they went ashore to view the local attractions but nothing seemed to impress them.

One year, my sister, who is a travel agent, arranged a fully guided tour of Switzerland. As they traveled from canton to canton, their harassed guide diligently attempted to find something with which he could really stir the hearts of this blasé American couple. In despair he played his last card—the magnificent panorama of the Alps from Lausanne. "Isn't it the most beautiful view you've ever seen?" prodded the guide.

"Oh, I don't know," said my mother. "Take away your lakes and your mountains, and what have you got?"

Miami is God's country. . . . He's the only one who can afford it! It's the land of the palms. . . . all open. It's got hotels and motels. Some motels are built so poorly that you can hear the lady next door changing her mind. When you get to Miami, you'll know it. No matter how hot it is, the women who have them will be wearing their mink coats.

—Myron Cohen

Mummies are Egyptians that were pressed for time.

From a brochure sent to University of Colorado alumni, advertising a Danube cruise: All meals are included during your Blue Danube cruise. In fact, while in Europe, you will enjoy all meals except three lunches and three dinners.

When you look like your passport photo, it's time to go home.

—Erma Bombeck

The FBI is trying to figure out how this Unabomber guy traveled around the country. Well, it's pretty simple. He detested advanced technology, and he liked explosions. Obviously, he took Amtrak.

—Jay Leno

If you like to spend your vacation in out-of-the-way places where few people go, let your wife read the map. —Jack Carter

One of the main troubles about going to Europe is that no one wants to hear about your trip when you get back home. Your friends and relatives are rife with jealousy and are not only sorry you went to Europe but deeply regret that you came back.

—Art Buchwald

When my parents were in Switzerland, my sister, who had arranged their tour, phoned them one day and inquired, "How's the food at that hotel I sent you to?"

My dad's reply: "There was a man here yesterday who simply raved over it. But this morning the attendants came and took him back to the asylum."

My pastor Harold swears that in the part of Oklahoma his family hails from, there's so little water that you can tell when a school of fish is swimming upriver by the cloud of dust it raises.

I'll never forget the time I was flying over Milwaukee, and the pilot said, "We're now approaching the great city; let's set our watches back one hundred years."　—Jack E. Leonard

I know there's not a North Dakota. What you think is North Dakota is actually part of Canada, and it's so cold and bleak there that the Canadians are trying to pass it off as a part of this country.

　　　　　　　　　　　　　　　　　　—Lewis Grizzard

Sunday morning in Arizona is just like Sunday morning in Connecticut, only more bowlegged.　—Jack Douglas

The dough we spent on Disney World we could have saved instead; the ride the kids remember most was jumping on the bed.

　　　　　　　　　　　　　　　　　　—Charles Ghigna

And that's the wonderful thing about family travel: it provides you with experience that will remain locked forever in the scar tissue of your mind.　—Dave Barry

Further Reading:
New Mexico Tour Book, Albie Kerky
Still Looking for My Heart, Sam Francisco
Home of the Liberty Bell, Phil A. Delphia
Mobile Homes, Winnie Bago
Daddy, Are We There Yet?, Miles Away
Highway Travel, Dusty Rhodes
Uninteresting Road Signs, Bill Bored

The Pullman Sleeper, Bertha Buv
Swimming in the Arctic, I. C. Waters
Desert Crossing, I. Rhoda Camel
Maritime Disasters, Andrea Doria
Where to Find Islands, Archie Pelago
Round the World, Madge Ellen
Defunct Nations, Sophie Etunion
Scandinavian Photography, Matt Finnish
Nice Hotels, Mary Ott
East Coast Resorts, Nan Tuckett
Weekend in Hong Kong, Rick Shaw
As Solid As . . . , Rocco Gibraltar

■ Typos and Misplaced Modifiers

Proofread your work to make sure you don't words out.

—secretarial training guide

From a police blotter bulletin in the Elko, Nevada, *Daily Free Press*: "The suspect was arrested by a police officer at 10:41 P.M. yesterday at a service station on US 93, on a charge of carrying a concealed fireman."

Social announcement in the Malvern, Iowa, *Leader* for a retirement party: "Please, no gifts; just the honor of your presents."

In a letter from a summer camp director: Dear parents: We are pleased to announce the opening of registration. We are working hard and looking forward to the ultimate bummer experience for everyone.

From the Yeovil, England, *Western Gazette*: "The first swallow has arrived at Devizes. It was spotted by Police Constable John Cooke, of Seend, whose hobby is birdwatching, sitting wet and bedraggled on telephone wires."

413

Ad in the Three Rivers, Michigan, *Commercial:* G.E. Automatic Blanket—Insure sound sleep with an Authorized G.E. Dealer.

Classified ad: Man wanted to work in dynamite factory; must be willing to travel.

Ad in *Betavia Daily News*: "Odd jobs wanted by handy man, trimming hedges, shrubs, and others."

In an Ohio paper: "The operator of the other car, charged with drunken driving, crashed into Miss Miller's rear end which was sticking out into the road."

The Harrah, Oklahoma, *News* ran an article about the Folderol String Band, which was to entertain at a barbecue. The story explained, "These true sons of the Southwest have twanged their music all over Oklahoma and have been asked more than once to leave the state."

From an article in the Sun City Center, Florida, *Sun* on mosquito-borne encephalitis: "Physician Bob Craven, with the Atlanta-based U.S. Centers for Disease Control, said avoiding contact with mis-quotes is the best way to avoid the disease."

From the Tulsa, Oklahoma, *World:* "It is permissible to spank a child if one has a definite end in view."

In the Monterey, California, *Peninsula Herald*: "The area in which Miss Garson was injured is spectacularly scenic."

A Chicago restaurant menu offered: Today's Special—Dreaded Veal Cutlets.

From the Allentown, Pennsylvania, *Lentz Post News*: "Mrs. Jones, a strained elocutionist, will give readings."

From a *Business Week* article on the marriage rate and its effect on retail sales: "It should be at least a year or two before the bulge appears in the marriage figures."

In an English newspaper: "A committee of ladies, with Mrs. Roberts as leader, threw themselves into the tea, which proved a master-piece."

From a bulletin of the Tucson Art Center: Figure Class I. A studio course working directly from the human figure. Anyone wishing to take advantage of the model without instruction may do so.

From the New Bethlehem, Pennsylvania, *Leader-Vindicator*: "Obviously a man of sound judgment and intelligence, Mr. Rau is not married."

Society note in the Denver, Colorado, *Rocky Mountain News*: "She looked like the belle of a court ball with the gown and her hair piled high on her head."

Help-wanted ad in the *Washington Post*: "Widower with school-age children requires person to assume general housekeeping duties. Must be capable of contributing to growth of family."

From the Jacksonville, Florida, *Times-Union*: "The sewer-expansion project is nearing completion, but city officials are holding their breath until it is officially finished."

From the Hastings & St. Leonards, England, *Observer:* "House to let. Furnished with period pieces from an unfortunate period."

Real estate ad in program of The Barn Playhouse, New London, New Hampshire: "For Sale. Business site in large city. Busy intersection with traffic light out of order. Just the right spot for doctor or lawyer."

Philadelphia department store ad: For you alone! The bridal bed set . . .

Road sign in Atlanta, Georgia: CAUTION! Water on Road During Rain.

Sign just outside a bridge construction job: No Unauthorized Trespassing.

Sign spotted in Jacksonville, Florida: Pool is open 24 hours. Please do not enter the pool at any other time.

In the vestibule of a Tennessee funeral parlor: For sale: hearse with 1968 body.

On a self-service elevator: Eighth floor button out of order. Please push five and three.

Try our cafeteria. Courteous and efficient self-service.

In the *Toronto Star*: "Marijuana Issue Sent to a Joint Committee"

Classified ad in *Entrepreneur* magazine: "Publicize your business absolutely free. Send $6."

At a canoe rental shop at Lake Hopatcong: No tipping allowed.

A classic of its kind was this sign in an army mess hall in Britain. Printed in big black letters across the exit, it read: Kindly Let Those Who Are Going Out First.

That sentence drove us crazy, and I thought it would never be topped. But it was, in a San Francisco bar. I overheard a guy who was being pestered to death by a frightful bore snap, "If you don't get out of here and leave me alone, I'll find somebody who can!"

From recent newspaper ads:
- Ground Beast: 99¢ lb.
- Fully Cooked Boneless Smoked Man: $2.09 lb.

From a help-wanted ad in the *Atlanta Journal & Constitution*: "Law firm needs secretary. Excellent benefits, including tension."

A notice in the Bridgeton, New Jersey, *Evening News*: "Elder Valese, pastor of the Soul Stirring Church, Brooklyn, will speak here at eight o'clock. She will bring a quart with her, and they will sing appropriate selections during the service."

Classified ad in Raton, New Mexico, *Raton Range*: "Dairy Queen seeking person with supervisory and fat-food restaurant experience."

From the social column of the Asheville, North Carolina, *Citizen:* "A musical program was presented during the afternoon. Mrs. Melvin Tilson, accompanied by Mrs. C. Fred Brown, sank two numbers."

Ad submitted to travel guide: Cocktail lounge. Continental cuisine. Mid-Evil atmosphere.

 The following correction appeared in a small-town paper: "Our paper carried the notice last week that Mr. John Jones is a defective in the police force. This was a typographical error. Mr. Jones is really a detective in the police farce."

Ad from Fremont, Nebraska, *Tribune:* "For Sale—Young dressed hens. Absolutely clean and ready for the rooster."

From the Andrews County, Texas, *News:* "Refreshments of cake squares, iced in pink and glue, were served."

From the personals in the *Tacoma News-Tribune*: "Due to illness of the owner, Milton's Barbershop will be operated by a competent barber until owner's return."

The following are real classified ads taken from newspapers around the country:
- Two female Boston Terrier puppies, seven wks old, perfect markings, 555-1234. Leave mess.
- Wanted: Unmarried girls to pick fresh fruit and produce at night.

- For Sale—Eight puppies from a German Shepherd and an Alaskan Hussy.
- Great Dames for sale.
- Dog for sale: eats anything and is fond of children.
- If you think you've seen everything in Paris, visit the Pere Lachasis Cemetery. It boasts such immortals as Moliere, Jean de la Fontain, and Chopin.
- The hotel has bowling alleys, tennis courts, comfortable beds, and other athletic facilities.
- Sheer stockings. Designed for fancy dress, but so serviceable that lots of women wear nothing else.
- Modular Sofas. Only $299. For rest or fore play.
- Our bikinis are exciting. They are simply the tops.
- Illiterate? Write today for free help.
- 50% Off Our Rockers!
- Tires Slashed 30%
- '83 Toyota hunchback—$2000
- Star Wars job of the hut—$15
- Georgia peaches—California grown—89¢ lb.
- American flag—60 stars—pole included $100
- Tired of working for only $9.75 per hour? We offer profit sharing and flexible hours. Starting pay: $7–$9 per hour.

The *Portland Oregonian* ran an article about a volcano in Iceland, including this passage: "No one was in danger from the eruption; the sparsely populated region is uninhabited."

■ Vegetarians

I was a vegetarian for a while, but I quit because there are side effects. I found myself sitting in my living room, starting to lean toward the sunlight.

—Rita Rudner

I didn't fight my way to the top of the food chain to be a vegetarian.

I thought I could do my own small part to save the planet by becoming a vegetarian. Actually, I did it not so much because I love animals but because I hate plants. I still like to hunt, though. In fact, I've found that plants are a lot easier than animals to sneak up on.

—A. Whitney Brown

I'm a Volvovegetarian. I'll eat an animal only if it was accidentally killed by a speeding car.

—Ron Smith

■ War

In 1787, George Washington led the convention that wrote the United States Constitution. He spoke little during this historic meeting. Then someone suggested that the Constitution set a limit of five thousand men in the army. Washington could be quiet no longer. "If that is so," he said, "let the Constitution also say that no foreign army should ever invade our country with more than three thousand troops."

—Melvin Berger

Sometimes I think war is God's way of teaching us geography.

—Paul Rodriguez

MX missiles—they changed their name. They call them the Peace Keepers. A multiple-warhead hydrogen bomb called the Peace Keeper. What do they call a sledgehammer? The Finger Massage? Is napalm now Dry Skin Remover? Let's be consistent. It's not mustard gas—it's a really strong antihistamine!

—Will Durst

I grew up in a tough section of Chicago. I heard that a captain in an infantry unit made up mostly of draftees from our neighborhood summoned one of his lieutenants. "Better look up the pre-induction record of Private Genovese," he said. "I've noticed that every time he fires his rifle on the range he wipes off the fingerprints!"

You can't say civilization isn't advancing; in every war, they kill you in a new way.

—Will Rogers

Shooting the breeze down at the Veteran's Hospital, a trio of old timers ran out of tales of their own heroic exploits and started bragging about their ancestors. "My great grandfather, at age thirteen," one declared proudly, "was a drummer boy at Shiloh."

"Mine," boasted another, "went down with Custer at the Battle of Little Big Horn."

"I'm the only soldier in my family," confessed vet number three, "but if my great grandfather was living today he'd be the most famous man in the world."

"Why? What'd he do?"

"Nothing much. But he'd be 165 years old."

 **W**e have women in the military, but they don't put us in the front lines. They don't know if we can fight, if we can kill. I think we can. All the general has to do is walk over to the women and say, "You see the enemy over there? They say you look fat in those uniforms."

—Elayne Boosler

How to tell if your neighbors are militia members:
- When you say, "Good morning," they reply, "That's what the government wants you to believe."
- They are always blending into the bushes.
- When you visit and pick up the remote control, they scream, "Don't touch that!"
- They don't mow the lawn—they blow it up.
- When a car backfires, they barricade themselves in their home and demand to see a negotiating team.
- They ask to borrow a cup of nitro.
- Their last yard sale attracted Libyan arms dealers.

—Scott Craven in Arizona Republic

Watch closely. I'm going to do this only once.

—Kamikaze flight school instructor

Further Reading:
Drafted!, Abel Boddeed
Fistfights, Donny Brooke
I Hate Fighting, Boris Hell
Keep Out!, Barb Dwyer
Military Rule, Marshall Law
Pentagon Press Release, Colonel O'Truth and Lotta Lies
Military Defeats, Major Disaster and General Mayhem
In the Trenches, Helmut Wearer
When's the Revolution?, Millie Tant
Making Explosives, Stan Wellback
Nuclear Explosives, Adam Baum
Okee-Dokee, Roger Wilco

■ Weather

My friend Margie tells me that the Street Cleaning Department in Fargo has come up with a foolproof method for getting rid of snow. They call the method "August."

Weather bulletin broadcast by a TV station: "Severe thunderstorm watch until 4:30 this afternoon. Stay inside. Do not use any electrical appliances. Please stay tuned for further information."

Question: What normally follows two days of rain?
Answer: Monday.

—Ron Dentinger

There are two seasonal diversions that can ease the bite of any winter. One is the January thaw; the other is the seed catalogues.

—Hal Borland

Timing has a lot to do with the outcome of a rain dance.

—Texas Bix Bender

A fellow down south was sitting on his porch holding a small piece of rope. "What's that?" asked a stranger.

"That's my weather vane," was the reply.

"How can you tell the weather with that?" inquired the stranger.

"When it goes to-and-fro, it's windy. When it's wet—it's raining!"

—Joe Laurie Jr.

It was so hot I seen a cow lying on her back giving herself a shower.

—Homer Haynes

In Arizona, I overheard two ranch hands discussing the effects of a drought on their herds. "Our cattle are so thin," one said, "that we don't brand 'em anymore—we just photocopy 'em."

—John E. Kovacs in *Arizona Highways*

Barry Goldwater, the Arizonan, once expressed his envy of the state of Minnesota with its many inland lakes and waterways: "Out where I come from, we have so little water that the trees chase the dogs."

—Bob Dole

The differences between the way residents of various parts of the United States and other places in the world deal with the weather have been noticed as follows:

60 degrees   Californians put their sweaters on.
50 degrees   Miami residents turn on the heat.
45 degrees   Vermont residents go to outdoor concert.
40 degrees   Californians shiver uncontrollably; Minnesotans go swimming.
35 degrees   Italian cars don't start.
32 degrees   Water freezes.

426

30 degrees	You plan your vacation in Australia.
25 degrees	Ohio water freezes; Californians weep pitiably; Minnesotans eat ice cream; Canadians go swimming.
20 degrees	Politicians begin to talk about the homeless; city water freezes; Miami residents plan vacation farther south.
15 degrees	French cars don't start; cat insists on sleeping in your bed with you.
10 degrees	You need jumper cables to get the car going.
5 degrees	American cars don't start.
0 degrees	Alaskans put on T-shirts.
-10 degrees	German cars don't start; eyes freeze shut when you step outside.
-15 degrees	You can cut your breath and use it to build an igloo; rednecks stick tongues on metal objects; Miami residents cease to exist.
-20 degrees	Cat insists on sleeping in pajamas with you; politicians actually do something about the homeless; Minnesotans shovel snow off roof; Japanese cars don't start.
-25 degrees	Too cold to think; you need jumper cables to get the driver going.
-30 degrees	You plan a two week hot bath; Swedish cars don't start.
-40 degrees	Californians disintegrate; Minnesotans button top button; Canadians put on sweater; your car helps you plan your trip south.
-50 degrees	Congressional hot air freezes; Alaskans close the bathroom window.
-80 degrees	Polar bears move south; Green Bay Packer fans order hot cocoa at the game.
-90 degrees	Lawyers put their hands in their own pockets.
-100 degrees	Hell freezes over; Clinton finally tells all.

Further Reading:
Downpour!, Wayne Dwops
Geez, It's Hot!, Mike Hammeldyed
Not So Hot, Luke Warm
I Hate the Sun, Gladys Knight
The Big Wave, Sue Nami
Many Are Cold, But Few Are Frozen, Minnie Sota

■ Weddings

I think my life as a humorist began when I was four and was asked to participate in the wedding ceremony of my mother's cousin Jo. My mother wrote this account:

As Lowell was coming down the aisle, he would take two steps, stop, and turn to the crowd (alternating between bride's side and groom's side). While facing the crowd, he would put his hands up like claws and roar. So it went: step, step, ROAR, step, step, ROAR, all the way down the aisle. As you can imagine, the crowd was near tears from laughing so hard by the time he reached the pulpit.

Little Lowell, however, was getting more and more distressed from all the laughing and was also near tears by the time he reached the front of the chapel.

When asked what he was doing, Lowell sniffed and said innocently, "I was being the Ring Bear."

Her whole family hates me. During the wedding ceremony when they asked, "Is there anyone here who objects to this marriage?" her side of the family stood up and started forming a double line.

—Ron Dentinger

My wife was wrapping an odd assortment of gifts to take to a bridal shower: an antique pitcher, an electrostatic dust wand, a box of brownie mix, and a blue-flowered candle. I asked her what the strange collection was all about. "It's traditional," she replied. "Something old, something new, something bar-coded, something blue."

■ Weight

A new study shows that three-quarters of all Americans are overweight. In fact, it is so bad that three-quarters of all Americans are nine-tenths of all Americans.

—Conan O'Brien, *Late Night with Conan O'Brien*, NBC

You guys—you gain thirty pounds, and we call you cuddly. We gain an ounce, and you call us taxis. Then you don't call us at all.

—Carol Siskind

Fat people don't think like thin people. We have our own way of thinking different. Did you ever go up to a fat person on the street and ask them where something is? They tell you: "Well, go down to Arby's. Go right past Wendy's, McDonald's, Burger King, Taco Bell, KFC. It's the chocolate-brown building."

—Roseanne Barr

Inside every fat person there's a thin person screaming, "I'm hungry!"

—Brad Stine

You know you're getting fat when you can pinch an inch on your forehead.

—John Mendoza

Further Reading:
Two Thousand Pounds!, Juan Ton
Eating Disorders, Anna Rexia

■ Wisdom
If fifty million people say a foolish thing, it is still a foolish thing.

—Anatole France

Common sense gets a lot of credit that belongs to cold feet.

—Arthur Godfrey

You've got to be willing to give up good to get great.

—Kenny Rogers

A man who wants to lead the orchestra must turn his back on the crowd.
—Max Lucado, *And the Angels Were Silent*

Trust everybody in the game, but always cut the cards.
—Texas Bix Bender

Compromise: A deal in which two people get what neither of them wanted.

If you are sure you understand everything that is going on, you are hopelessly confused.
—Walter Mondale

GREAT TRUTHS ABOUT LIFE LITTLE CHILDREN HAVE LEARNED
- No matter how hard you try, you can't baptize cats.
- When your mom is mad at your dad, don't let her brush your hair.
- If your sister hits you, don't hit back. They always catch the second person.
- Never ask a three-year-old to hold a tomato.
- You can't trust dogs to watch your food.
- Don't sneeze when someone is cutting your hair.
- Puppies still have bad breath even after eating a Tic-Tac.
- Never hold a dust buster and a cat at the same time.
- School lunches stick to the wall.
- You can't hide a piece of broccoli in a glass of milk.
- Don't wear polka-dot underwear under white shorts.

GREAT TRUTHS ABOUT LIFE ADULTS HAVE LEARNED
- Raising teenagers is like trying to nail Jell-O to a tree.
- There's always a lot to be thankful for if you take time to look for it. For example, think how nice it is that wrinkles don't hurt.
- Every seven minutes of every day, someone in an aerobics class pulls a hamstring.
- The best way to keep kids at home is to make the home a pleasant atmosphere . . . and let the air out of their tires.

- Families are like fudge: mostly sweet, with a few nuts.
- Middle age is when you choose cereal for the fiber, not the toy.
- If you can remain calm, you don't have all the facts.
- Eat a live toad first thing in the morning, and nothing worse can happen to you the rest of the day.
- You know you're getting old when you stoop to tie your shoes and wonder what else you can do while you're down there.

What's right is what's left if you do everything else wrong.

—Robin Williams

Every man is a fool for at least five minutes every day; wisdom consists of not exceeding the limit. —Elbert Hubbard

■ Wishes

A secretary, a paralegal, and a partner in a city law firm are walking through a park on their way to lunch when they find an antique oil lamp. They rub it, and a genie comes out in a puff of smoke. The genie says, "I usually only grant three wishes, so I'll give each of you just one."

"Me first! Me first!" says the secretary. "I want to be in the Bahamas, driving a speedboat, without a care in the world!" *Poof!* She's gone.

In astonishment, "Me next! Me next!" says the paralegal. "I want to be in Hawaii, relaxing on the beach with my personal masseuse, an endless supply of piña coladas, and the love of my life." *Poof!* She's gone.

"You're next," the genie says to the partner.

The partner says, "I want those two back in the office after lunch."

On a wishing well: Wish carefully. No refunds!

A struggling salesman is walking along the beach in Malibu when he comes across a salt-encrusted piece of metal. He works for an hour or so to remove the salt. Lo and behold, it is a very old oil lamp. The guy starts to buff it to remove the corrosion when *poof*—a genie appears!

This genie, like all genies, is so happy to be freed of the lamp that he grants the guy three wishes.

"Genie, I wish to be a dollar richer than Bill Gates," says the guy. The genie isn't sure who Bill Gates is until the guy tells him to check *Forbes* magazine. When the genie calls up *Forbes* from inside the lamp, he learns that Bill Gates is indeed the richest man in the world.

"Guy," the genie says, "you will forever be a dollar richer than Bill Gates. What's your second wish?"

"Genie, I want the most expensive Porsche made: Fire engine red, on-board GPS, and the finest audio system ever installed in an automobile."

"That's easy, guy," says the genie. He waves his hand, and the best car anybody has ever seen pops out of the lamp. The genie then asks the guy for his third wish.

The guy mulls the problem over and over. He just can't decide what to wish for. "Genie," the guy says, "I can't think of anything now. May I save the third wish for later?"

"Gee, guy, this is most unusual. But you hold the hammer—I can't escape from this lamp until you make a third wish. Call me when you're ready." And whoosh, the genie disappears back into the lamp.

The guy carefully picks up the now-ever-so-valuable lamp and places it in the trunk of the fire engine red Porsche. He turns the radio on to balance the sound and makes all the other adjustments needed to get his great audio system customized to his ears. After that, he pulls off the beach and heads south along the Pacific Coast Highway. Soon he's doing sixty, then seventy, then eighty. The Porsche handles perfectly.

The guy is so happy that he begins to sing along with the familiar commercial on the radio: "Oh, I wish I was an Oscar Mayer wiener . . ."

Further Reading:
Genie in a Bottle, Grant Wishes
Say the Magic Word, Abby Cadabra

■ Words
I'm not bad—I just spell that way.

CAPSULE COURSE IN HUMAN RELATIONS
- 5 Most Important Words: "I am proud of you."
- 4 Most Important Words: "What is your opinion?"
- 3 Most Important Words: "If you please."
- 2 Most Important Words: "Thank you."
- Least Important Word: "I."

—Paul Pride

A few years ago, the telephone company in a midwestern state, after publishing a directory with certain abbreviations, received this letter from a subscriber: "Gntmn: Yr abbr of our town of Commerce as Comre in ur br new tel drctry is unfr, unclr, unplsnt, unecsry."

Why is abbreviation such a long word?

Among the English language's many puzzling words is "economy," which means the large size in soap flakes and the small size in cars.

Since we say a herd of cattle, a pack of wolves, and a pride of lions, maybe it should be:
- a piddle of puppies
- a wince of dentists
- a lurch of buses
- a wrangle of philosophers
- a shrivel of critics
- a descent of relatives

If lawyers are disbarred, and clergymen defrocked, then doesn't it follow that:
- electricians can be delighted
- musicians denoted
- cowboys deranged
- models deposed
- tree surgeons debarked
- and dry cleaners depressed

Almost everybody knows that lions travel in prides, that pups come in litters, that elephants en masse are referred to as herds, and that fish navigate in schools. But you'll have to dig into James Lipton's unique book *An Exaltation of Larks* to find that in their time and fashion, good folks have referred to:
- an ostentation of peacocks
- an impatience of wives
- an unction of undertakers
- a sneer of butlers
- a twinge of dentists
- a tantrum of decorators
- an indifference of waiters
- a descent of relatives
- a no-no of nannies
- a babble of barbers

—Bennett Cerf

Did you hear about the van loaded with copies of *Roget's Thesaurus* that collided with a taxi? Witnesses were astounded, shocked, taken aback, surprised, startled, dumfounded, thunderstruck, caught unawares.

—*Inprint,* England

The late Will Rogers once heard a talk about author-lexicographer Noah Webster. "Webster," observed the lecturer, "had amazing command of the language. Audiences were spellbound by his mastery of words. His English was just perfect."

"Mine would be, too," interrupted Rogers, "if I wrote my own dictionary!"

—Bennett Cerf

To encourage better spelling, somebody on the *Chicago Daily News* put up this notice on the bulletin board: "Let's set our sights high. Let's learn to spell JUDGMENT correctly. Let's repeat to ourselves each day, 'Today I will spell JUDGMENT without an E.' Who shall be the first to announce this accomplishment? Praise be unto him. Deranged."

Right next to this a reporter pinned up: "Dear Deranged, I tried to spell judgment without an 'e' and it came out judgmnt. Now I'm in a prdicamnt. Confusd."

DEFT DEFINITIONS

Antacid: Uncle Acid's wife.

Antelope: How she married my uncle.

Arbitrator: A cook that leaves Arby's to work at McDonald's.

Avoidable: What a bullfighter tries to do.

Baloney: Where some hemlines fall.

Bernadette: The act of torching a mortgage.

Bottom: What the shopper did when she found the shoes that she wanted.

Bucktooth: The going rate for the tooth fairy.

Burglarize: What a crook sees with.

Butler: A solemn procession of one. —P. G. Wodehouse

Cantaloupe: When you are unable to run away to get married.

Cartoonist: What you call your auto mechanic.

Castanet: What they did to fill the role of Frankie Avalon's movie girlfriend.

Catatonic: Feline pick-me-up

Celtics: What a parasite salesman does.

Concert: A breath mint for inmates.

Consist: A growth on an inmate.

Content: A fabric shelter for inmates.

Control: A short, ugly inmate.

Convent: How inmates get air conditioning.

Counterfeiters: Workers who put together kitchen cabinets.

Crestfallen: Dropped toothpaste.

Cross-eyed teacher: A teacher who loses control over his or her pupils.

Decrease: De fold in de pants.

Demote: What de king put around de castle.

Despise: De persons who work for the CIA.

Detention: What causes de stress.

Dictator: Another name for Richard Spud.

Dilate: When a person lives longer.

Dioxin: What you say before you kill a herd of buffalo-like cattle.

Dreadlocks: The fear of opening the deadbolt.

Endorse: Last one in the race.

Palisade: Royal retainer.

Palindrome: Michael's private airport.

Grateful: Fireplace needs cleaning out.

Humdrum: Beehive.

Impeccable: Unable to be eaten by a chicken.   —Ray Hand

Inverse: Rhyming.

Patriot: Irish punch-up.

Represented: The hated insurance salesman.

Stalagmites: Miniature German prison guards.   —Spike Milligan

Supervision: 20/20 sight.

Universe: All-purpose poem.   —Ray Hand

■ Work

If you ever need a helping hand, you'll find one at the end of your arm.
                    —Yiddish proverb

In labor news, longshoremen walked off the docks today. Rescue operations are continuing.   —George Carlin

Americans work hard to buy labor-saving devices, so they'll have more time to work hard to buy more labor-saving devices, so they'll have more time.

Will Rogers predicted World War I wouldn't last very long because his brother-in-law joined the Army, and he never held a job for over two weeks.   —"Senator" Ed Ford

I like work. It fascinates me. I can sit and look at it for hours.

—Jerome K. Jerome

Efficiency: The knack of getting someone to do a job you dislike.

There's no limit to the amount of work a man can do, provided, of course, that it isn't the work he's supposed to be doing at that moment.

—Robert Benchley

And there was the street cleaner who was fired because he couldn't keep his mind in the gutter.

—Ron Dentinger

It's impossible to thoroughly enjoy doing nothing unless you have a very great deal of work to do.

—Abe Martin

He does the work of three men—Larry, Curley, and Moe.

—Ron Dentinger

The best work in the world is done by people whose bosses don't know what they're doing.

When the other guy is laid off, it's a recession. When it happens to you, it's a depression.

Speaking before the annual meeting of the National Alliance of Business on October 5, 1981, Ronald Reagan said, "I heard of a fellow who had been unemployed for a long time, and a few days ago he found a job at a china warehouse. He'd only worked there a couple of days when he smashed a large oriental vase. The boss told him in no uncertain terms that the cost would be deducted from his

437

wages every week until the vase was paid for. And the fellow asked, 'How much did it cost?' The boss told him three hundred dollars. And the fellow cheered and said, 'At last, I've found steady work!'"

Further Reading:
Laid Off!, Gwen Home
Unemployed, Anita Job

■ Writers and Writing

He writes so well he makes me feel like putting the quill back in the goose.
—Fred Allen

One day novelist Arthur C. Clarke was reading a newspaper when he saw a story he wanted to share with his friends.

"During a crash landing of a commercial airliner, one passenger in the news story had been quoted as saying, 'I was reading an Arthur C. Clark novel, and it took my mind off the potential disaster.'

"After the story was printed, I sent clippings of it to all of my pals, including one of my dearest friends, the late, great science-fiction author Isaac Asimov. I included the following note:

'Dear Isaac,
If only he would have been reading one of your novels, he would have slept through the whole thing.'"
—David Naster

From the moment I picked your book up until I laid it down, I was convulsed with laughter. Some day I intend reading it.
—H. Aaron Cohl

I write for *Reader's Digest*. It's not hard. All you do is copy out an article and mail it in again.
—Milt Kamen

If writers were good businessmen, they'd have too much sense to be writers.
—Irving S. Cobb

A literary party is four authors and their wives who live in the same suburb and loathe each other.
—Frank Taylor

I suppose that this is another of those young writers who are worth watching. Not reading, just watching.
—Dorothy Parker

Somerset Michamud sat happily typing the final pages of his new novel. In the yard, his six-year-old son had just tripped over a tree root and broken his leg. The boxer puppy had chewed up Mrs. Michamud's best curtain, the twins had spilled a can of paint in the parlor and were now trying to pull each other's hair out, and the nurse had given notice. Mrs. Michamud called out to her husband, "Lunch is almost ready. How far have you gotten with your manuscript?"

Mr. M. answered, "It's going like a house afire. The hero is just proposing to the heroine."

"Give it a happy ending," begged Mrs. M. earnestly. "Have her say 'No.'"
—Bennett Cerf

Writing a daily newspaper column is like being married to a nymphomaniac. The first two weeks, it's fun.
—Lewis Grizzard

Some authors, I am told, write out their books in longhand. That's because they never learned to type. That's why Edgar Allan Poe wrote all that weird stuff. His hands and fingers were always hurting him. The pain became so intense he began to see talking ravens.
—Lewis Grizzard

An impetuous interviewer once asked the five-foot-two Truman Capote, "Very seriously, Mr. Capote, how would you describe yourself?"

Capote scratched his ear for a moment and said, "Well, I'm about as tall as a shotgun and just as noisy."

I once had an old friend of mine who believed he was the greatest writer of his time. One day while he was seated on a hotel lawn, he struck up a conversation with a fellow seated next to him.

"What do you do?" the fellow asked.

"I'm a writer," my friend said proudly.

"Have you written anything recently?"

"As a matter of fact, I have. I've just completed the greatest play of the century."

"Is that right? What did you call it?"

"I've entitled it *Hamlet*."

"*Hamlet*! You must be joking. Didn't you ever hear of a fellow named Shakespeare?"

"Isn't that strange," smiled my friend. "They asked me the same question when I finished *Macbeth*."

—Myron Cohen

One day in a conversation with Oscar Wilde, Welsh poet Lewis Morris bemoaned the fact that the press never published any of his work. "It's a conspiracy of silence, Oscar. What should I do?"

"Join it," said Oscar.

—Art Linkletter

An editor is one who separates the wheat from the chaff and prints the chaff.

—Adlai Stevenson

Sir Arthur Conan Doyle, author of the famous Sherlock Holmes stories, once hailed a cab in Paris. He threw his handbag inside and climbed in after it, but before he could say a word, the driver said, "Where to, Mr. Conan Doyle?"

"How do you know I am Conan Doyle?" asked the author in surprise.

"Well," said the driver, "I had read in the newspapers that you were on vacation in the south of France; I noticed you getting off a train that came from Marseille; I see you have the kind of tan that bespeaks a week or more in the sun; from the inkspot on your right middle finger, I deduce you are a writer; you have the keen look of a medical man, and the cut of clothes of an Englishman. Putting it all together, I felt you must surely be Conan Doyle, the creator of the great detective, Sherlock Holmes."

Conan Doyle burst out, "But you are yourself the equal of Sherlock Holmes since you recognized me from all these small observations."

"There is," said the driver, "one additional fact."

"And that is?"

"Your name is lettered on your handbag." —Isaac Asimov

One sour book reviewer noted that my previous book, *An Encyclopedia of Humor*, included selections from over two hundred sources. This led him to remark, "If you steal one man's stuff, it's plagiarism. If you steal that of several men, it's research." Then he paraphrased a Dorothy Parker description of anthropologists and called me a "lazy fellow who likes to spend a quiet evening at home raiding a good book."

RULES FOR BETTER WRITING

- Verbs has to agree with their subjects.
- Prepositions are not words to end sentences with.
- And don't start a sentence with a conjunction.
- It is wrong to ever split an infinitive.
- Avoid clichés like the plague. They're old hat.
- Also, always avoid annoying alliteration.
- Be more or less specific.
- Parenthetical remarks (however relevant) are (usually) not needed.
- No sentence fragments.
- Contractions aren't necessary and shouldn't be used.
- Foreign words and phrases are not *apropos*.
- Eradicate and eliminate superfluous unnecessary redundancies.
- One should never generalize.
- Don't use no double negatives.
- Eschew ampersands & abbreviations, etc.
- One-word sentences? Eliminate.
- Analogies in writing are like feathers on a snake.
- The passive voice is to be ignored.

- Eliminate commas, that are, not necessary. Parenthetical words however should be enclosed in commas.
- Never use a big word when a diminutive one would suffice.
- Kill all exclamation points!!!
- Use words correctly, irregardless of how others use them.
- Understatement is always the absolute best, most fantastic, and exciting way to put forth ideas.
- Use the apostrophe in it's proper place and omit it when its not needed.
- Eliminate quotations. As Ralph Waldo Emerson said, "I hate quotations. Tell me what *you* know."
- If you've heard it once, you've heard it a thousand times: Resist hyperbole; not one writer in a million can use it correctly.
- Puns are for children, not groan readers.
- Go around the barn at high noon to avoid colloquialisms.
- Even if a mixed metaphor sings, it should be derailed.
- Who needs rhetorical questions?
- Exaggeration is a billion times worse than understatement.

At the Redding Bookstore in northern California, a husband and wife from Oregon on their way to Yosemite, were browsing. They came upon ten copies of Homer's *Iliad*. "Wonder why they stock that book so heavily?" mused the wife.

The husband replied, "Probably a local author."

Further Reading:
Leo Tolstoy, Warren Peace
Lewis Carroll, Alison Wonderland
Ah, Thor!, Ty Till